WE BECAME
LIKE A HAND

WE BECAME
LIKE A HAND

~

A Story of Five Sisters

Carol A. Ortlip

BALLANTINE BOOKS
NEW YORK

Disclaimer: For the first two years of my life, I sang alone, with occasional accompaniment provided by my parents. Then, one by one, my sisters joined in, the songs we sang growing full and vibrant. The following story was influenced by many voices, and not just the voices of my sisters. Because it is a work of nonfiction, some names have been changed out of respect for those who experienced life differently than the way I have documented it here.

This is not just my song, my story. But it is the one I choose to sing.

A Ballantine Book
Published by The Ballantine Publishing Group

Copyright © 2002 by Carol A. Ortlip

www.ballantinebooks.com

Library of Congress Cataloging-in-Publication Data is available upon request.

ISBN 0-345-44342-X

Text design by Holly Johnson

Manufactured in the United States of America

First Edition: April 2002

10   9   8   7   6   5   4   3   2   1

For my sisters,
Kate, Shari, Danielle, and Michele

THE WINDY WATERS

The windy waters dance at night
In circles by the shore.
They whisper to the trees in sight,
"Come join the ocean floor!

The sky is wild and full of life,"
The waters tell the trees.
"Forget your many years of strife
And feel the easy breeze.

"Lift the roots that hold you down,
For they are tired and worn.
Let the sun become your crown
To hide you from the storm."

With ancient grace and peaceful pride
The bounded figures know
That with the eagles of the tide
They are not free to go.

To leave what they have always been
And blow it to the sea
Will give the trees a way to swim
But will not make them free.

The windy waters dance at night
And the white moon seems to know
The ocean can teach the trees to laugh
But never how to grow.

SHARON ORTLIP

Table of Contents

~

Our lives, blessed and frequently confused by the mysterious behavior of parents who had been given the wrong tickets to a marriage, began on the Palisade Cliffs in Fort Lee, New Jersey. We were perched there, in our world of flower gardens and wind, surveying the landscape carved out by glacier and then built up by human hands. Small, brittle lights glistened from across the Hudson River in Manhattan into our bedrooms at night. Tales of Revolutionary War battles that had been fought on the very rock where we were about to sleep merged with the stories of what lay in that wicked city beyond the river. Our sacred cliffs held us aloft, above the realities of humanity, past and present.

There were five of us children in all, five girls born within seven years to Paul, an artist, like his parents, and Miriam, wife, mother, and psychologist, graduating with high honors and a master's degree from Ohio State University. Getting married was a chance Mom took in the hopes of finding love, of which she had always felt deprived. Their mothers arranged the initial meeting of our parents. When Dad and Mom accepted this fate, caught up in the romance that a long-distance written correspondence can evoke, they soon discovered nothing existed for them to dream about together, except for the creation of children.

As each new sister arrived, the bond among us grew stronger, especially after our mother left. We became like a hand, fingers moving and behaving on their own yet functioning together. By the time Michele was born, the fifth and last cellular creation of our parents during their doomed thirteen-year marriage, the hand was complete, a final balance achieved. Each one of us was essentially placed, becoming the sister the rest of us had been waiting to welcome into this world.

Into my first-born consciousness, the cliffs came toward me in the light of each day, steepling up out of the Hudson River and ending in front of our living room window, which faced east, toward the morning sun. In my young mind, they had been cut out by the hands of God, or perhaps torn out by a giant's teeth or laid out by a masterful magician as curtains for mythical creatures to hide behind.

Then came my sisters, created by fairies who lived in Manhattan and retrieved by my parents, who always went over to the city to bring back the next one from the hospital, the factory where I imagined my sisters were made. What my mother's large belly had to do with their creation I didn't discover until preadolescence, when an older neighborhood girl told me what parents really did to produce babies.

Say either word now, "sisters" or "cliffs," and the thunder in my heart begins. These storms of remembrance rain warm and passionate, the smashing brilliance of lightning strikes bringing memories into the light.

Cliffs and sisters, residing in skin, bone, and cell. I tell this story in honor of both. I also tell this story in honor of everyone who has come from the land of sisters. You'll remember.

I

~

The Cliff Years: 1954–72

Kate, Shari, Danielle, Carol, Michele
Displaying photographs of Julie Andrews, 1966.

THE GRAND MARSHAL

The parade is beginning. I sit myself on the back hood of the designated turquoise convertible, the top down and squashed flat. Al, the driver, adjusts the mirrors and his black felt hat, one of the five or so that he received from Frank Sinatra, whom he was pals with and worked for back in the 1950s. Al's been in ninety-six movies, mostly appearing in the role of Italian mobster. I can certainly understand why. Distinctly Italian-looking, especially his nose, his face displays the stereotypical features of a Sicilian thug, particularly when he snarls, which is only when the car will not respond the way he thinks it should. Al likes to smile, and he is doing a lot of it right now.

Just before we pull away from the curb, edging forward into the lead car position, Al tells me he was denied a driver's license at his most recent test. I am tempted to ask him why the parade officials, which include law officers, are allowing him to drive me, the Grand Marshal of the Heritage Day Parade 2000 in Fort Lee, New Jersey, the length of the parade route, approximately 1.2 miles. But

I stifle the question. After all, he is clearly enjoying this experience enormously.

Al took a particular liking to Gemma, my life partner of ten years, who is walking along on the sidewalk, and the two of them looked like family, long lost, now found, as they stood side by side, chatting amiably before the parade began. Gemma is half-Italian and she could easily pass for Al's daughter or granddaughter.

As soon as we begin moving, I'm not worried about Al's driving. The pace of the parade is so slow, it would be difficult for anyone to veer off course, even Al.

Everyone along the parade route seems to know Al. As our dusky aquamarine convertible creeps along, with the rumpled white-and-brown Grand Marshal banners hanging off either side and flapping in the late September wind, they shout, "It's Al! Hey, Al!" They also shout out, as they point at me, "It's the Grand Marshal," and then, after they have gotten a good look at me, "Who is she?"

There is no program handed out explaining who the participants are. For the most part, you can tell who is in it by the costumes or the signage or the uniforms. There is no reason anyone would know who I am unless they recognize me from years ago or the parade organizer has told them who I am or I've told them who I am. All together, the number of people who know me tops off at around fifteen, give or take five or six people. The Grand Marshal was supposed to be someone else: my father. A lot more people would have known the Grand Marshal if it had been him.

This year, the Heritage Committee is honoring my family for our artistic contributions to the Fort Lee, New Jersey, community. It all started seventy-five years ago, in the 1920s, when my grandparents, Williard and Aimee, purchased and renovated a restaurant called Gerth's Belvedere, which had been built on the Palisade Cliffs and was frequented by wild bohemian types, into living and painting space. After settling in, my grandparents unleashed their talent and their seven children into the unsuspecting town. Paintings created by my grandparents have long since been taken down and put up on other walls far from Fort Lee, but the Fort Lee Firehouse is still home to a mural my father painted, which honors firemen everywhere. Have a civil suit tried in the Fort Lee courthouse and you'll be sure to see dozens of portraits my father painted of judges and mayors, their eyes following you no matter which way you turn.

Although Fort Lee has changed significantly, growing exponentially in all directions, there is a strong core of people who are striving to hold onto its heritage, thus the Heritage Day parade and the creation of the Fort Lee Historical Museum. Along the walls of the refurbished stone structure, just a block away from where our house on the cliffs once stood, three of my father's paintings are now on display in a permanent collection. The museum is where I wind up at the end of this day as Grand Marshal.

Why am I Grand Marshal? My father asked me to represent him and our family, after facing the fact that he wasn't in good enough health to attend. Living in Florida now and recently diagnosed with what is known as "old person's leukemia," Dad would rather sit these kinds of events out. Just a few years back, he not only would have shown up; he also would have jumped into the role of Grand Marshal with his unique brand of silly enthusiasm. What about Kate? Michele perhaps? Kate lives too far away, and, to be truthful, she isn't exactly parade material; I'm sure she would agree. Michele is way too pregnant, even though she is definitely parade material. (I'm writing her in as Grand Marshal for next year, and, who knows, maybe Dad will be well enough to join her then.)

In the end, though, I'm glad I got to be Grand Marshal. It is as

I ride along the parade route, with Al as my navigator and Gemma as my compass, that I get to wave through to memories of an old Fort Lee. These memories appear like canvasses, painted by my father and my grandparents, arrested moments of history flying out and away into this altered terrain. I can see Old Man Yoman holding his age-worn pipe; the old abandoned Kinstler house gasping with the winds of emptiness; Shari and Danielle pushing their baby carriages down the lawn at the far end of our garden; Michele's upturned face rising into a huge bouquet of recently picked lilacs; Kate sitting placidly in a rocking chair, holding a curly-haired doll that looks just like her; the carousel at Palisades Amusement Park, packed with the bright faces of swirling children; Dad standing on the cliffs as a boy, his hand gently resting on the back of his beloved goat, Go-go; and the Manhattan skyline in the early evening.

These images are forever held in a breathless dimension, viewed by those of us who have come to the parade and by those who could not be here but have not forgotten life on the cliffs. I'm sure that microscopic bits of cliff rock are still embedded in my palms, where they have been for over twenty-five years, and as I wave to those who have come here to remember, the cliffs are surely moving within me.

I wave for my family. I wave for the cliffs. I wave for those who are here today.

But mostly, I wave for my sisters, Kate, Shari, Danielle, and Michele.

I

~

FADE IN, FADE OUT

It is mid-April in northern New Jersey, magnolia time. Every year Dad cuts a few sprigs of magnolias and paints a portrait of them with the view of the river as background. While he paints and our mother sits, three of my sisters and I spend as much time as we can in the arms of our beloved "Maggie," the graceful, venerable magnolia tree that grows in the middle of what we call the castle woods. Our house adorns the top of the cliff, five hundred yards or so above an actual castle that was built during World War I by a German spy named Knoche. I have many questions about this spy named Knoche: It takes a long time to build a castle; why didn't anyone figure out that he was a spy during the time the castle was being built? How was it finally discovered that he was a spy? What did he look like? Did he live by himself? Did he have friends? Did he have children? The fact that he existed at all and probably walked the very woods where my sisters and I now carry out our adventures gives the castle woods a vibrant sense of foreboding, as if old spy Knoche could materialize at any moment and scare the wits out of us. Maggie, sleek and bright, rises up out of this mythical thicket, urging us to do one thing: climb.

And she is perfect for climbing, each branch placed almost steplike for our experienced climbing legs. I reach one of the top branches quickly. Surrounding me are the freshest blooms, the tasseled centers hurling their scents toward my nose. I shut my eyes and plant my face in the nearest blossom. My arms and legs are totally familiar with Maggie's branches; if they weren't, I would certainly sway from magnolia swooning and fall out of her. I've already fallen out of a tree once, and I am determined not to let it happen again. The scent of magnolias enters my bones hypnotically, and I remain in this state for a good five minutes, the scent taking me to past lives, to dreams, out of my body right into the flower. I know my sisters would agree. I peek up over the petals to find Kate, Shari, and Danielle face-first in a blossom, eyes closed, smiles shimmering.

There is a game we play here among the earliest spring blossoms: "the shoe game." Since I am the one perched at the highest point, one of my shoes is designated as "the shoe." I remove my right shoe and get ready to throw it down to Danielle, who remains on the ground for this round. Although barely three years old and not always able to negotiate the knobby and rocky earth of our cliff domain, she is old enough to play the shoe game as the "groundy."

Our climbing training starts early here on the cliffs, and usually it begins at the rock slide over in the evil woods below Mr. Thompson's garden, out of which we steal rhubarb every spring. Our rock slide, frequently at the center of our games, becomes a waterfall or a tunnel or a great stream of volcanic lava. Danielle can already scamper up the face of the rock slide without any help from Shari, Kate, or me; she's obviously a natural climber. Michele, only one year old, is still too young for her initiation onto cliff rock. But soon. She's inside today, with Mom. In the back of my mind, I keep track of the position of the sun and the length of the shadows. Dad has been asking me to keep a check-in schedule going for Michele on the days that he goes to work at the university. We can't leave Michele alone for too long with Mom because Mom hasn't shown any interest in taking care of her at all. Mom was so attentive with Danielle when she was a baby, but she isn't the same with Michele. What we'll probably find when we get home is either Michele in the playpen, sucking on a bottle that has been placed on that small rubber bottle holder shaped like a chopped-down tree, or Michele playing quietly with a toy, and Mom watching television alone in the playroom.

I've been very aware of Mom's and Dad's behavior lately. They never talk with each other unless it is about boring scheduling stuff. Dad still takes her into New York City for doctor visits, leaving us with baby-sitters. I've overheard all kinds of phone conversations between Dad and doctors, Mom and doctors, Dad and his friends, Mom and her friends. I've heard words and phrases like "treatments," "divorce," "in the dark," "utter chaos,"and "can't take it." All I know is, my sisters and I have got to keep quiet and not upset anyone, especially Mom. She might wind up back in that mental hospital again.

Danielle yells up, "Throw the shoe!" I toss it to her as softly as I can, but she still can't catch it, letting it drop to the ground. After a half-dozen attempts, Danielle gets the shoe to Shari, who is just a little way up a side branch. We cheer and cheer. Danielle stands pigeon-toed, kicking the dirt at her feet and looking down in humble yet proud acknowledgment. Shari then flings the shoe to Kate, who has shimmied up a narrow branch that is on the opposite side of Maggie from where I am. If Kate isn't able to grab it the first time, the whole process will start again. I close my eyes, wishing for a lucky first toss. I hear Kate exclaim, "Got it!" We cheer and cheer. Then, of course, Kate must try to get the shoe back to me. It's a hard maneuver: Kate must throw the shoe at a really awkward angle, above and behind her head. Wrapping both my legs around the branch for stability, I extend both arms to Kate. She winds up and lets the shoe fly. One of the shoelaces gets caught on a small branch and the shoe falls toward the ground. The shoe hangs in the air, shoelace attached to this branch. Kate disengages the lace and tries again, this time tucking the laces inside the shoe. She makes a great throw that is about one inch short of my hands, but I stretch with determination and snatch the shoe out of the air, almost coming dislodged from my spot. My sisters gasp as I reorient myself. We cheer and cheer and cheer.

Because we are successful on our first round of the shoe game, it's agreed that we can have one more adventure before going home. We head for the rope-swing-of-no-return, which is farther down the cliff below the rock slide and within sight of the old Kinstler place. This swing, put up by older cousins during a summer visit, soars out over an impressive abyss. Kate once walked in front of the swing as someone began her initial and powerful descending swoop. She was hit by the swinging body and flung out into the air, landing facedown beside a boulder that was bigger than our station wagon. We sighed in relief as she raised her head and began crying: no broken bones or torn skin. After that, the swing became a legend and even more of a draw to kids from all over the neighborhood. They regularly come down the tricky path just to get a look at it hanging there, almost nooselike.

Standing at the rope swing, looking up at our house sitting atop the Palisades, I always feel a great surge of anticipation and joy because I know there are still at least a hundred million glens, crevices, rocks, springs, wells, bluffs, or trees to explore. There are easily a billion games to play, a zillion characters to become, and we can do it all right here beneath the protective, watchful gaze of our house.

Michele is where we left her, in the playpen. Her bottle long since emptied, her diaper looking uncomfortably soaked, and her face blotched from the tears already wasted, she looks up at us through the wooden slats with the expression of someone abandoned. Mom is in the playroom, watching a soap opera and smoking Salems. She turns her head to watch as Kate and I take care of Michele, changing her diaper and straightening up the playpen. Kate and I are both good at changing diapers now. I ask Mom if we can take Michele out into the yard. "It's a beautiful day, Mom." She shakes her head "yes" as we head to the grassy yard by the small brown shingled playhouse Dad built for us. It can hold all of us if we jam ourselves inside. We spend the next couple of hours here, playing games that incorporate a baby (deftly played by Michele) into the plots. Kate and Danielle pretend they're either mothers or aunts while Shari and I offer ourselves as variations on the male theme: fathers, neighbors, or uncles. This is a natural coupling order that evolved during the first summer Danielle was old enough to understand the game of "house." Kate and I easily became a duo, with Shari and Danielle slipping right behind as the second couple in command. Somewhere during the development of my partnership with Kate, Shari, Danielle, and Michele became "the kids," clumped together for convenience' sake, especially as Kate and I became more responsible for them, talking about them as if they were our children.

We have the most well adjusted family ever; everyone, including the mother, is in the best mental condition possible. We are extremely mentally fit and will never need treatments or visits to a mental hospital. We're so mentally fit, our neighbors (played by Shari and Danielle) come over to watch us and ask for advice on how to become healthy and stay that way.

Dad arrives home from his job teaching art classes at Fairleigh Dickinson University in Teaneck and finds us all observing Kate as she demonstrates the proper techniques for being a healthy mother. (Rule # 1: Never watch soap operas.) I notice Dad's eyes scanning us as he approaches. Turning to view us as Dad might see us, I suddenly realize how filthy Michele has gotten, how bedraggled Danielle is, how grimy we all are. Ashamed that he has come home to find us this way, I start brushing Michele off, which is a waste of time. Dad ignores the fact that we're a mess, though. He kisses each one of us as if he hasn't seen us in weeks, picks Michele up, and heads inside.

"Where's your mother?" he asks, all of us pushing up close after him.

"Watching TV," Kate responds.

After Dad changes Michele's diaper and washes off most of the dirt that is covering practically every inch of her little body, he starts preparing dinner, all the while making animal faces and noises for Michele's entertainment. The rest of us assess Mom's mood (she's definitely in a bad one, we can see from the full ashtray), wash our faces and hands, and then draw with our beloved twenty-four-color Crayola set. Mom eats alone from a tray Dad provides in the playroom while Dad, my sisters, and I eat at the dining room table.

"Whatja do today, girls?"

"We played, Dad," I report.

"Anybody go on the rope swing?"

"No, Dad," I lie, but it's not a total lie. We didn't let Danielle go for a ride on it.

"You girls be careful," he softly instructs.

I'm not sure what Dad would do if he found out that we had lied and gone on the forbidden rope swing. He has only hit me once, and that was when I took Shari down to the Hudson River during a hurricane to show her the rats I had discovered earlier on a walk with some school friends. When Dad discovered (Danielle spilled the beans) our absence, he ran down Old Palisades Road to come get us. Shari and I were already on our way home, and we intersected Dad at the bottom of the hill. Dad's face was the reddest I'd ever seen it. He grabbed my hand and, holding it as hard as he could, whacked my bottom with enough force to lift my feet off the asphalt. I didn't cry or respond in any way, because I knew I deserved this punishment.

My sisters and I have to lie sometimes. We have come to understand that Dad has plenty to worry about and telling him about certain activities would just make life worse for him. Like our climbing skills, learning how to protect our parents from needless worry begins early, so when he asks about the rope swing our faces go blank with just a nip of sincerity: in protective mode, we can convincingly shake our heads with "Oh no, Dad." Somehow we know that it's not really what you would call lying. Of course no one has formally instructed us in the ways of parent protection. We watch and we learn. We protect and we climb.

A few days later, my sisters and I, returning from playing on the cliffs after school, enter the house to find Michele not with Mom but with Mary Octer, the German housekeeper Dad has hired to help out when he can't be around. She seems to be coming over a lot more recently.

"Where's Mom?" I ask nervously.

"You'll have to ask your father when he gets back," she answers curtly.

We know not to ask again. Mary Octer doesn't like to be asked questions twice. I'm pretty sure I already know the answer. Mom's gone back to the mental hospital, the fortress known as Greystone. The other question we have is, "Why?" The first time she went, Dad told me it was because she was sad. That's what I don't understand. I don't think she should be sent to that scary place just because she is sad. We'll cheer her up. I know we can. We just need to figure out what will make her happy again.

Before Dad gets back, Kate asks me if I think there's a mental hospital for sad kids. I suppose there is, but I don't tell Kate that. I don't want her to think that we'll end up there. I know that my sisters and I are sad, but we've been trying with all our might to be happy, especially in front of Dad, Mom, schoolteachers, relatives, and, now, Mary Octer.

It's late when Dad gets home. All the kids are asleep except for Kate and me. Kate helped put Danielle to sleep and I soothed Shari until she was close enough to falling asleep that I could confidently leave her. Michele went right off to sleep as Mary Octer sang her lullabies. I almost fell asleep, too, but made myself stay awake so I could see Dad.

"You girls still up?" Dad asks through a forced smile. He looks tired. Neither Kate nor I ask about Mom, and he doesn't volunteer anything, yet. I suspect that he will call me into the studio tomorrow to break whatever news there is about Mom. That's been the routine ever since all of this business started with her. Dad calls me into the studio after school and explains the latest. It's as I thought:

Mom is definitely sad again and needs help from those special doctors at Greystone. They are going to "pull her out of this thing,
Carolina."

As I gather my sisters around me and repeat what Dad has
said, they eye me doubtfully.

"What is she in, Carol?" Shari wants to know.

A few weeks after Mom has gone back to the mental hospital and
Maggie has dropped the last of her spongy petals glazing the ground
beneath her with a rust-colored mush, it's lilac time. In May, my
sisters and I sell bunches of lilacs up on Lemoine Avenue in front
of the A & P, the first supermarket in town. A red wagon filled
with tied branches of lilacs that we have cut from the bushes that
form the borders of our yard serves as our vending stand.

The four of us (or five when Michele joins us later) sit behind
the wagon, backs against the wall of the A & P, smiling meekly and
solicitously at the passing lilac lovers, of which there are plenty.
This particular year lilac time falls on Mother's Day and we almost
can't keep up with the demand. We hustle back and forth, replen-
ishing our supply at least five times in one day. Our lilac bushes
never seem to become depleted from our harvesting; there are always enough blooms for us.

Returning home from our day's work, we meet on the red Oriental rug in the living room to count our earnings and talk about
the lilac-selling events. Shari wants to know why so many people
seem sad even when they're in the middle of giving flowers to their
mothers. Kate wants to resolve the pricing issue: should we let people try to talk the price down or should we say, "The price is
fixed"? Danielle wants to give the lilacs away for free to anyone
who seems even the least bit sad. I want everyone in the world to

be happy, especially Mom, so we make a special bouquet for her; we're going to visit her at the hospital tomorrow.

My sisters, Mary Octer, and I wait on a bench just in front of the building where Dad has gone to get Mom. Michele is the only one making any noise; the rest of us sit silently, swinging our legs, Danielle holding the bouquet of lilacs. Mary Octer tells us to stop fidgeting. We do.

We look up to see Dad guiding Mom out of the building by one of her elbows. He brings her over to the bench and we get up immediately, allowing her to sit alone, kind of like a queen might sit before her subjects. Shari and Danielle present the bouquet to Mom, their little voices squeaking out, "Happy Mother's Day." Mom looks from one face to the next; she seems to be searching for something. The five of us grouped closely together (Dad and Mary Octer are standing off to the side respectfully, giving us this moment with Mom) simply watch and wait for a clear signal of dismissal. We're not sure what to do with Mom anymore. Some of us used to know what to do with Mom: Kate, Shari, Danielle, and me especially. Mom used to touch us gently with her fingertips, which usually meant she had a smile ready for one or all of us. We would look at her then and keep looking until she smiled back. She used to reach for us, too, inviting one or more of us into a long, tight hug. I guess she doesn't know how to do these things anymore because she is so sad.

Danielle darts over to Mom and kisses her cheek. This compels each one of us to kiss her, too. Holding Michele closely, I dip her over so she can kiss Mom's face. Mom responds with a small smile, and then the five of us start making our way over to Dad and Mary Octer. I turn to look at Mom, our eyes meeting for a second. In the time it takes for me to blink, she averts her face and brings the lilacs up to hide behind. I swing around, turning my back to her, hesitating slightly. I want her to call after me, to stretch out her arms for some kind of Mother's Day embrace. When she doesn't, I shake away my longing and rejoin my sisters.

Danielle takes Mom's hand and we all get into the car. Today's treat will be lunch at a local diner in Parsippany. Some treat. Everyone is so nervous (except Michele, and even she is probably able to pick up the tension), the food on our plates remains in little untouched blobs, barely poked at by forks or registered by anyone's attention. The only one to eat is Michele. I want to ask Mom questions, but none of them seem appropriate. ("What do you do in the mental hospital, Mom? Do you have any friends?") My sisters and I act as happy as we can, which is very difficult to do because we're not saying anything. We sit in the diner booth with goofy smiles on our faces. I'm positive that anyone looking at us would have to conclude we were a family of mentally unfit people, even after all that practicing. The only person who looks normal is Michele, and that's because she's a baby. A couple of times during this torturous meal, Mary Octer looks at us quizzically and shakes her head. She probably thinks we're being rude, making fun of Mom and the entire situation, which we're not.

I start feeling giddy. My cheeks are beginning to ache from holding them in a smile. I'm tempted to fling food at Kate or, worse, Mary Octer. Under the table, I kick Kate's leg. She scowls at me. I pinch Danielle, who is sitting next to me. She barely reacts, keeping a smile scratched into her face. I can't take much more of this; I ask to be excused so I can go to the ladies' room.

"Does anyone else have to go?" I ask in a helpful older-sister voice. Every sister (except Michele) nods with a big "yes." The four of us haul off to the bathroom, where nervous jabber begins and is sustained until we finish with this concluding purpose: "Let's make Mom smile somehow." We certainly try. A couple of times I think I see Mom's mouth beginning the side curve toward a smile, but it never turns into a full-blown, genuine smile.

Little, oh so little, did my sisters and I know about what our mother was enduring behind the medieval-looking walls of Greystone. Looking back now, I realize Mom never could have smiled, painfully aware of what she was heading back into. When Mom finally told us many years later about what really went on behind those cold stone walls, my sisters and I were incredulous. It couldn't have been that bad, we had been insisting for over a decade. In an unwavering monotone, Mom described one of her ordeals. During the ten-week second visit, she was being administered insulin, which was one of the chemical shock treatment choices of that time, and one night, unmonitored, almost slipped into a coma and died. A male attendant who found her lying unconscious on the linoleum floor of the bathroom pulled her up off the floor by her breasts and dragged her back to bed, where he administered the antidote. Somewhere in the middle of her description, my sisters and I, with the creeping disintegration of our necessary denial, silently and guiltily acknowledged the truth.

I imagine as Mom walked out the door of Greystone, turning to see the door closing behind her, she must've thought to herself that she would never allow herself to be treated so cruelly again. Soon after she returned home with renewed determination to change her life and pick up where she had left off after graduating from college, Mom got herself a job in Manhattan giving IQ tests. It was there that she met a man named Frank and a whole new romantic, intellectually stimulating life and, eventually, a different type of mental incarceration began for her.

———

My sisters and I meet Frank one night when Dad is away. It's summer, the magnolia, lilac, and wisteria long since shriveled up, turned to brown husks by the sun. Michele has just turned two years old, and I'll be nine soon. On a particularly hot and dense evening, Mom announces that a man from work is coming over to help with some important papers. We view them from the playroom as they sit at the dining room table, supposedly working. Some work. They are mostly staring at each other, barely glancing at the papers sitting in front of them, which is leading me to conclude that this talk of work is just another story from the mouths of adults who think children aren't capable of figuring out what is really going on.

I hear this man, who asks us to call him Frank, suggest that we all go for a drive to the river since it's such a lovely night. Mom goes to check on Michele, who is asleep in her crib. I can't believe my ears when I hear this man say that we can go anyway: "We'll only stay long enough for a quick stroll. The baby won't even know we've been gone." I'm horrified. Horrified and scared to refute him. He might get mad at me or my sisters, and who knows what he will do? He seems like the mean type. I look to Mom for a sign that she will resist his suggestion, but she doesn't and so we all leave for the river, except for Michele who remains in her crib, asleep.

Mom and the man from work walk to the end of the dock by the river while Kate, Shari, Danielle, and I squirm together in absolute unconditional concern for Michele. We stare at the two of them, and I am hoping that all of our collective worry will crash through their blocked heads to a place of sense. It's then that we see them kiss. Oh, great.

"They're kissing," Shari whispers loudly.

"Mom, can we go now?" I yell out in the middle of their unbelievably obnoxious, stupid kiss.

The man, trying to be polite I guess, says that it's probably a good idea. "Don't want to leave the baby for too long." C'mon, c'mon, c'mon. Let's go.

Michele is still asleep when we get home, thank God. I watch the man walk to his car after their "work night." I wish with all of my internal organs that as he drives home, wherever that may be, he and his car are swallowed by a huge hole in the ground and that we never have to see him again. It is as he drives away that my loathing for Frank begins to settle.

Dad is packing up our blue station wagon, named Cindy With Guts, for our annual summer trip to our cousins' house in upstate New York. The letters of our license plate are CWG 740, and somehow Dad came up with the name Cindy With Guts. As far as we're concerned, Cindy With Guts is the best car in the world: she is royal blue, reliable (she's never broken down), strong, and very familiar. When we ride in Cindy With Guts my sisters and I feel utterly safe and excited, because getting into Cindy With Guts usually means that we're heading for adventure with our Dad at the controls. My sisters and I actually believe Cindy With Guts has a soul; we make sure she is treated respectfully. We write songs for her—Dad does, too—and we sing them when we go on trips. Some of our best times have been traveling along in Cindy With Guts, together, crunched up in our blankets in the back, singing, "Oh, how we like to go for a ride and see the country far and wide . . ." from the Alvin and the Chipmunks television show.

This time is no different; we are heading for one of our favorite places in the world: our cousins' house. Everything would be great, except for the fact that a secretive and still very sad Mom is coming with us. She doesn't seem like part of the family as she climbs into Cindy With Guts. Sitting in the passenger seat, Mom looks totally foreign, and Cindy With Guts knows it, I can tell. If Cindy With Guts had an ejector seat, Mom would be flying right out the top into the fishpond, and we would be on the road without her.

My sisters and I stay at our cousins' long enough to play out our anxiety. The sheltered world of this remote upstate New York village, where the majority of my father's family lives, offers my sisters and me relief from the stress of constantly trying to make sense of the confusing state our lives have been in with Mom and Dad. Here we are free to let go of our rehearsed posturing and our careful, observant stances that have practically lifted the spontaneity right out of our bodies. We run crazed through the pine-needled landscape with cousins of all shapes and sizes but only one religious inclination. I get to spend time with my favorite cousin, Priscilla. She is just about the right age (a little over a year and a half older) to be my older sister, and sometimes she acts like one, bossing me around as I imagine an older sister might, but it's all right; I like it. Our play is not without supervision of the Methodist kind, but our aunts and uncles seem to understand that what my sisters and I are in insane need of is uninhibited play (with Methodist suggested behavioral rules of conduct as guidelines of course). And so we play, kindly and cooperatively, but with ruthless passion.

Mom sits it out, barely interacting with my father's side of the family, who are the only relatives to be found; all of Mom's kin are in Ohio. There are plenty of aunts and uncles to take care of Michele, so Mom can sit it out. When we come in from our well-mannered yet rumbly games, Mom is lying on a couch, reading. It's clear that the other adults don't know what to do with her, either; everyone just leaves her alone.

On our last night, Dad, Mom, my sisters, and I are gathered up for the annual photograph. It is the last one ever taken of us together as a family. We sit all pushed together, each of us looking washed out and desperately posed. It's easy to see that the expressions on our faces are not smiles but grimaces.

Home again, home again, and Shari heads into a mischievous spell, which may have contributed to sending Mom out the door, finishing off the final phase of her fade-out.

One day, Shari gets out the Vaseline and, with her hands, spreads it all over the stairs leading from Dad's studio up into the kitchen of our house, one of the two ways to get inside. She's been trying to figure out how to make an indoor waterfall for weeks; finally, she does. Danielle is right there with Shari, spreading Vaseline with total assistant zeal. They don't tell anyone, so no one is able to warn Mrs. Gaihard, a kind elderly woman who is in the generous habit of bringing fruit to cheer up our mother, not to come in this way. Mrs. Gaihard speaks in a heavy Dutch accent and usually calls out a grand, "Halloooo!" when she enters our house. Today we hear a grand, "AIEEEEE!" followed by a huge thump as she hits the stairs and slides down. She lands face-first at the base of the stairs, fruit mashed and scattered. The thump and screech rouse Mom from her cementlike state and she stands at the top of the stairs staring at the awkwardly splayed Mrs. Gaihard, who is sputtering, "Dun't come down dose steps. Dere ess somesing on dem."

Shari and Danielle are nowhere in sight, and so Mom turns to me. I smile and shake my head, trying to silently convey to her that I know nothing about this, even though that isn't entirely true.

"Where is Shari?" she inquires with clear and potent rage gathering in her face. This is certainly the most animated I've seen her in a long time, and I'm almost happy about it, except for the fact that Mrs. Gaihard is lying wounded at the bottom of our stairs, fruit squashed against her nylon-stockinged legs and Vaseline slathering her black orthopedic shoes.

"Go get her," Mom commands with a directness I hardly recognize.

Shari and Danielle are out behind the playhouse. Kate and I march down to them like the little parental unit we have become. We stand, hands on hips, glaring at them.

"You're in trouble," Kate warns.

"Why?" Shari asks. She has already focused on the next adventure and has practically forgotten the waterfall.

"The stairs, Shari? Remember?" I fill in.

"The waterfall?" she asks.

"Yes. Mrs. Gaihard just slid right down the stairs. She's hurt."

Shari instantly starts to cry, which makes Danielle cry, too. Great. Now I'm totally confused about what to do. How can I turn them over to Mom? She could fly off and whack them with a hanger like she did to me when I was five years old and poured water into my pink pajamas with the attached feet to see if the feet would hold water. They didn't.

"I'll talk to Mom; you go hide. Kate, you hide with the kids."

I don't hear a thing as I enter the house. No Mrs. Gaihard howling. God, maybe she's dead; Shari would really be in trouble then. I run up the back staircase, rounding the corner of our living room to find Mom back in the playroom, watching television, without the slightest wisp of anger or sadness on her face. Michele must be asleep in her crib: no sounds from her. I race to the top of the studio stairs, in a state of fear: Mrs. Gaihard is gone—she must've gone back to her house across the street—and lying in her stead at the bottom of the stairs is a small, neat pile of damaged fruit.

As I pass the playroom on my way back outside, I say quietly in Mom's direction, "Shari is very sorry, Mom."

She moves her head so slowly toward me, I'm not sure it's moving at all. "I know she is, Carol." She begins to say something else, her lips opening just a crack. Say it Mom. Please. Say something to me. Say something. Please. Her mouth closes, and she looks away.

There is nothing I can do. There is nothing I can do. There is nothing I can do. There is nothing I can do.

I collapse right there and start to cry, not loud enough for Mom to hear, not loud enough for anyone to hear.

2

~

OUR MOTHER, GONE

Mom is sobbing. She sits alone with a cigarette in her fingers, ashes falling into an ashtray one of us has made for her at school. Dark, straight hair pulled back tightly, she looks as if she is wincing. I want her to stop crying—her face so splotchy and puffed I can't look—but she won't stop, and nobody can help. We've tried. Dad is standing behind us, his arms crossed over his chest, arm hair poking out from under his flannel shirt. He is impassive. I try to muster up some tears, but I just can't, or better, I just won't. I hate my mother right now with all of my blood. I hate her for crying for what seems like years. I hate her for making Dad so angry and distant, for making all of us so jittery that we can't sit or stand or play or do anything without worrying if we are disturbing her. I want my mother to die or go away, back to the mental hospital even, anywhere, just as long as it is away from us.

At Christmas, my sisters and I always open our presents in the living room beneath the big windows that face east, our view of the
Hudson River and New York City unobscured this time of year.
The silver buildings appear closer in the winter, as if magnified by
the cold and frigid air. Dad's paintings hang on every wall; the one
nearest me is of the old Kinstler place down the cliff. Boarded
up and hollow, it was abandoned years ago by the family, and that
is how Dad painted it. The room seems abnormally quiet for a
Christmas morning. Maybe it is because both our parents are subdued, standing to the sides, viewing us as if we are behind glass, on
display in some department store window. I keep glancing around
to see what they are up to. At first I think they might have a large
present for one of us hidden somewhere, like a bicycle for Kate or a
big doll for Michele, and are plotting the exact moment to spring
it. But they aren't talking to each other at all; there can be no plot
brewing. Dad occasionally jumps in making animal noises or silly
faces, pretending he is about to steal one of our presents away.

Somewhere in the middle of the morning, I turn and both our
parents are gone. I don't say anything, not wanting to draw attention to their absence and take the chance of scaring my sisters.
When Dad returns a few minutes later, I ask where Mom went, to
which he replies, "She's moved to New York to live for a while."
From the way he is talking, his eyes averted and his voice barely
audible, we can tell that he doesn't want us to ask any questions,
and so we go back to opening and playing with our presents, the
image of Manhattan in plain sight.

It takes Kate and me about a week to figure out that our mother
hasn't been escorted back to the hospital again with the promise of
recovery and return. We come to understand, after piecing to-

gether information that has filtered down to us from what Dad isn't saying about her and what friends and family are saying about her, that Mom has finally roused herself from the sleep of the weary, disenchanted, and hormonally disabled long enough to get herself out the door and into Manhattan. The fact that she chose Christmas morning ultimately does not matter. When would it have been a better morning to leave?

Awkwardly my sisters, my father, and I begin shifting the weight of our bodies into the empty space Mom has left behind. We had gotten used to sliding around her as if she had been living on an island, separate from us. We would watch her from across our distance, constantly wondering if the moment had arrived when reaching out for her was possible. We had spent a lot of time in silent observation of her face and posture, waiting. Occasionally she would venture toward us demonstratively, taking one or, sometimes two, of us into her arms for an embrace or a story. When she behaved effusively, I shrank back, afraid she might hurt me or one of my sisters in a crazy gesture of pent-up love; she wasn't expressive often, and I stopped myself from doing things that would cause her to respond emotionally. I encouraged my sisters to restrain themselves as well with my finger to my lips in a "Shhh" or great shakes of my head in a "No. Not that." Now here is all this space to navigate. How should we move and behave?

Accompanying our growing realization that she is gone are new questions and doubts. Dad attempts to explain our mother's departure with these words to Kate and me: "Your mother doesn't love me anymore." That explanation does not exactly satisfy us, and consequently, in the sister conferences that follow, unanswerable questions continue to erupt.

Many decisions about our fate are made without us, as is done in most families when the welfare of children is being considered.

We were told, years later, that our father was adamant about keeping the five of us together despite the financial demands of raising five girls on his own and despite the fact that aunts and uncles from both sides of the family were volunteering to take one or two until "things calmed down." There was even talk about Mom taking Danielle and me (we had always been, up until the time of her departure, the most "cooperative") to live with her in Manhattan. But Dad would have none of it; his position on this subject was unshakable, as if he knew intuitively that we needed to stay together, no matter what.

Our mother's visiting schedule is determined without us, too, and soon after she leaves she is back, bearing groceries and the ingredients for our favorite dishes, like blueberry turnovers, macaroni and cheese, and hamburger stew. As soon as I see my mother walk through the door, I am set on making it difficult for her. How dare she just come right back into the house without a word of apology or explanation, even if she did have a sickness called depression? I will not speak to her, and after a few weeks of what I consider a charade I convince my sisters that we really do not want Mom coming to visit us anymore: "Right, kids?" In the well-established sibling structure, I am, at age nine, the powerful and mighty top kid. Although I have been in charge for some time, ever since Mom left, my role has taken on clearer definition and become more of a necessity. Someone has to be the leader, and I'm the obvious one to do the job. My sisters comply with just about every decision I make, especially the ones that have to do with Mom; I feel really important every time my sisters look at me as I hand down my rulings. The only thing that bothers me is when Shari says, "You are so serious, Carol," which she says often.

I ask Dad if we can speak about Mom. We sit on stools, and I tell him that Kate, Shari, Danielle, Michele, and I don't want to see Mom anymore. He does not try to convince me otherwise. He simply asks, "Are you sure, Carol?"

It is a damp, cool Saturday morning when Mom comes back again. Dad meets her at the studio door and they speak quietly. We can hear their voices, soft as gauze, raveling and unraveling in the air between them. I cannot make out the words, only the tones. I suddenly and urgently want to race down the stairs and scream, "No. Wait. You can visit. We don't mean it!" But I remain where I am, huddled with my sisters, thinking about my mother's back and how many times I have seen it receding into some vanishing point. Then Mom and Dad's talking stops. We rush downstairs to watch her walk away. Mom's solemn figure, in a black-and-white checkered coat, rises slowly as she leaves the yard, reaches the driveway, and gets into the passenger side of a car that we haven't noticed before. She doesn't look back. I recognize the car; it belongs to Frank.

"It's Frank, remember?" I whisper low and intense into Kate's ear. "That mean man from Mom's office, who kissed her on the dock by the river." Kate gives me a nod, acknowledging that she remembers, too.

They drive away. I feel triumphant and miserable. The studio door shuts. No one speaks.

Mom returns the next week. It seems she will not take "no" for an answer. She comes in, puts the groceries away, goes into the living room, sits down on the couch in front of the TV, and lights a cigarette. I command loudly and defiantly, "Okay, you guys, we're all going outside to play. C'mon." I grab Michele, two and a half years old by now, dress her in a coat, hat, and gloves, and drag her into the yard. The other three follow reluctantly. We halfheartedly play "Huck," a game fashioned after a story Dad has been telling us, a story about a kid named Huckleberry Finn. We begin with our usual launch of the raft into the muddy, swirling waters of the Mississippi River. I pole us out into the current. We wait for someone to come up with the day's conflict: the river beast to kill, the pirates to destroy, or the storm to survive. Then the moment comes when Kate performs her first ever act of mutiny: She gets up and goes into the house to sit with Mom. I look at Shari, Danielle, and Michele, trying not to show the doubt and apprehension that are growing in me. But I know they can sense it, too.

"Dani, will you go and ask Mom a question?" I ask with a voice still filled with some command. "Ask her if we are the reason she left."

The three of us wait silently until a few minutes later, when Danielle comes running out yelling, "It wasn't us, Carol. We didn't do anything wrong. Mom says so!" Danielle's face, usually so quiet and passive, waiting for someone to tell her what to do, is ignited with excitement, little explosions of relief animating every cell in her body.

My sisters look at me expectantly. "Okay, you guys, let's go in," I whisper. I pick Michele up and we all go into the house, where Kate and Mom are already eating hamburger stew.

"Would you like some lunch?" Mom asks.

I nod, but I'm still not talking. Everyone else is chattering all at once.

I am talking to my mother by the following weekend. I figure it's the least I can do since she is bringing us so much food and

so we sit, finding each other's eyes in our discomfort and smiling weakly. As we sit, a question rises and falls, not fully formed; it comes from within our tension. Finally, I get hold of it: If we are not to be mother and daughter, then who are we to be? I do not ask this question of my mother. I never have.

When Mom and I say goodbye that Saturday, just before she heads back to Manhattan, we hug. It is the first time in weeks that we have touched. Perhaps Mom believes we have crossed over the trouble and can be close again. Maybe she is hopeful and goes back to her small white apartment and white cat with a smile on her face and tells Frank that she has finally reached me. What Mom doesn't know is that in our silence, in our separate breathing on the half-moon couch, my feelings of love for her sink away. I know, deep inside, that I no longer have a mother the way I used to. I know that today is the day I let her go.

～

I remember the afternoon during the summer of my sixth birthday when I told Mom about Anthony. It seemed that her body grew bigger and bigger before my incredulous eyes as I watched her respond to my words. I was not used to her so strong and sure; none of us were. I had finally mustered up the courage to tell her what Anthony, a baby-sitter my parents called in once every few months, had been doing for the last three years to my small body with his pudgy fingers, under my blankets at night. Once I told her, she ignited, transforming into a screaming bird of prey, talons and beak ready to shred flesh. She charged forward to find my father, her fingers pressing a cigarette so hard it dented. I didn't follow her but waited with Kate, Shari, and Danielle.

We were a compact unit of four then, comfortable with

one another, sitting together as if we had always been sitting together, not even bothering to speak. Danielle, just about one year old, watched with the focused attention of someone who is already gathering important family information. Shari was the only one getting squirmy, until she found her two middle fingers and began to suck on them.

Mom was back within minutes, her body already gone slack again after her few minutes of bristling up. She had another cigarette gripped between her fingers and was standing in front of us as she reached for Danielle, who cooperated instantly, slipping effortlessly into the hollow between Mom's large breasts. Danielle looked over at each of us, and then the four of us settled back into our practiced calm.

"Anthony will never baby-sit again, Carol," Mom reassured me.

Anthony was not mentioned again until he returned years later, when I was thirteen. Why he thought it was all right to come calling again remains a disturbing mystery. I was suspicious when he said he was stopping by to ask for a schedule of Dad's painting classes. Mom was visiting on a Saturday, after our parents' divorce, when Anthony turned up at the front door. When I heard his raspy, deep voice, I ran for the safety of a bedroom closet, where I stayed until I was sure he was gone. Mom's voice, a bullying force, turned Anthony around and back to where he had come from, which, in my imagination, was a cave hidden away in some dark, isolated mountain. She closed the front door and sat back down on the couch.

"You can come out now, Carol. He's gone. And he is ugly," Shari said after getting me from the closet.

"Thank you, Mom," I said, gazing at my mother curiously. But she was already sitting stiff like uncooked lasagna strips, looking satisfied and, once again, distant. I was hoping that the warrior Mom was still present, because I wanted so desperately to meet her. Mom smiled to herself, not a warrior's smile, and lit another cigarette with voracious intent, unaware of the admiration that had, just moments ago, been inches away from her grasp.

～

There is the falling away of the damaged skin. Then there is a deep inhalation of new air, an expansion of the chest, and the turning toward the love that is right in front of me, the love of my sisters. Journeys had always begun and ended with them; now there is everything in between. Dad provides the framework in which we find our love, our truth, and our way into our new life, but in this role he is required to do and say things that make him squirm with discomfort.

One night he comes down from his studio after he has been on the phone for at least an hour. We are beginning to think he has a new girlfriend. He spends a lot of time on the phone, and if one of us picks up the receiver he swiftly says, "I'm on the phone, girls." We are never able to hear who is on the other end of the line, and we speculate about who it might be: "Maybe it's one of the ladies taking his painting class," or, "Maybe it's a lady from the university," or, "Maybe it's one of the nude models with the big breasts."

He has already put the younger three to bed in their bedroom downstairs. I think he is going to attempt kissing me and Kate good night, something he rarely does anymore since we are getting too old for good-night kisses. He stands in front of us, moving his weight from one foot to the other, and says, "Carol, could I talk with you for a moment?"

Puzzled, I give Kate a quick look of panic and follow Dad into his studio. I sit on the stool he offers. He looks tired. His bushy, tangled eyebrows are drooping so low, they practically cover his eyes altogether, and the whites of his eyeballs are bloodshot. He sits down at a table and holds his head in his hands, which are still spotted with oil paint. Suddenly I am afraid he has some awful news to tell me, like he's sick or dying. He clears his throat. "I'm all right, just tired. Man, oh man. Listen, Carol. I gotta ask you something. You just let me know, Okay? Do you know about women bleeding?"

This last part he asks quickly and very quietly, so quietly, I'm not sure I have heard him correctly, but I don't want to make him repeat it. So I say, "Yeah, Dad, I know all about it. They showed us a movie at school." I don't tell him that tucked away neatly, beneath some underwear in one of my drawers, are a package of sanitary napkins that I bought at the A & P and a belt that I bought at a drugstore with the guidance of a school friend.

"Good. You'll tell Kate and the other kids?"

"Sure. You're going to sleep now, Dad?"

"Yeah, I'm gonna hit the hay. You and Kate get some sleep now. Good night, Carolina."

We hug briefly and I leave him to his studio. I look around. He has put his head back in his hands again, and I wonder if he will fall asleep at the table.

Dad doesn't often reveal that he is tired. We usually see him lit up, pumping through the days, keeping everything and everyone cheerful. If we happen to show any signs of feeling lonely, tired, or confused, he says things like, "Gotta keep smiling, girls," "Let's see that smile," or, "Keep it up." We learn not to speak too much about Mom, Frank, or anything bad that happens at school. The five of us talk with one another about our problems, unless Kate or I decide that Dad has to know. He knows all about my tonsillitis because I complain about my sore throats; Dad says my tonsils will have to be taken out soon. I keep saying, "No, not yet." We also learn that Dad doesn't have a whole lot of money and it is better if we don't ask him for it unless we need it for mandatory school events.

In the summer, he takes us to his job at Palisades Amusement Park. He paints different park scenes for Mr. Rosenthal, the owner of the park and gets paid for each canvas Mr. Rosenthal likes. My sisters and I get to ride the carousel over and over again for free as Dad paints it from many different angles. We feel like queens as we ride the brightly colored and lacquered horses, waving at one another from across the round expanse, the popcorn-and-cotton-candy-scented wind blowing our hair back into streaming ribbons. When we get the spins from riding in circles for too long, Dad lets us explore, as long as we stay together and check in with him every half hour. We wander all over the park. We peek through the big gray fence and watch the swimmers in the "World's Largest Salt-water Pool"; a machine makes giant waves that are big enough to knock over the small children who are playing in the water. We stand beneath the Cyclone, the "World's Largest Roller Coaster," and listen to people laughing, an undulating mix of excitement and fear.

Whenever and wherever we find Dad painting, there is usually a crowd standing around him, observing his exuberant techniques. He holds a palette and several paintbrushes in his left hand, thumb through the hole of the palette as he paints the canvasses with his right hand. He hums, talks, and dances, pursing his lips and making faces while speaking like Donald Duck or some other cartoon character; these antics are intended to hold the attention of his subjects, young and old. They do.

Dad was born to paint. I've often heard him say that he never thought of doing anything else with his life, something I have always envied. His parents, Williard and Aimee, were both painters, their genes and talent thundering full-strength into my father's cells and psyche. Out of seven children, three of our aunts and uncles turned out to be artists. Two of our aunts are painters, living in that upstate New York town where Methodists reign, and one of our uncles is the director of a boys' choir and an accomplished organist.

In midlife, our grandparents became religious people, born again into a life of fervent worship and proselytizing. Dad grew out from under the heavy religious indoctrination, wanting more than anything else to be a true artist, something he felt his father was but discarded when he took up his soapbox ministry. Williard would take my father to camp meetings and to the streets, where, I believe, my father must have experienced his most embarrassing moments as a witness to my grandfather's religious performances. Grandfather was a master showman. He set up pulpits on street corners all over Fort Lee. Using colored chalk, Grandfather told and drew the stories of Jesus, the disciples, the resurrection, and the light. All of his energy was poured into those street corner sermons. Dad listened and, I imagine, humiliated, would sometimes beg my grandfather to stop. But Williard was swept away by the provocative and powerful desire to save souls, to try to bring them into the fold, thus freeing them from the temptations of cruel mortality.

Sometimes I leave my sisters with Dad and sit alone in front of the funhouse, watching "the Crazy Lady." She is an animated painted, wooden statue that bends up and down at the waist as she revolves around on a conveyor belt. She laughs and laughs with a wide-open mouth, red flesh of her throat exposed, a dark, menacing hole in the middle of all that red. Her face is distorted, cheeks shoved up against her forehead bones, her eyes nothing more than nails glinting under the lights and her lips like viscous, mangled snakes, coiled around that awful mouth. But the most mesmerizing aspect of the Crazy Lady is the sound of her laugh. It is a cross between the laughter of Dad's friend Les, when he is drunk, and a dog named Gus, who howled and moaned in our hallway all night until we gave him back to the pound after owning him for less than a week. I could listen to the Crazy Lady laughing for hours, and I am not sure why. Maybe it is because her madness is visible and no one makes me turn away or whisper in front of her.

It is around this time, in the late summer, that our parents have the only blatant fight we witness. Mom and Frank have, behind everyone's backs, gotten married and been hired as surrogate parents, at a new mental health clinic in Pennsylvania where the patients live with the therapists, and they want us to start visiting them at this clinic as soon as they settle in. Dad hates being kept in the dark more than anything. "Stop treating me like a child, Miriam!" he yells, and then slams the phone down, pounding into the playroom. Picking up a big red fire truck, he heaves it across the room, smashing it into a wall. Shari, Danielle, and Michele, who have been playing in the playroom, run downstairs to hide in their bedroom. Kate rushes after them in a motion of protection. As Kate leaves, she passes a look to me that means, "I'll take care of the kids. You stay here." I nod and peer around the corner of the playroom. I can't see Dad, and that makes me nervous. I think maybe he is about to throw something else, and I don't want to see him do that. I slip downstairs to find Kate and the kids sitting on the edge of Shari's bed, shaking.

"Is Dad going to throw something else?" Danielle wants to know.

"No, Dani," Kate answers.

"Why is he so mad?" Danielle wants to know this, too.

"It's because of Mom. He's not mad at us," I state emphatically.

Kate and I confer in a corner of the room, trying to come up with a plan. Dad's uncharacteristic display of rage has altered our sense of reality, our sense of security.

"What if he does it again?" Kate asks.

When I can't come up with an answer, we decide that the best thing to do is run away. Kate and I pool all our gift money and all the money we have saved from selling lilacs. We pack clothes for each of us, bundle them in some towels, tie the bundles to sticks the way we imagine hoboes do, and then set out for New York City.

My-eleven-year-old body is trying to keep a four-year-old Michele balanced, piggyback style, while we walk through our neighborhood toward the George Washington Bridge, which is about a mile away. I grip her tightly and try to reassure her, while Kate, Shari, and Danielle take turns carrying the hobo luggage, including mine. Less than two blocks from the house, I decide that Michele should be left with Nancy and Earl, some friends of the family who live on River Road, for safekeeping. The plan is to drop her off, explaining that we are only going for a short walk and will be back soon to retrieve her. As I go over my plan with my sisters just outside the door to Nancy and Earl's ground-level apartment, Michele starts to cry. "I don't want to stay with Nancy and Earl. Don't leave me behind!" she is screaming as we knock on their door.

"We'll be back to get you in a couple of days," Kate whispers as the door opens.

Nancy and Earl seem to fall for our story, even though it must seem strange to them that Michele is hysterical as we leave. With teary eyes we say goodbye and walk the rest of the way to the bridge.

We arrive at the entrance to the pedestrian walkway that crosses the bridge and stare, first, at the formidable journey that lies before us and, then, at one another. I breathe in a blast of hot air before I shrug my shoulders and step onto the walkway. My sisters follow, and as we walk we discuss strategy.

First, we will find an apartment, someplace inexpensive and within walking distance of the bridge so we can get home if we need to. Then, I will find a job as a waitress, obviously lying about my age, telling my future employers that I am a mighty fifteen. Kate, Shari, and Danielle will stay at home, taking care of the apartment and doing chores, until each one of them is old enough to get a job, too. After we are settled into our new place and have a little money stashed, we will go and get Michele. It seems like a good plan and we try to believe in it, until about halfway across the bridge; it is then that we stop and reconsider the situation. We are only halfway across the bridge and already very tired.

"Is this bridge safe?" Danielle asks.

"Yes."

"Won't Dad come looking for us and get mad when he finds us?" Shari asks.

No answer.

"What if you can't get a job, Carol?" Danielle asks another question.

"I will."

"What if Nancy and Earl call Dad when they find out we

aren't coming back in a little while to get Michele?" Shari asks another question.

"We can't leave Michele! We have to go back!" Danielle shouts loudly.

"Carol, we have to go back. Danielle's right," Shari says, obviously conflicted about her allegiance.

"Carol, let's go back," Kate says.

I admit our plan is not going to work, and we turn around. On the way back, we decide that if things ever get that frightening at home again, we will run to the Fort Lee Public Library, where we feel safe. There we will rest and make a plan.

Michele is elated to see us as Earl and Nancy, naive of any trouble, hand her over. They ask us to stay for something to drink, but we say no, blaming it on fatigue, which is the only true part of the story. It seems that we have been gone forever, and we are more than relieved to see our house rising up to greet us as we crest the last hill. Down Federspiel Street we run.

When we get home, Dad is talking on the telephone in his bedroom. We can hear his voice, low and quiet, and we sense that he is no longer angry. Later, when he comes out, he seems giddy and doesn't ask us where we have been, he doesn't even know we have run away. We never tell him.

What we do tell Dad, the neighbors, our relatives, friends, teachers, our mother, and ourselves, for months, is that we are "just fine."

About a year later, we are still fine and we smile for Dad's camera on a cold spring Easter afternoon. I am a little over twelve years old, and this is the last time I tolerate putting on an Easter bonnet that Dad has purchased for me, holding a small begonia plant, and posing for a photograph in our yard. We are just home from Baptist Sunday school where Dad has been bringing us for the last few years, to "get a little religion and a little discipline." Every Easter we receive begonia plants from the Nowack sisters, the matrons and dedicated Sunday school teachers of the First Baptist Church of Grantwood, and every year Dad takes photographs of us lined up in our top to bottom order, holding the plants. I despise the smell of begonias and try keeping the pot as far away from my nose as I can. After the group shot, Dad takes a photo of each of us alone. He gets copies made and sends them out to aunts, uncles, grandparents, and friends. It is probably his way of showing the world that we are all doing well. "The annual photographs of 'the girls' have arrived. They look so good, so healthy. Paul made it work after all," these relatives and friends are sure to say.

After the photographs are complete, Dad tells us he has a surprise: "Go get changed and meet me in the kitchen." I have already guessed what it is: smoked shad, for it is that time of year when the shad head up the Hudson River to spawn. Every spring Dad goes down to the river, one of his favorite places to paint, and buys a smoked shad from one of his fisherman friends. Smoked shad brings with it the hope of a change in the weather. We always reach for it with the cold fingers of children who are ready for the thaw.

We rip off our Easter bonnets, throw the dresses on our beds, put on the first comfortable clothes we can find, and run into the kitchen. Dad has already laid out the shad on the table, oil-soaked brown paper right on the wood, no plate, no plastic wrap. We gather around and Dad picks out the first piece after removing the skin and some of the bones. He gives the piece to me. For a second I feel guilty, and I am about to hand it to Michele when Dad nudges the fish toward my mouth and I am inclined to eat it. I am not aware of who gets the next piece; all of my senses have been invited into that first bite of fish. Soon everyone has a piece and we are silenced by our eating. I wish someone had taken our photograph at that exact moment: There is a wooden table with a wide-open smoked shad lying on oily brown paper. A father with big hands and a wide-open face, in joyful concentration, carefully divides up the fish. Five girls in rumpled shirts, hands oily and opened wide, are eating and laughing, on an Easter day.

Once we've eaten, we girls head to the cliffs for another day of adventuring. A few hours later, satiated and still smelling of fish, we scramble in through the porch doors. It is cold by evening, and we decide to light a fire in the fireplace. Later, after Dad has kissed us good night and gone up to his studio, I haul out mattresses, as I have done in the past, and position them in front of the fireplace and we sleep together, dreams and bodies interconnected as the cold seeps in around us.

I believe it was during the nights we slept together that our deepest bonding occurred. I believe our sweet and precious dreams, floating innocent and bright in the cool air, mingled and took on new life. I will always believe that our combined dreams took us lovingly into landscapes where only sisters go. We learned our sister language there. We learned our sister strength and grasped the significance of our love; it was this love that comforted us during the fledgling years. Deep and consistent as the Hudson River below us, which had always set our course and sense of direction, this love was enduring. This love was all of life.

3

~

AFTERMATH

We're resting in the attic bedroom at the mental health clinic where Mom and Frank work now and we visit every other weekend. I can hear Mom's footsteps as she approaches the attic door, and within seconds she'll ask if one or all of us, except Michele, who is the youngest and doesn't do a good job yet, would mind giving Frank another rubdown. I, for one, am sick of it and just might refuse this time, but I'm positive he will keep harassing us until he gets his way. We've already massaged him half the day, it seems. Since I'm so good at "cracking" his big toe, I know he'll make me do that over and over as he lies on the bed watching television, gripping his filthy rag of a pillow, occasionally sucking on it.

Shari whispers that she is going to pretend to be asleep and burrows under her blankets. Frank has been bothering Shari lately. Why he picks on her so tenaciously is baffling, although we have our theories, the best being that Shari has become very vulnerable and is the most sensitive to his verbal attacks. Ever since she turned nine, Shari has begun questioning everything, especially her own self-worth. Although Frank hurls his insults at all of us, Shari is the main focus of his attacks. He thinks she could use a few years of confrontational therapy, the kind that they practice here at the clinic, where the patients live with therapists who have been trained to take on the role of parents. With a little too much eagerness, the doctors and "parents" invent ways to shove insanity into the faces of the patients. Like Joe, who thinks he's Jesus: Frank and his cohorts constructed a body-size cross made of wood, which Joe now must carry with him wherever he goes. But Joe doesn't appear to mind; he lugs it around wearing a large, beatific smile.

As Mom opens the door, Kate, Danielle, and I exchange glances; it is in those glances that the decision is made. Danielle and I were the last ones to touch Frank, and Kate knows it. But of course, she doesn't want to give him another full-body massage. Danielle and I will not give in. Reluctantly Kate rises and meets Mom on the attic stairs without Mom having to utter a word of request. Danielle and Michele stay with Shari to protect her and keep her company. I pass the door to Frank and Mom's bedroom on my way to the living room and pause to listen. Maybe the massage has turned into a lecture on vocational intention; lecturing is one of Frank's favorite pastimes, and now he has even more cause to torture us with these monologues.

At the encouragement of some friends who have been working for years in modeling and commercials, Kate and I started doing the same, actually making some decent money, some of which we give to Dad to help out with family bills. As soon as he found out about it, Frank began badgering us relentlessly with the reasons that careers in the performing arts would be disastrous. "You'll both wind up becoming fruits. Is that what I've taught you? How to become fruits?" Kate and I don't understand what he means by "fruits," and we don't ask him to explain. Just to get him off our backs, we tell him neither of us has any interest in going professional. We try to convince him that we have much loftier and more serious aspirations, but he doesn't want to be convinced and the lectures continue.

All I can hear is the low throbbing of the TV. I slip downstairs to find Joe sitting in the living room with the cross placed on his thighs. When he's not in the bedroom that he shares with two other male patients, this is where Joe can be found. Two female patients inhabit separate bedrooms upstairs; the house has been full, five patients in all, as long as my sisters and I have been visiting. Joe mumbles something about persecution as I flop into the armchair that faces a huge TV screen. He must've just turned it off.

"Jesus," I ask, trying to sound as respectful as possible, "would you like to watch a little television."

I turn it on. All I can find are golf games and old movies. I see Jesus' face flicker off and on as I try to locate an interesting program. Soon his face goes slack. Jesus has fallen asleep, his body slumping over onto the cross. Danielle comes down the stairs and wants to go outside, so we leave Jesus and head to the fields behind the clinic, where no one can ask us for massages.

When we return, Mom is sitting in a chair at her spot by the kitchen window, smoking. Stained-glass window hangings and blown-glass figurines form a backdrop for her head. This is where Mom can be found when she isn't reclining on their bed upstairs; she rarely ventures out of the house anymore. In front of her on the counter there is a small notebook where she writes lists of the tasks she must complete. After one is finished, she crosses it off with a swift and heavy stroke of her pen. She is chewing on her lips, looking especially anxious, so I ask if something is wrong.

"Frank is having one of his headaches. He wants to know if

you could rub his head, Carol, just for a little while," she replies, looking down timidly as she speaks. I want to tell her to rub his greasy head herself, but that would just make the tension between her and me even worse, and besides, Frank hates the way Mom massages and never asks her to do it.

I walk into the darkened bedroom to discover Frank lying on the bed moaning, with a Q-Tip stuck up his right nostril. He presses it against some inner membrane trying to reach a nerve ending, which will stop the headache. A bottle of prednisone is placed, cap removed, on the dresser next to the bed. He's been taking steroids for as long as we've known him, popping them into his mouth a few times a day. He's had these "cluster headaches" ever since he met our mother, arguing that it's because of her that he has them at all. Recently he also started injecting himself with Talwin, a non-narcotic painkiller, but I don't see any signs that he's used it today; there are no needles or vials around. He has not heard me enter the room, and when I sit down on the bed he turns toward me and lets out a long, pitiful sound. He slowly opens his eyes. When he sees it's me, he shifts his body so I can fit in above his head into a position conducive to massaging his neck and shoulders. After a few minutes of jamming fingers into the base of his skull, I ask if it is helping. Frank has fallen asleep. I carefully slide out from behind him, looking back to see that the Q-Tip is still hanging from his nose. I wonder if I should yank it out, but I don't want to wake him and so I leave him that way.

Hours later, after we've finished dinner, Frank is still lying down, one hand placed over his eyes, the other clutching his pillow. He looks as though he has been airbrushed with a thin spray of gray dust. Mom has brought his dinner: boiled cow tongue (sliced really thin) and pickles and mustard, but he hasn't touched it. He stares at the TV, which blinks out the faces of two news anchorpeople. Without warning Frank says, "Those two really want to get some. Right, Miriam?"

"Yeah, right," she answers in a vain attempt at sarcastic nonchalance.

I roll my eyes at Kate, who has been watching the news, too. Frank's opening line could be the beginning of an onslaught of comments about the sexual desires of not only the news anchorpeople but everyone he knows and doesn't know, including him and our mother. I don't want to hear for the hundredth time about how much my mother likes fucking Frank or about how big his penis is. "Tell them how big it is Miriam," or, "Tell them how much you like doing it, Miriam," he likes to boast. I could leave now or take my chances; I want to watch the news, without commentary. I look at Frank, trying to gauge just how weak he is feeling. He has the pillow up to his mouth; with his right hand he kneads the pillow while his tongue lightly licks the dirty material. The pillow has not been washed in years; he won't allow it. Apparently he's had the thing since he was a child. Frank remains quiet, all talk of sex over for now. I stay.

That night, I try to imagine Mom and Frank French-kissing. It makes me want to vomit. I wonder if Kate ever imagines stuff like that, but I don't want to ask her in front of Shari, Danielle, and Michele. I force myself to think of more pleasant things, like the outfit I'm saving money to buy or our tentative plans for summer vacation, before finally falling asleep.

The next morning Frank is rejuvenated. He immediately starts talking with me about dating, which he thinks I should be more actively pursuing. He says I'm old enough to start seeing boys, unless of course I don't like boys, in which case I'm a pervert and dating would be a waste of time.

"But, Frank, I'm only thirteen."

"That's old enough. A friend of ours has a son, Dave, who is about your age. I thought we'd invite him to go with us on the boat some Saturday. What d'ya say?"

I feel compelled to agree with his plans, and so it's all set. The next time we're down for a visit, we'll all go out on Mom and Frank's small houseboat, which is parked, set on top of its trailer, outside the back window. Frank calls Dave and his father, who graciously accept the invitation.

When the five of us girls arrive home in Fort Lee the next day, we feel like we've just been released from the confines of a place where there wasn't enough oxygen. Frank goes on to Long Island, where he will visit his aging parents. In two weeks he'll be back to pick us up for another weekend visit in Pennsylvania.

It takes a long time to settle Shari down on this return from the clinic. She keeps asking if we think she is crazy, and we insist that she is not. I find her crying in her room with Danielle sitting next to her on the bed, stroking her forehead. Her diary lies open on the floor, its pages crowded with words and images.

"Why did Mom have to marry him? It was a big mistake," she sobs, her white-blue eyes magnified by the tears. Danielle and I gently get her up; it's time for dinner.

Before she leaves the room, Shari grasps the carved wooden horse necklace that she keeps around her neck at all times. She stops at the doorway, where she touches the wall three times and then exits. None of us question Shari's need to perform these rituals and none of us thought they were in any way strange until Frank labeled them "compulsions" and began his private talks with her, in which, as Shari describes it, "he asks me dumb questions that I never have an answer for." She used to be slightly insecure, but now, thanks to Frank, she's worse than ever.

~

I dream that I am looking for Shari as I walk along a woodland path. I am calling out her name into the trees and grasses. The path is lined with cobblestones. Winding upward into the hills I can see its direction, coursing farther into the distance. There is a light moving toward me from behind a large, gnarled tree. I stop to let it reach me; it is Shari, thin blades of light spinning off from her body into the sky. She tells me these are "quills" and lets them touch me as she moves away again. I am left alone on the cobblestone path, hands clenched around tiny remains of Shari's "quills," which continue sizzling into my flesh because I will not let them go.

~

At school, my friends hound me for stories about the weekend, knowing we went to the "loony bin." I am reluctant to tell the stories, thinking I will be set apart from them if I divulge anything. There was a time at the start of our bimonthly visits when I couldn't wait to go into the boldest details about the clinic and its inhabitants. Now I am sickened and guilt-ridden by what I'm witness to and feel that by telling the stories I am somehow condoning what happens there. I ask my friends never to mention stories of the clinic to my father, who is unaware of them. When he asks, we simply say everything went well, and he does not push for more. I am convinced that if we told him about what goes on at the clinic he would either have a heart attack or fly into a rage and not let us go there again, which I'm beginning to think might be a good thing. Our visits to the clinic seem to be upsetting my sisters and me more and more. I cannot tell Mrs. Burns, our new housekeeper, about our visits, either, for I know she would feel obligated to tell Dad.

Mrs. Burns (or Migga, as Michele calls her because she has a hard time pronouncing the "Mrs.") despises our mother, for "running off and leaving her babies," and would use what ammunition she could to discredit her and even keep us from seeing her altogether. Most of the venom aimed at our mother comes from women who are or have been active mothers. Right in front of us they say things like, "How could she do such a thing to her own children?" or, "She should be slapped," or, "What kind of a woman is she?" or, "They shouldn't be allowed to see her at all." When the kids ask Kate and me if we think Mom is bad, we answer, "No, she still loves us." This is the answer we've become accustomed to saying. We learn to repeat it to ourselves whenever doubt arises, whenever we see or hear things at the clinic that I suspect we shouldn't be allowed to see or hear. Kate and I have occasionally dared to speak about the clinic and Frank during late-night discussions on the half-moon couch, after Dad has put the kids to bed in their room. We make whatever sense we can of everything and vow that we will never abandon our own children or marry bastards like Frank.

I am about to read out loud to my eighth-grade English class a composition I wrote about being motherless. My teacher, Mrs. Ciampi, insists I read it because it is "competently wrought." I must stand and, with legs I'm sure will not support my weight, propel myself up. I'm the final reader of the day, as if the subject matter weren't enough to make me a nervous wreck. With a breathy, quiet voice I begin. Mrs. Ciampi asks me to read louder. I look around hoping to find a sympathetic face, but all eyes are cast down. They know the situation. I am not the only child of divorced parents, but I am the first to have written about it. I begin again. My voice finds a strength buried in the words that tell of my anguish, my feelings of "being left alone at a banquet, the flowers wilted and the lights faded." As I read, I realize that this composition is not about my mother but about some fantasy mother I wish I had. The words begin to get heavy, a wave of sadness rising into my throat. Suddenly all I want to do is cry. I know that if I start crying, though, I will not be able to finish reading, and so I swallow hard against my tears and they subside. Everyone is quiet as I end with the line, "And now when I need her most, she isn't here." Everyone's been holding their breath; there is a roomful of exhalations. Mrs. Ciampi asks if there is any feedback. A few kids say the usual, "It was very good." One of my best friends, Harriet, whose parents are still married, says, "It's just that it's so sad, Carol," and looks at me as if she thinks this is the biggest tragedy she's ever heard in her entire life. I want to scream, "Stop looking at me that way, Harriet. It's not that big a deal!" As we solemnly shuffle out of the room, Mrs. Ciampi calls me over to her desk and asks if I'm all right. Then she asks if I would like her to call my father and tell him about the composition; maybe he needs to know how I'm feeling, and maybe he would like to know what a good writer I am.

"No, Mrs. Ciampi. Please don't call my father. He knows how I feel," I lie as my neck grows red and hot. I walk into the hall wanting to run from the school, home to a cliff hiding place where I could be alone.

When I do get home later that afternoon, Migga announces that I've gotten a call for an audition. It is for an acne scrub commercial. An audition is the last thing I want right now; all that prepping and posturing feels like too much work. I look at the paper where Migga has written the information down, hoping Kate can go instead, but it's for thirteen-to-fifteen-year-olds who must be able to play a guitar, which I do and Kate doesn't. After looking over the directions, I realize it's a simple trip to the television studio: the A-train down to 42nd Street, a short walk over to an office building on 45th Street and Ninth Avenue. I'll be able to do this.

Migga comes over and stands next to me, placing her arm on my shoulder. She wants to know if I can go into New York City by myself. I assure her that I can, citing the other times I've managed without a stage mom or dad. She pushes me back at arm's length and looks me over with her watery brown eyes as if to make sure she sees a girl capable of the trip. Migga is all soft and doughy in her blue housedress with a Kleenex stuffed up under the left sleeve. There are times when her consistency is just right, exuding a comfort I have missed and long to be near. Other times she comes in too close and I want her to get away from me, but I never say anything to hurt Migga.

I ask her if she has mentioned to Dad that I have an audition the next day. She hasn't had the chance; he's been teaching at Fairleigh Dickinson University all day and then had a meeting with NASA officials about going aboard a recovery ship to sketch the astronauts returning from space. I am unable to corner him as he walks through the door; Kate nabs him first with news and requests of her own. Then it's time for dinner, baths, homework, and bed, and by the time I arrive at the gray door that separates his bedroom and studio from the rest of the house I can hear him talking on the phone. I knock gently. No response. I knock harder.

"I'm on the phone." His muffled voice is barely audible. I can either stand here and try again, leave it until morning, or pick up the phone on our end and tell him that I need to speak to him. He doesn't like us to do that, but sometimes we have no choice; Dad talks for hours at a stretch to a mystery person, who we suspect is a lady from one of his painting classes. Dad acts goofy after she's been around. We can see her and the other ladies walking across the yard, down into the studio where they learn how to paint with oils. From our vantage point in the kitchen, which is situated below the yard line, the ladies appear headless until they reach the last set of stone steps before the red studio door.

When Dad finally unlocks his door and emerges into the kitchen, I am turning off the lights in the living room, getting ready for bed. I tell him about the audition and he asks if I need a little cash to get over to Manhattan. "You be careful Carolina. Nothing could be finer than to be with Caroliner in the morning," he croons, then sidles over to try to kiss my neck the way he used to when I was about two.

"Dad," I whine and push him away.

He says good night, then, "You got what it takes, my little poet," winking at me as he returns into his inner sanctum.

～

When I was three, I stood at the very top of my world, on a wedge of cliff overflowing with bright grasses as thick as my fingers. At only three, I was already as sure of my feet on cliff rock as I imagine a young goat would be. I stood surefooted in my white sandals as I looked out across the now-familiar land called New Jersey. The blue-and-gray river was below; it had the consistency of clay from this height.

Dad and Mom both called the dark line of buildings

across the river, "the city." I tried to repeat terms like "the city" back to them all the time, and I also tried to make up new words. I wanted to tell them new things about the sky, the river, the grasses, and the city.

My father and his friend Dan Mahoney, whose long name I really liked to say, were standing near me and also looking out at the view. While they talked to each other, I looked all around me, naming everything in front of me. There were "tree" and "river" and "house" and "sky" and "clouds," too many things. Dad and Dan Mahoney stepped closer next to me and listened. I was trying to find the best words to say to them so they would know, too. Dad picked me up so I was sitting on his shoulder. I felt like I was sitting in the clouds. While the three of us were looking up at the clouds, I said softly, "The clouds are watching over the river today."

Dad and Dan Mahoney laughed, and Dad hugged me tighter. Dan Mahoney said, "She is going to be a poet." I had never heard the word "poet." It must be something good because both my father and Dan Mahoney seemed really pleased.

As soon as we got inside the house, I ran up to my mother, who was giving Kate apple slices in her high chair. Still holding onto the new word I had just learned, I blurted out "poet" right at the side of my mother's face so she would really hear it.

"Poet," my mom repeated back to me, turning away from the high chair and looking right at me.

"Poet," I said one more time so everyone would hear it, even the people who lived in my father's paintings. And then, in one dancing happy moment, Dad, Mom, Dan Mahoney, and I all said the word "poet" together.

～

Every girl at the audition has a mother by her side. In moments like these, I wish I had one, too. I try smiling by way of a general greeting. Most of them look at me with suspicion; they don't know what I'm doing. I feel like an aberration, a child formed outside the norms of audition waiting room society. There are no seats left, so I stand, propping my guitar against the wall. As soon as I've found a suitable position a few of the mothers go back to coaching their daughters on how to achieve stellar audition behavior. It's as though their droning fills the room with waves of rhythm; it becomes like a chant: "Smile, dear." "Speak clearly and directly to them." "Never clear your throat." "Give them your best angle." "Don't hold the audition script in front of your face." "Be polite." "Be nice." The girls being lectured pretend to be listening to their mothers, but I suspect that they are also dying to yell, "Shut up!" At this moment, I do not want a mother.

After I have read over the script, handed to me by a young woman holding a clipboard, at least fifteen times, it's my turn. I am met by the staring faces of seven people, all sitting on stools, as I walk into the audition room. I introduce myself, take a breath, and then recite the lines from the script, a testimonial about the acne product, which has little scrubbing grains that grind pesky blackheads right out of the pores. When I'm finished, a kind-looking bearded man wants to know if I can perform any songs. They want me to sing a song, stop singing the song, and then recite the lines from the script, all the while looking like a soulful young teenager. I take out my guitar, tune it up, and begin singing "Dona," a sad song about a calf being lead to the slaughter. They listen intently, letting me sing the entire song, which is really long. When I'm finished singing and reciting the lines, the kind guy asks if I know any more songs. I choose a song I recently composed, which ends with the chorus: "Oh, Lord, oh, Lord, can't seem to hold my head above this sinking ground. Oh, Lord, oh, Lord, faces melt before my eyes and slowly start to drown." I've closed my eyes, and when I open them each member of the group is smiling or nodding. "Is your mother here?" Mr. Kind asks. When I tell them I'm alone they raise their eyebrows and begin to speak quietly to one another. I'm escorted back to the waiting room by Mr. Kind, who thanks me, touching my arm gently in a gesture of what seems like sincere caring, and walks off, humming the chorus to the song I wrote.

When I get home the next day, Migga tells me that I got the job, without a stage mother in sight.

We go to visit Mom and Frank for an extended weekend while Dad goes off to sketch the action on board an aircraft carrier bound to pick up astronauts returning from the moon. When Frank arrives to pick us up, he is exuberant. He has just purchased a batch of new eight-track tapes and can't wait to hear them. Most of the way to the clinic, he talks about classical music, the great composers, opera, and the great opera singers. He says that he's read about opera singers and that they have the hardest job in the world: they have to learn a new language, learn all these difficult musical passages, get dressed in heavy clothing, and go out onstage in front of thousands of people who expect them to sing their lines perfectly.

I can think of many other jobs that seem much more difficult than opera singing, and I say so. There is a chorus of agreement from my sisters. Shouts of "garbageman," "lion tamer," "window washer of skyscrapers," "doctor," "farmer," and "dentist" ensue. Our enthusiastic and loud contributions on the subject of hardest jobs in the world last all the way to the Pennsylvania/New Jersey border. Frank even asks Michele what job she thinks is the hardest job in the world. She answers with "artist." We pause and wait for Frank's response, knowing full well he doesn't regard "artist" as a viable profession and also knowing this will give him an opportunity to reiterate his judgement of our father. On more than one occasion, Frank has made it clear that he thinks Dad's work as a painter is not "real" work: "Only fairies and wimps call themselves artists. Your father just isn't smart enough to do anything meaningful with his life." I vow that if he says something about Dad now, I'll tell him I'm carsick and have to vomit, and when he pulls over I'll hit him in the head with one of my shoes, I swear. But Frank says nothing, leaving the space for one of us to encourage six-year-old Michele in her young conviction.

As soon as we get to the clinic, Frank dashes upstairs to the bedroom with his tapes, putting on Mahler's Symphony no. 7. He cranks the volume and flails his arms about the room in mock conductor fashion. The music changes the shape and demeanor of Frank's face; all darkness and doubt recede back behind the hairline, transforming his expression into one of serenity.

Frank has also purchased some pornographic reel-to-reel films, and after dinner he excitedly announces that he's going to show one in the den for the benefit of two male patients who he claims are "sexually screwed up." With his overwhelming power of persuasion, he suggests that Kate and I join him and the patients in the crowded, stuffy room, saying we would probably learn a lot from the movie, too. The title of the film is *The Traveling Salesman*. As soon as the movie comes on, I begin to feel nauseous. A fat, dark-haired man knocks on a door. He is carrying a suitcase. The door opens and an attractive young woman, wearing only pink underwear, answers. The man places the suitcase on the floor and reaches for the woman, who responds with apparent glee. She immediately pulls down his pants, exposing his penis. I have never really gotten a good look at a penis before, and now, as I gaze in puzzlement at the penis of the "traveling salesman," I wonder if they all look like rain-bloated worms.

I am sitting next to Kate, who is wearing the same look of horror that I am. I elbow her and she gives me a frown. I don't think I can stay for the duration of the movie; it's making me way too uncomfortable, especially since we're sitting with a couple of nervous kooks. I don't want to seem squeamish; after all, this is sex, I guess, and I'm supposed to find it desirable.

When it's over, Frank tells the two patients to go to their rooms and jerk off. The guys shuffle off to their bedroom, where I suppose they will do what Frank instructed them to do. Kate and I wonder if we're going to be commanded to go to our room and jerk off, too, although neither of us is sure what it means. When Frank asks us what we thought of the movie, we simply shrug. We don't hear any noises as we pass the patients' room on our way upstairs, and so later, after talking about it, we conclude that jerking off must be a quiet activity, and maybe one that two people can do together.

The next day we're slowly cruising in Mom and Frank's houseboat along the coastline off Highgate, New Jersey. It took Mom, Frank, and my sisters two hours to get to the Jersey shore from Pennsylvania, but we left early, so we could have as much of this summer's day on the water as possible. Dave, my prospective first boyfriend, and his father followed behind us in their car and are now showing their appreciation by exclaiming how beautiful everything is. I have never felt so awkward in all my life. Every time Dave comes near me, I'm sure that I blush. What a setup. He's nice-looking and polite and at least tries to have conversations with me, though they invariably collapse into stilted small talk. My sisters keep teasing me as we all sunbathe and continue filling our glasses with disgusting lukewarm soda.

At one point Dave goes down to the bathroom and when he comes back I notice with absolute embarrassment that his penis is bulging out from under his tight trunks. I want to say something or give him a subtle eyes-to-the-groin look that will tip him off to the state of his private parts. Doesn't he feel the wind blowing against it? I can't tell if anyone else notices, but soon it is apparent that Frank has noticed something else Dave has done. He comes up from the galley and in a big, reproachful voice says, "Dave, ya peed all over the head. You dip. Don't you believe in opening the lid of a toilet before you pee in it for God's sake." Frank guffaws and then he turns to Dave's father and taunts, "Don't you teach him anything?" The two of them seem to think the whole thing is a great joke, and they laugh obnoxiously.

Meanwhile Dave has disappeared, probably to go back to the bathroom and clean it up. When he returns, everything is where it should be, and for that I am grateful. Dave's face has turned red in humiliation. I go to him and say, "I did the same thing the first time I used the stupid bathroom." He smiles in quiet thanks. After that, I actually like him more, and I don't feel so desperately alien.

As we say goodbye, Dave's father asks me if I would like to join them for dinner the next evening. I say yes.

At the Black Bass Inn, the three of us struggle through the meal, making the best of our limited knowledge of one another. Every so often, Dave's father pretends he sees an old friend at the bar and leaves us alone. We find out that there are a number of things we have in common: we both like to draw and watch TV.

He's no good at telling jokes, but I laugh at the ones he attempts to tell anyway. He's pretty good at asking me questions and shows a keen interest in anything having to do with my modeling and TV commercial career. Overall I'm satisfied with my first date with a boy and can imagine doing it again.

When we get home, Dave walks me to the back door while his dad waits in the car. We're standing next to the houseboat, saying good night, when Dave leans over and kisses me on the lips. We hear the sound of giggling and look up to find the faces of my sisters peering down at us from inside the boat. They have been hanging out in there, something we frequently did to get away from the patients and Frank. They are witnesses to my first good-bye kiss. I smile and say, "Thanks for a really nice time." Dave slips away.

My sisters climb out of the boat with the speed of tree monkeys. "He kissed you. He kissed you," they tease. I try to remember the sensation of the kiss itself; it was soft, quiet, and considerate.

We go upstairs to Mom and Frank's room. I'm feeling elated and relieved about my first date, and I want everyone to share this mood with me, even Mom and Frank. Two other therapists whom Mom and Frank have become friendly with, have come over to watch TV. Before anyone can utter a word or question about how it went, Frank blurts out, "Hey, what's that dripping down between your legs?" and laughs, looking around at the others. No one else is laughing. I spin around so I can run out of the room, but Frank is quick. He grabs me by the shoulders and attempts to keep me in the room. I reach around for one of his arms, gouging my nails into his skin. He lets go; I run to the door, turn, and scream, "Fuck you!" with all the fury from my ruined first kiss. Dave has vanished and been replaced by the "traveling salesman."

My sisters and I run upstairs to the attic. Someone slams the door. I throw myself on my mattress and cry. My sisters gather around me, each one touching some part of my shaking body. "I hate him. I hate him." My sisters keep their hands on me until this round of tears is spent.

At breakfast the next morning, the atmosphere in the kitchen is tense. Even the patients seem on a different kind of edge. Jesus asks me if I need a blessing placed upon me, and Marvin, an autistic man usually totally oblivious to everything going on around him, rocks over to me and offers to get me some juice.

Finally, Frank makes his appearance. I sit with my face averted. The kitchen becomes quiet. Mom sits on her chair by the window, writing out her list for the day. Frank is strangely silent. I've never known him to go even five minutes without a comment. He rises to leave and, as he passes behind me, places his hand on my head, messing up my hair. An apology perhaps? No thanks. He'll have to do a lot better than that.

I never return Dave's phone calls, and after about a month of trying to reach me he stops calling.

I am standing in the bedroom listening to my mother try to defend Frank's behavior of the night before. I watch her face as she talks, and I wonder who this woman is. I feel as if I have never seen her before in my life; her mannerisms seem unrecognizable. I know she is delivering this monologue so I will forgive Frank, but she is wasting her breath. I don't know how to forgive such an act; no one has ever treated me this way. She begins by telling me that he is an only child, something I already know. His Czechoslovakian parents immigrated and have never understood the culture very well and continue to rely on Frank for translations of all things American. Frank never had a sister or brother to relate to, so he learned to live within his own world in order to survive his strict upbringing. His old-fashioned parents embarrassed him constantly in front of his friends, his mother, Vera, showing up at the playground, calling out, "Frankiecoo, Frankiecoo!" He was subsequently dubbed "CooCoo" by the cruelest boys and taunted until he didn't want to go to school anymore. His parents have despised my mother from the beginning, blaming her for his headaches and most of his other problems. He is still under their scrutiny, the pressure on him to be the perfect Czech son continuing to drive many of his actions.

Then Mom proceeds to tell me a story about Frank that she seems to think will elicit my sympathy. When Frank was a young boy, he had a canary that he loved dearly and even slept with at night. He would hold it close to him so that he could feel its little breath blowing against his cheek. He whistled to it when he got home every day from school and would run up to its cage to let it out. One night Frank rolled over onto his beloved canary, smothering it to death. When he woke up the next day and found the lifeless body of the bird lying next to him on the pillow, he wailed in helpless sorrow. He didn't speak for weeks, and his parents claim he was not the same Frankiecoo after experiencing such intense grief.

I want to feel compassion for Frank, but I can't. I wish Mom had told me this story some other time, when I could have been open to its meaning, but she has picked the wrong moment and it is too late. I turn away, knowing that in my turning away I am once more rejecting her.

My sisters and I are back home. It's late summer and we're alone; we haven't seen Mom and Frank for weeks, and no one has asked to see them. We're too busy missing Dad. Migga has left for the night, but not before we convinced her that it was perfectly safe to leave. Both Kate and I pleaded our cases, insisting that we were old enough to take care of Shari, Danielle, Michele, and the house for the night. Dad is still on the aircraft carrier and will be gone for another few days. We watched on TV as the space capsule plunged into the ocean, and when they showed scenes from the deck of the carrier we strained to find our father among the scurrying people. We couldn't spot him. Dad called from the carrier, but the connection wasn't very good, so we could only make out a few words. I heard him say, "Weather fine . . . you girls . . . Mrs. Burns is . . . love you . . . ," and then his voice faded into a surge of static.

I am sitting in the dark, looking out at the river. The porch doors are open, letting in the late-spring air. A large boat is going up-river; I can see its lights slowly moving north. Kate is in the house with the kids. Their voices are steady, with an occasional burst of laughter, Shari's boiling up over the sound of the others with a throaty resonance. I've already told Michele three episodes of "Melancholy Valley," a story I made up and began telling her years ago, about a group of animals who are always fighting but have forgotten why. She loves the story, especially when it's emotional, and so I end each installment with a tear-jerking dramatic scene.

Michele can't fall asleep tonight; she's constantly asking for Dad. Talking to him just made us miss him more, and Michele is the one who seems to miss him the most when he goes away. I thought Kate and I would be able to take care of things, but at the moment I'm not so sure. Maybe I'm not as mature as I believe I am. I was beginning to think I understood this world or at least pieces of it. There was a shape to it, one I was getting used to.

I'm worried about Shari, that her compulsions might get worse and worse until Frank has a good excuse to bring her to the clinic for a round of confrontational therapy. I know that Frank is going to continue saying awful things to me and my sisters and that I will be forced to hurt him. I haven't gotten my period yet, and I'm almost fourteen. My curiosity and desire for sex might just be ruined, and maybe I'm too disgusted to even try finding out. I'm incapable of taking care of my sisters and fear that everything I'm worrying about will one day make me go insane, like my mother.

I watch the river, trying to concentrate on its simple, silvery form. Danielle pokes her head out of the bedroom door; she looks as worried as I feel. I motion for her to join me. She sits on the floor, resting her head against my legs. For a little while she allows me to comfort her as I play with the short strands of dark hair, twirling them around in my fingers. I know Danielle will get up and go back to the others soon just to make sure they are safe. I want to ask her to stay longer. She would do it gladly, but I know Danielle well enough to let go of her hair. As she gets up, she asks me if I think Shari is going to be all right. Looking into Danielle's eyes gives me all the strength I need to say, "Absolutely," and mean it. She whispers good night, leaving me to the shadows.

I awake into the muted partial light of deep morning. My sisters are asleep; at least I think they are. I carefully get out of bed so I won't wake Danielle, whom I share a bedroom with now. Kate has a bedroom to herself; Shari and Michelle share another one. I move silently through the living room on my way to the bathroom, not wanting to rouse any of them. The characters who inhabit the living room walls are already awake; the ten or so paintings that my father has chosen to display here seem alive in the wavy light that has escaped from Manhattan and been diffused by river molecules that rise unencumbered at this time of day. Even the painted landscapes tremble, and I squint in dreamy anticipation of words or movement from one of the images.

There are two portraits in particular that, with those spectacular penetrating eyes, appear to be on the verge of saying something important as they stare at me. I stand waiting for them to speak; maybe they can help me understand this life, offer solutions or words that would soothe. But, of course, they do not speak, and I move away, knowing that they never will.

4

~

DONUTS

Shari is laughing so hard she loses hold of herself, practically fainting as she sinks down onto the floor. There is no use trying to pull her up now. The best thing to do is leave her, let her finish out the laughter, until it has moved completely through her body. This round was set off by a look from Danielle. Shari, Danielle, and Michele were putting on a play for me and Kate, another episode of *Oh, Dolly*, which is about an emotionally fragile young woman who, with her pushy mother, is on the prowl for a boyfriend. Danielle pursed her lips, crossed her eyes, and flared her nostrils, propelling Shari into hysterical laughter; sometimes we all go with her, but never as far. Now we lie down on the floor next to Shari as she laughs, surrounding her like sentinels, making sure she stays with us, making sure that the laughter doesn't take the breath right out of her.

Shari once entered a laughing jag at the Fort Lee Diner and fell out of the booth. That time we brought her back by shaking her as quickly as we could for humility's sake. Everyone in the diner was staring, probably thinking we were stoned hippies. A waitress was on her way over, probably to tell us to leave, but she saw that we had Shari back in her seat, compliant and ready to order a tuna fish sandwich or something else that, of course, she wouldn't wind up eating.

Sometimes I wrap myself around her as she laughs, wanting more than anything else to know what it's like to be Shari when she has given herself over to it. I imagine it must be an escape from the confines of her overactive mind. I hope she can take me with her someday; maybe I can lose my mind that way, too, lose my mind to laughter.

"Oh, God, Dan. Do it again please. Please!" Shari shrieks in between gasps for air.

Danielle looks at me, then at Kate, and we both give her the "Don't do it" face. We fear if Shari goes off again she might just slip away for good.

As hard as we try to minimize the influence of Frank's prognosis for Shari's future mental health, we (mainly Danielle and I) sometimes believe she could be going crazy. We simply will not allow Shari to go over the edge, and Shari usually convinces us that she is far from nuts, but sometimes it's difficult to believe her, especially when she laughs as thoroughly as this.

"I am an artist, you guys. Artists are supposed to be slightly crazy and have weird habits. Frank is a jerk. He doesn't understand artists at all."

At nine, Shari already knows with precision who she is. I adore her for this conviction of who she knows herself to be. It is never who she will become, it is who she is. Kate and I certainly flounder around about "who we will be when we grow up." That seems standard. Shari has always known. She has always expressed herself creatively, making mud sculptures, Vaseline waterfalls, and poison ivy hats. Kate and I agree that Shari's direct line to her creative side is probably why she is so close to Dad; they both seem to have oil paint in the veins. It's "Look at that composition," or, "Look at the color of that sunset." Dad always knew he wanted to be an artist; he never questioned it. Shari sometimes says she wants to be a psychologist as well as an artist so she can help artists deal with their agony.

～

"It's hamburger stew for dinner," Mom announced, taking out the formidable pressure cooker. As she placed it on the stove, I cringed back and away. Although ecstatic to hear about Mom's dinner choice (hamburger stew with black olives, corn, and tomatoes is our favorite dish), I couldn't help but feel extremely nervous as she pulled out that pressure cooker. I watched my mother carefully as she placed all the ingredients into the metal canister, twisting the lid into place. I just knew that the pressure cooker was going to explode someday, and I waited in heightened anticipation of that moment, always behind a wall that allowed me a peeking vantage point. Kate stood near me, clearly sharing my anxiety. Shari and Danielle were oblivious because they were still pretty young. They only turned to look once when the whistle started to squeal on top of the pressure cooker. The cap jiggled all around, the steam escaping in a thin, narrow spray.

I couldn't believe how close Mom stood to the pressure cooker, staring at it with spellbound fascination. There have been a few times when it looked as though Mom was going to stick her hand straight into the steam. Her hand, shaky and tentative, began to rise up toward it until, as close as a few inches away, she pulled it back at last. If she had ever stuck her hand into that steam, I knew that I would have to run over and pull it out. But it never happened.

It wasn't long before the stew was finished cooking. Kate, Shari, and I gathered around the low turquoise table that was shaped like a lily pad as Mom put plates down for each of us. Danielle was too young for this kind of hard food; she sat in her high chair eating mashed carrots. Mom was sitting on a stool at the counter, distractedly separating the olives from the other ingredients. She took maybe three bites of the remaining pile, which consisted of the corn, hamburger, and tomatoes, and then pushed her bowl away. As quietly as possible, Kate and I finished our dinner, doing everything we could to keep Shari quiet, too, but Shari didn't like to be quiet. She was a noisemaker who didn't seem to understand yet how quiet Mom liked it to be.

Kate and I took our plates and Shari's plate to the sink. By the time we got back to the table, she had already made a mess—milk poured onto the napkin, which had been decorated with pieces of black olive that she had picked from her plate before it was taken away. She was very happy with her creation. Kate and I tried not to make a big deal of it because we didn't want her to get in trouble with Mom.

Mom came down from her stool and looked at what Shari had made on the turquoise table. It was a face: black olives for the eyes, mouth, and hair and a stray piece of corn for the nose. Mom smiled at Shari, whose mischievous eyes had convinced her to smile many times before.

"It's beautiful, Shari, but you need to clean it up now, dear."

Shari wanted to leave it there, so Dad could see it, too, and to our surprise Mom agreed. Then Mom picked up

Danielle and sat in front of our new TV set without turning
it on. Kate went over and turned it on for them. Shari was
asleep when Dad came home, but Mom had already swept
the napkin, milk, and olive creation into the garbage can.
Dad would get to see many more of Shari's creative expressions
in the years that followed. Even at three years of age, Shari
seemed to know that she was an artist, too.

～

Kate and I wait patiently on the half-moon couch as Danielle
touches up the talcum powder on her face for the second half of
Oh, Dolly. The talcum powder has the effect of making Danielle
look like a girl who has been drained of blood or a clown who has
lost all hope. These plays frequently have to do with the insane, a
theme we are always trying to make sense of.

Danielle takes the stage: the red Oriental rug in our living room.
She sucks in her cheeks, tilts her head, and stares vacantly into space,
all the while clutching a beat-up black handbag. Michele, as the
mother, leads Danielle around. Their purpose is to locate a boyfriend for Danielle's character. It's obvious that this will never happen. Danielle's character is so crazy, no one with even a smattering
of sense would see her as a prospective romantic partner. The plot
is always the same. Arm in arm, they do find a guy, who is somehow always played by Shari. "He" gets hoodwinked by the cun-
ning, manipulative mother to sit on a bench with Danielle and
talk with her. After maybe two minutes of trying to speak with her,
the guy realizes this woman is not operating with all of her facul-
ties. "He" eyes her suspiciously. It is usually at this point that Shari
loses it, laughing and crashing to the floor. I can certainly understand why. All the fleshy planes of Danielle's face are flattened by
the powder, her lips, nostrils, and eyes exaggerated by poorly ap-

plied makeup. She has played this part too many times, I think to myself; she's too convincing as this haunted and bereft girl. We are unable to take our eyes from her face; it's either laugh or cry. Kate and I practically fall off the half-moon couch with our involuntary choice, laughter, but clutch each other, remaining steadily upright. This time Shari stays focused and is able to stay in character until the end of the skit. As the guy, she gets up and runs away, leaving Danielle alone on the bench. It's heartbreaking. She sits, seemingly unaware, until her mother swoops in to rescue her.

"We didn't like him anyway," the mother reassures.

The two of them shuffle off the rug and right out of character. I, for one, am relieved when Danielle's face relaxes back into Danielle's real face. With her face still covered with powder, Danielle becomes an audience participant along with Kate as Shari, Michele, and I perform, *Oh Well, What Can You Do?* This skit takes all of five minutes. The basic plot is, as with *Oh, Dolly,* always the same, with new circumstances revolving around a familiar predicament that needs to be solved. Today's installment has to do with a birthday party to which no one comes and at which the main character, Mindy, played by Michele, is left alone with her stuffed animals, her parents, and an uneaten birthday cake. This leads to the eternal final question, always spoken by Mindy, "Oh well, what can you do?" Obviously, nothing.

This is the last production of the day. We rearrange the furniture and tidy up the living room in preparation for the arrival of Migga Burns and her new boyfriend, Bill. Kate and I can't fathom how an older woman such as Migga can have a boyfriend, as she calls him. We didn't know adults could have them, although we now think that Dad has what we call a girlfriend for lack of a better term. It's definitely one of the ladies from Dad's oil-painting class, and her name is Mary. He's introduced my sisters and me to her and not to any of the other ladies from the class. We've seen Dad and Mary walking together down and up the studio path, Dad tenderly holding one of her elbows, unlike the obligatory way he used to support our mother's elbow. Our father is not a boy and neither is Bill, although he sometimes acts like one, we have to admit. We thought boyfriends and girlfriends belonged to the young.

Migga and Bill are coming to stay with us during another one of Dad's painting trips, this time to Vietnam. I protested at first, insisting I could take care of my sisters myself, but Dad said he really wanted Migga around, especially since it was summer. He also said something just before he left that made me awfully suspicious of Migga, Bill, and Dad.

"I know you girls are going to have a really good time on the trip."

"What trip, Dad?"

"Oh. You know, a little summer trip."

After kisses, hugs, and a lot of tears, Dad was gone, with not another word spoken about a "little summer trip."

Migga and Bill arrive bearing bags of groceries. That first night we have a feast and over dinner Migga announces that we are going on a long trip. The final destination will be a surprise until one of us figures it out. Neither Kate nor I feel so good about this, and our faces must reveal our misgivings, for Migga and Bill keep trying to assure us that it will be fun this way. We eventually fake our approval so they can stop attempting to convince us and so Shari, Danielle, and Michele will stop watching our faces and relax.

While we are packing for the trip (Migga tells us to make sure we bring along our bathing suits, Hint #1—some hint; it happens to be summer everywhere in the Northern Hemisphere) Mom calls. Shari picks up the phone first and is thus the one to break the news to her about the mystery trip. I hear her voice shift; it goes up a level and becomes strained. Frank. I race into the kitchen and gently take the phone away from her. "Let me talk to him, Shari. It's okay." She smiles weakly, her face already gone a color resembling cliff rock. She stands near me as I blurt into the receiver, "Yeah, Frank?"

He wants to know where we are going. He wants to know whose big idea this is and don't we know how much pain Mom goes through because of things like this. His voice is even and hard, stirring a fury in me that feels like it could escalate out of control. I clench my fists and teeth as Frank asks, "Do you know where you're going, Carol?"

"No, Frank. I'm going to hang up now. We have to pack."

"Wait a minute. Say goodbye to your mother, for Christ's sake."

Mom asks if I know when we'll be back and I answer, "No." Mom doesn't ask to speak to Migga. What would be the point of that? Migga hates Mom and tries, through the use of seemingly subtle questions about Mom's mental status, to make us question her authority: "Has your mother been forgetting your names lately, girls?" was the most recent question Migga asked us. Mom's voice is fading, getting feathery and thin. I struggle to stay calm. I can't help her. I can't help her. I can't help her. "Bye, Mom." "Bye, dear. I love you." "Love you, too."

I'm not sure what to do or where to go when I hang up the phone, so I go to check on Shari. She is in her room, tracing the bedspread pattern with one of her nail-bitten fingers. As I sit down on the bed next to her, I try pushing the presence of Mom and Frank off the back of my neck where I fear they will become embedded, but it's too late. The physical tension from the phone conversation descends, lodging itself in my throat; I spend the next few days suppressing the urge to scream. I look Shari in the eyes to see where she is; how far did she go into self-deprecation this time? Her eyes are clear and she doesn't turn from my gaze. She hasn't gone far. I take her hand.

"C'mon, Shari. I'll help you pack." Neither one of us tells Migga that Mom called. What would be the point?

Climbing into Cindy With Guts, we head onto the southbound lane of the New Jersey Turnpike. Without Dad at the helm, the usual sense of joyful expectation is missing. My sisters and I crawl into our established traveling positions, hoping to find remnants of our last trip with Dad tucked in the corners of the car. Kate and Danielle start a license plate game: whoever shouts out a word starting with the first letter that appears on a license plate gets a point. The game fizzles out after just a few rounds and we start to lamely sing our practice songs from the singing lessons we attend every Saturday with Lela Holiday.

Dad has been religiously taking us to Lela's Riverside Drive apartment building for the past two years. In his vain attempt to corral our singing talent into a quintet with seasoned performing skills, he perseveres, imagining us becoming the next Lennon Sisters. His efforts are not totally wasted on us. Our voices have certainly become stronger and more refined and we've learned some pretty snappy show tunes, but when it comes to performing in front of strangers we're a bust. We are too self-conscious and, unable to invoke the muses of stage, always end up standing stiffly in one of two linear formations. Although when we do our annual Christmas performance at the Salamagundi Club, an artists' club in Manhattan that Dad belongs to, we liven up, presenting ourselves with moments of genuine animation.

Migga comments on how nice we sound, but I don't believe her. She's swallowing hard and too often, a sure sign that she's bending the truth. We stop singing and start waving at passing drivers. It takes us what seems like years to get out of New Jersey. In Maryland, I ask Migga and Bill when we'll know where we're going. Bill says, "When we get there," smiling slyly over at Migga, whose smile with those big teeth can't cover up the fact that she's a little uncomfortable with this whole thing.

Last night, Kate and I discussed our theories about this trip before going to sleep. We decided it's a plot to get back at Mom, but we're not sure who is the mastermind behind it. It couldn't be Migga; she doesn't have a devious brain cell in her head, although she's pulled a couple of tricks on us that surprised the "chickens" out of us, as Michele would say, and has said some pretty wicked things about Mom. We concluded that it had to be Dad. But for the life of us, we can't understand why he would use this trip to torture Mom; it's just not like him.

"Does Dad know where we're going?" I ask Migga.

"Of course, Carol." She looks positively shocked, as if my question is an insult. "We would never take you girls on a trip without your father knowing about it."

"Why are you taking us on this trip?"

"We told you. So you girls could have fun."

As we pull into the parking lot of a motel in Virginia, Michele asks, "Is this where we're going?" Bill and Migga just laugh.

Bill books two rooms. None of us can believe it: a motel, we never stay in motels. Who is paying for this?

My sisters can't fall asleep no matter how many stories I tell from the cot that has been set up next to Kate and Danielle's double bed. In the middle of my intentionally boring narrative, questions and comments fly out from the mouths of my sisters.

"Do you think Dad's thinking about us right now?" Michele asks.

"Yes," Kate answers.

"Do Migga and Bill have enough money to pay for the motel?" Shari wants to know.

"I hope so," I answer.

"Do you think Mom and Frank are mad at us?" Danielle asks.

"No," Kate says.

Finally, each one drops off, leaving me awake and staring at the ceiling.

Just as I'm about to drift off myself, I hear a low mumbling coming from one of the beds. At first, I can't make out who it is, then the voice rises up more clearly, and I know it is Shari and she is insisting, "Stop the music. Stop the music." With that, she gets up from the bed, makes her way to the door, and begins to fiddle with the lock. I get to her before she is able to negotiate an escape. I lead her carefully back to the bed, making sure not to wake her. The last time I found her sleepwalking, I inadvertently woke her up and she wouldn't stop crying. She lies back down, and I stroke her forehead softly until her breathing becomes steady and deep. The lights on the ceiling from the cars going by the motel diminish as this long night lengthens. I'm not sure when I finally fall asleep; I am listening, counting the measured rhythm of my sisters' breathing until I'm assured that I, too, can let go.

We make it to Georgia the next day, the hours bouncing off the car as we find our road trip pace. Everyone is more relaxed, so we can be focused on our games, songs, and stories without being distracted by doubts.

In Georgia, we stay at an old hotel, the trees covered with Spanish moss, which none of us have ever seen before. We stand in awe of the draping tresses that hang off of every branch.

No one has any trouble getting to sleep in our Georgia hotel room. I tell stories in a southern accent, which has a lulling effect on my sisters. Right before falling asleep, Danielle whispers something about calling Mom. She doesn't want to worry anyone. I'm sure the thought of Mom sitting on her stool by the window chewing her nails has been eating away at Danielle ever since our departure. Kate tells her that we'll try calling Mom in the morning.

We forget all about calling Mom the next morning when we find out that Migga and Bill are gone. Kate wakes me by shaking my shoulder and whispering loudly, "Migga hasn't come in for us and it's eight-thirty." We pad next door to their room and knock. By this time Shari, Danielle, and Michele have joined us, rubbing their eyes and smelling of hotel pillow disinfectant. There is no answer. I tell my sisters to wait in the hotel room while I go and ask at the front desk. The very sweet yet suspicious woman who comes to the desk when I ring the bell informs me that Migga and Bill left about a half hour ago, instructing her to tell us not to worry, they would be back soon, and we should stay put.

"Did they say where they were going?"

"No, honey. But they left these donuts for y'all."

Back in our room we eat donuts and watch TV, none of us willing to give a voice to the fear that is creeping into every bite of donut. After an hour, I go back to the front desk to ask the lady if she has heard anything from Migga and Bill. Not a word. She asks if I'm all right, and of course I say, "Yes."

It's not long before Migga and Bill finally turn up, both of them gushing with their secret. Migga is holding a small bouquet of flowers and her face is bright red. She motions Bill to speak and he motions her to speak. "C'mon, Migga; c'mon," we urge.

"We're married!" Migga shouts out with a force none of us knew she had. We're totally silent; the TV is the only thing making any kind of noise.

"To each other?" Michele wants to know. Everyone laughs.

Migga grabs Michele, giving her a thick hug as she says, "Of course, dear." I can only conclude that adults are weird. I know Kate feels the same way—she looks at me with her eyebrows raised and her mouth twisted into a lopsided smirk.

We finish our donuts, but the mood has shifted to one of celebration. Bill asks Migga to dance. I ask Shari to dance. Kate asks Danielle and Michele to dance. Bill tries to bend Migga backward and kiss her in an apparent attempt at suave and debonair behavior. Migga turns red again, sputters an unintelligible word, and pushes Bill away. We all stop dancing and begin to pack up.

As we pull out of the hotel parking lot, Bill looks over at Migga and says in his best southern accent, "Want to go to Florida for our honeymoon, honey child?" A honeymoon with five children along? I, for one, have never heard of such a thing, but I'm not going to refuse to go now, honeymoon or not. We didn't ask them to get married, for heaven's sake.

We arrive at the Sunrise Golf Village in Fort Lauderdale later that afternoon. A huge blue-and-pink concrete arch with the words "Welcome to Sunrise Golf Village" and a large replica of a golf ball balanced at the apex of the arch stretches over the entrance to the development of little houses. Bill tells us that one of the houses belongs to him and that he bought it ten years ago when houses in Florida were cheap. Did Bill buy this house because he plays golf? He didn't bring any golf clubs with him. He stands proudly in front of his house as we climb wearily out of the car, legs practically giving way from lack of use. "Is this where we're going?" Michele asks. Everyone nods.

After a tour of the house, which takes about three minutes, I ask if we can walk around the neighborhood. Migga and Bill tell us to be back by six o'clock and we head off. At the end of the block is a house that we immediately notice is empty. There's a FOR SALE sign jammed into the ground of the front yard, and the house has the scraggly look of an orphan. A fence runs along the perimeter of the yard, and I poke my head over it, discovering a built-in pool. The gate opens easily, no lock. Quietly we sneak in.

My sisters start yelling upon reaching the pool; there must be one hundred small frogs floating belly-up in various stages of decay. I scream at the sight, too loudly, and my sisters turn to stare at me. This uncharacteristic sound momentarily stuns them. I can see I've scared them just as much as this pool of rotting amphibians has, and they wait to see what I'm going to do next. I know that if I scream again or fall apart in any way they could temporarily lose their confidence in me, so I don't scream.

I look around the backyard and see a pool net lying against the fence. I survey the scene, trying to figure out where we can dump the dead frogs. There's a small metal shed that has been set up against the back wall of the house. Kate scopes it out and finds that the door slides open without a problem. It's empty except for a few rusty hand tools. I give the pool net to Kate, who starts nabbing the frogs and tossing them into the shed. Without looking at them, I pull out the frogs with my hands and add them to the growing pile in the shed. Shari, Danielle, and Michele remove as many as they can before getting grossed out. There are a couple of frogs that have become stuck to the side of the pool and must be pried off with a stick. They fall apart into slimy fragments, making removal a difficult process.

For some reason we've become obsessed with ridding this pool of dead frogs and we don't quit until all visible remains have been eliminated. The filter has come on while we worked, and there's the faint smell of chlorine hovering above the water. Despite the fact that the pool is probably still swimming with dead frog germs, we all jump in, fully dressed. It seemed like exactly the right thing to do.

On our way back to the house, dripping with slimy water, Kate stops and exclaims, "Oh my God, you guys. Look at us!" We're not a pretty sight. We decide that we'll tell Migga and Bill that we ran through a sprinkler somewhere in the Sunrise Golf Village. Danielle is uneasy about this. She insists that we walk around the village until we find a sprinkler to run through which, thankfully we do. We get home in time for a dinner of packaged macaroni and cheese. Migga and Bill are totally satisfied with our explanation that we simply couldn't resist the temptation of a sprinkler on such a hot July evening.

They have already set up our sleeping quarters, a tiny room with mattresses jammed in so tightly there is no space to do anything other than sleep and crawl around on the mattresses, which, of course, we do. After an hour of playing, tickling, and mattress romping, Migga breaks in and tells us we're going to the beach come first light of day the next morning and that we all need to get a good night's rest. We hadn't noticed it was so late.

Before we fall asleep Danielle asks that we remember the frogs, the ones heading for the pool, the ones about to jump in not knowing there is chlorine, not knowing there are concrete walls that they will never be able to scale.

"We'll go save them in the morning," Kate says, which in fact we attempt to do. As Migga and Bill pack up the car, we run out of the house, telling them we want to say good morning to a little girl we met the night before. We did say "hi" to a little girl last night and plan on saying "hi" to her this morning, too; it's not a lie.

There are at least fifteen frogs in the pool by the time we get there, five of which have already died. We save the others, taking them across the road to a drainage stream that doesn't smell of chlorine, has gentle grassy slopes for easy frog access, and has frog pools of all shapes and sizes.

We're running back down the street to the house, when Danielle stops abruptly and says, "We're going to have to move here so we can keep saving the frogs. Who will do it when we go back to New Jersey?"

"We can't stay in Florida because of the frogs," I respond rather abruptly and without much sympathy.

Danielle turns and runs as fast as she can to Bill's house. We find her crying in the mattress room. Kate consoles her and explains the reasons that we can't stay in Florida.

"Dad would miss us if we stayed in Florida. We would have to go to new schools, which might not be as good as the ones we go to now. We would miss our house and it would miss us if we stayed in Florida. And we would never see snow again."

Danielle nods in acknowledgment even as she continues to figure out a way to save more frogs. Migga comes in and asks what's wrong. Shari tells Migga that Danielle's feelings got hurt, but that everything is all right now, and the rest of us get ready to leave for the beach. Shari stays behind with Danielle for a couple of minutes to help her get through this. I look back to see Shari whispering into Danielle's ear. Standing next to me is Michele, who is carefully watching them, too.

Michele is happiest when totally immersed in Shari and Danielle's shenanigans. When they don't include Michele, it's difficult to comfort her; she doesn't understand why they want to spend so much time alone, and any explanation that Kate or I offer just seems to make Michele feel worse. How can we explain that theirs is a partnership forged years ago, with its own language, rules, dreams, and pain? Kate and I have both admitted, but only to each other in discussions on the half-moon couch, that we have also been jealous of Shari and Danielle's relationship. We don't know what Shari says to Danielle to bring her out of her sadness; she just seems to understand how to make Danielle feel better.

I go to them now, after the frog incident, knowing Danielle will accept my apology for being insensitive about the frogs without resistance. We finish getting ready and leave for a long white sand beach in eastern Florida.

There is one photograph that survives our trip to Florida: the five of us are lying at the water's edge, squinting up at Migga and Bill, whose shadows are visibly cast over us. When I look at the photograph, I can actually recall the sensation of the water running up over my legs and the way the bathing suit dug into my body. I can remember how much I loved my sisters, how our games and schemes pulled me back from adolescence, long enough to be with them as a child again. We were free of thoughts spent in contemplation of anything other than play. To this day, I hate wearing bathing suits and sometimes frogs can still elicit feelings of guilt; we didn't get to save nearly enough of them.

Dad was waiting for us when we got home, bearing gifts from a different sea. Holding out his arms to us as we, even Kate and I, ran to him, he asked with a smile, "Did you girls have a good trip to Florida?"

"Yes!" came our chorus of replies.

"I knew you would."

II

~

Splinters: 1973–76

Kate, Danielle, Michele, Shari, Carol
Singing at a cousin's wedding, 1970.

GOODBYE TO OUR HOUSE

Dad is at the door at last
And with sad children mounting fast
And kissing memories in chorus sing,
"Goodbye, goodbye to Everything!"

To house and garden, trees and lawn,
The fishpond vine we swung upon.
Goodbye to the bee that gave me a sting.
"Goodbye, goodbye to Everything!"

Goodbye to the floods at the kitchen door
Whenever the rain would pour and pour,
Goodbye to the fires that kept me warm
From running in the outside storm.

Goodbye to the deep well way down the cliff,
Goodbye to snow fights that made my arms stiff,
Goodbye to the white dove with his small blue band,
Goodbye to every part of our land.

Goodbye to the splinters from our floor,
O ladder at the clubhouse door,
O cellar where the cobwebs cling.
"Goodbye, goodbye to Everything!"

Goodbye to the little blue men on the rug
Who snuck in the dark when we pulled out the plug,
Goodbye to our drawings all over the walls,
Goodbye to everything and all!

Rum goes the engine and off we go,
The trees and house smaller grow,
And last round the woody turn we swing,
"Goodbye, goodbye to Everything!"

But mostly goodbye to the heart of our land,
The warmth that will forever stand,
For peace and love it will always bring.
"Goodbye, goodbye, to Everything!"

SHARON AND MICHELE ORTLIP
(with a little help from Robert Louis Stevenson)

5

~

OVER THE CLIFF

K ate and I are doing our homework on the half-moon couch, minding what we can of our own business. It's not easy when the kids are giggling in the kitchen; it's the kind of laughter that indicates a plot is being unleashed, and most likely from Shari. Lately I find it difficult enough to concentrate on anything, especially on work that has no relevance to the traumatic social and emotional confusion plaguing every breath I take. Who is to help me? I can't think of one person to talk with, not even Kate. She might inadvertently spill it to Shari, Danielle, or Michele, and there it would become available to Frank. Any path that could possibly lead to him must be avoided. I am alone with my attraction to Mrs. Blake, my tenth-grade history teacher.

I remember the approximate moment when it became obvious that the cantilever of sexual desire had seesawed in a direction I had never anticipated: Mrs. Blake and I were standing outside the main office building at Greystone Mental Hospital in central New Jersey. For a social studies report I was investigating the conditions of three mental hospitals, and Mrs. Blake had agreed to be my sponsor. This meant she would accompany me to each hospital, a task she seemed more than enthused to do.

As Mrs. Blake and I stood on the lawn that day, I began telling her about my mother and the memory I had of waiting for her with Dad and my sisters on this very spot years ago. Kate had been the first to see Mom, emerging like a silhouette, silent and pressed flat against the ground as she slowly slid toward us. Everything about Mom, even her long black hair, was pulled back, like her skin had been stretched as tightly as it would go. It didn't look as though Mom could make any facial expression without tearing her skin apart. The only person who was able to reach through to Mom was Danielle, who took Mom's hand as if picking up a wounded bird. I saw Mom's fingers fluttering against Danielle's palm as we walked slowly to the car, Dad leading the way without a word.

Somewhere in the midst of the images that were returning to me with vociferous clarity, Mrs. Blake touched my hand. I turned toward her quickly, jarred back to the present by the prickling sensation on my flesh. Her eyes, all tender and glittery, blinked at me and encouraged me to go on. I blinked in return and became mute. She let her fingers rest on my hand for another few seconds, barely making actual contact; the infinitesimal weight of her fingertips pounded with intoxicating closeness. Heat suddenly and forcefully beat against the inside of my groin and vaulted into my neck and face. Mrs. Blake dropped her hand from mine and apologized for embarrassing me; she hadn't meant to make me feel so self-conscious and put-on-the-spot about such painful memories. I wasn't hearing much of what she said. I had turned away from her and was trying to gain some control of my legs, which didn't seem capable of holding me up. Mrs. Blake asked if I would be all right and placed her hand on my shoulder. This made me shudder noticeably; I honestly could not stop the involuntary response to her touch. She walked rapidly to the office, shouting back something about water as her blond head vanished inside.

I sat down on the grass without planning to, digging my hands into the earth beneath. Mrs. Blake must've thought that I was having an anxiety attack. If I was experiencing "abandonment angst," I wasn't aware of it. All I knew was that I wanted to kiss Mrs. Blake more than anything, certainly more than I had ever wanted to kiss Brian, my ex-boyfriend.

I held onto some blades of grass with one hand as Mrs. Blake gently handed me a cup of water. Carefully taking it, I sipped until I was able to calm down. In my mind, I was simultaneously begging her to stroke my hair and to get away from me. She said that I didn't have to do the interview with the director of the hospital that day if this experience was too hard for me. I assured her that I was fine and could go through with it. Later that night as I lay in bed fantasizing (ashamedly and exhilaratingly) about her, I berated myself for not canceling; if we had rescheduled, we could've spent another day together.

Now months into my secret love life with Mrs. Blake, I am ready to confess to someone. I almost told Mrs. Blake herself one day in her office; I came by on my way to class asking for a pen to borrow. Over the course of six months I had found both creative and not so creative reasons for turning up in her office, and she never seemed to mind or question my motives. She gave me a pen and sat studying my face, for what, I hadn't a clue. Instead of averting my gaze, which was what I normally would've done, I remained facing her, allowing us to fall into a silent and, for me, loaded moment, full of expectation. The words "I'm in love with you" entered my mind just as she opened her beautiful mouth to say, "How could your mother have left someone like you?" I shrugged automatically, used to fending off such questions, said, "Thanks for the pen," and wandered back into the crowded hallway. Mrs. Blake felt sympathy for me, sympathy, that was all. Although I already had known that sympathy was the basis of her acceptance of my attention, I had hoped that maybe some sexual desire existed in there as well.

What a total fool I have been and continue to be as I try to get focused on my homework. I scratch at my homework sheet as Kate seemingly concentrates on hers. Without realizing it, I have written Mrs. Blake's name all over my assignment. When I glance up at Kate's face to see if she has noticed, she asks, "Mrs. Blake?" All I can drag out is, "Yeah." Kate turns away, but not before she has given me a penetrating look of suspicion. The next time she and I would discuss my attraction for a woman would not be until college, when again I became distracted by a female teacher. For now I let my secret settle back into the deep recesses of my body where it won't have a chance of being discovered.

I look up to see Michele entering the living room, grinning and holding her hands behind her back. Neither Kate nor I are paying much attention as she inquires if either of us plans to wash our hair tonight. It is me who innocently responds, "I am." Before I know it, Michele has planted an aluminum pie dish of whipped cream on my forehead, the contents of which ooze up, down, and all over my hair, head, and face. As the dish lands directly on my already-trashed homework assignment, I look up at Michele through the whipped cream and calmly ask, "Why did you do that Michele?"

"Because Shari told me to."

Everyone is laughing, including me.

———

It is around this time that I have another bewildering dream about Shari. I mention it to Kate one night after Shari, Danielle, and Michele have gone to bed, but she can't make any sense out of it, either. I wonder if it's a dream precipitated by my old fear of losing Shari to an inner world that she tries to keep hidden from us. Lately we haven't been as concerned about Shari's state of mind. This is in part because Frank hasn't been around since a clinic tragedy prevented us from visiting the clinic every other weekend, as scheduled. One of Frank's favorite young patients hanged himself from a tree out in the back field, and Frank was the one who found him, swaying like a limp rag doll. Mom called the night it happened and told us that she has never seen Frank so withdrawn and despondent. At the sister meeting that follows my announcement of this news, Danielle suggests that we call Frank to tell him that we are thinking about him; we never do.

The dream about Shari and the feelings it rekindles are just more of the worrisome elements, along with my fading crush on Mrs. Blake, that are constantly gnawing at me.

~

I dream that my sisters and I are standing on the curb of a street in a city resembling New York but without the skyscrapers. There is a fire hydrant near us and an empty shopping cart. We are about to sing; a small crowd of people has gathered to listen. And then Shari slowly collapses to the pavement in what appears to be a faint. The rest of us kneel beside her, only to find that what remains of Shari is her deflated skin.

We are left holding an empty bag that only seconds before contained her.

～

Dad doesn't ask us to sing anymore. Like anything that isn't meant to be, the energy spent on our singing career slowly dissipates, leaving my father's dream unfulfilled. Kate and I agree that we wanted to make it big for his sake. We will continue to sing for him and for ourselves, and later Shari, Michele, and I would try to resurrect a sister singing group, it never happens.

Dad calls me into his studio on a day when my sisters are not around. The stoop where they usually listen is uncharacteristically void of their eager ears. I strongly feel the lack of their presence as Dad somberly removes his worn-out brown cowboy hat, runs a weary hand through his uncombed hair, and looks out at me with bloodshot eyes. We haven't had a studio chat in a couple of years, not since our "talk" about menstruation when I was thirteen. Instead of offering me the usual stool to sit on, he absently waves toward a chair at a low table where he always sits himself; we are now on the same level. He spreads his powerful arms out across the table; I can see that his fingernails are clean, which they always are. Paint and dirt can cake his hands and arms, but Dad makes sure his fingernails are free of any artistic debris. It doesn't take long before he brings a hand to his head and tucks his little finger down into the distinct crevasse between the bridge of his nose and his forehead. He closes his eyes as he sighs deeply. "Carolina, Carolina, nothin' could be finah, right, Carol?"

I smile and nod. Dad begins to speak. I can tell from the first few sentences that he will go off into a land of words that will eventually come together into a final phrase that will be what he wanted to say all along. Today he brings his vehement opinion about the waste of his father's talent into the warm-up monologue, and I settle in for a lengthy listen and wait. But this time, he doesn't go on. Suddenly turning toward me, he becomes still, watching my face. This makes me nervous, and I squirm in my chair. I don't remember his exact words, and I'm not sure I ever will. All I know is that within a few seconds I learn that we are being forced to move from our home because the property has been rezoned for high-rise apartment buildings. That means the taxes are way too high for him to keep up with, and we have about a year or two before we have to leave. Other houses on the block will start being razed within the month, so we should probably start saying good-bye to our neighbors, like the Stabiles and the Thompsons. Dad already has his eye on a house on Main Street; he'll take us to see it soon.

Pushing past the thickness of my disbelief, I find enough energy to get up from the table, hug Dad, and make my way to the porch, where I hold tightly to the railing, looking out at the river that has helped me stay steady all these years. It is up to me to tell my sisters. Simply imagining the expressions on their faces as I deliver this devastating news keeps me gripping the railing and facing into a cold wind. No matter how many deep breaths I take, I can't stop shaking.

Not even a month later, the old gray house at the end of Old Palisades Road next to Monument Park is coming down. My sisters and I stare at the growing rubbish pile from the sidewalk as savage machinery rips at the insides of the house; we are unable to move or speak. Shari kneels and begins to sob. We gather around her, our bodies becoming one form as we lift Shari up from the ground and slowly shuffle home. Looking along the length of our block, I count the houses; there are five more to go before the bulldozers get to our house. The first of many countdowns has begun.

Life turns gray. The realization that we must leave our home creeps into every motion, every task. When I speak, I feel unuttered words lying in wait just beyond tongue's reach. Mrs. Blake and other teachers ask what is wrong and I answer, "Nothing," because there are absolutely no words to express what it is I am feeling. I want to say something, have my emotions take shapes that could be spoken, but I cannot dig my way to them. Perhaps they are not words but more like guttural sounds. If I felt sure that someone could withstand the force of the noises I might release, then the screaming could possibly begin. As it is, I, along with my befuddled and subdued sisters, remain in a state of sleepwalking.

We go through the expected motions: going to school, doing our homework, eating, sleeping, and taking baths. My sisters and I are like the walking dead as we follow our well-worn trails to school, and I don't know how we wind up at school without getting lost. We present ourselves normally and this charade feels deeply familiar, the skins we wear slipping on and off with an ease mastered long ago.

Each morning we stop to inspect the progress of our block's demolition. We take enough notice to formulate predictions about when the bulldozer will strike down the next house. These daily stops take time and energy; invariably we are late for school and depleted of what little attention we had reserved for learning. All of my former concerns have fallen away; I care only for thoughts that keep me close to images of my home. Classmates speak, teachers instruct and advise, but all I can hear is the voice of the cliffs.

At home we begin to wander, the rooms swaying from the weight of our haunting. Sometimes at night I will find one of my sisters sitting alone in a room or on the porch staring into the darkness. Then together we sit huddled against the pain of this letting go. Two by two, alone or all together, my sisters and I head into the rhythm of emotional preparation for what lies directly in front of us: irrevocable grief. Little did any of us consciously know that this preparation would necessarily carry us through a deeper, more piercing grief, one that all the preparation in the universe could not have saved three of my sisters and me from experiencing.

About a month later, another house is down, the Stabiles'. As the vacant lot grows, so does the number of cars, workmen, and intimidating machines that fill it. Perhaps it is my imagination, but the men seem to swagger with excitement as they survey the potential of so much empty prime real estate. They spend a lot of time surveying; they stand around with hard hats on, though I can't fathom why—there is not a single obvious object threatening their heads except perhaps the anger we have been hurling at them every day. Some of the workmen try talking with us, but we ignore them, occasionally making rude comments, needing faces and objects to blame.

We begin to plan a strategy of protest, cardboard, markers, and sticks becoming the tools we use to express our feelings. Out of books filled with famous quotations and essays we borrow phrases, adding our own creative words to fill placards with lines of spirited intensity. Each evening, after the workmen have gone home to families we know they must have, love, and feed with the salaries they are making from destroying our world, my sisters and I plant signs in the loose, exposed dirt of the vacant lot. In the mornings the workmen are greeted with: "You call this progress, we call it insanity," "You tear down nature to put up filing cabinets of human lives," "Thank you for destroying our home." Every day, one of the older men working at the site carefully takes the signs down and places them respectfully underneath a large oak tree that will, of course, soon be turned into wood chips. A line of sturdy lilac bushes and some thick shrubs that run the length of the back wall of our garage make the perfect hiding place from which we watch the workmen.

When two more houses have vanished into what appears to be "thin air" (trucks come to remove most of what once existed), my sisters and I decide it is time for us to try more severe, guerrilla war tactics. The signs we have been using are not going far enough in conveying our sorrow and rage; only one old guy seems to be noticing.

We meet down beneath the safe branches of Maggie, the magnolia tree, and discuss the best possible ways we can sabotage the destruction, now that it's obvious the signs are not working. We all agree that messing with the machinery is way too risky and dangerous and could possibly get us into trouble with the law. None of us really understand what "the law" consists of exactly, but we're all afraid of it nonetheless; Shari is convinced that if caught, we would be separated, put in jail or in juvenile detention homes for really bad children, and kept inside so long that by the time we got out we wouldn't be able to recognize one another. That's enough to stop our fantasies of going near the bucket loaders and bulldozers.

After talking about our options for what seems like hours, we conclude that the only way to effectively get to the workmen is through their machines; there is no other way, even if it is dangerous and we run the risk of being sent to juvenile detention homes.

I come up with the radical notion of slashing random tires on the workmen's cars. No one thinks this is a good idea at all, especially Danielle and Michele, their faces curling up into looks of complete fright; they can't believe I would even suggest such a thing. Embarrassed and suddenly aware of how serious this could become, I take it back. I look at the faces of my sisters, earnest and so totally concerned with our plight; maybe we should just forget about these plans right now.

I catch Kate's eye. Before I can make the suggestion that we should quit, Kate offers, "Why don't we just let out a little bit of air from some of the workmen's tires every day?"

There is immediate agreement and enthusiastic jabber. I command with absolute, unwavering, and dictatorial conviction that Kate and I will be the only ones to do the actual air letting. Of course, there is protest from the other kids. The fear of incarceration is now long gone and has been taken over by their growing excitement. They want more than anything to participate in the actual act of this brilliant sabotage, but Kate and I are insistent that they continue to be the sign placers and be the ones who are on the lookout.

"Kate and I are the oldest and have to be the ones to take responsibility if we get caught, which we won't."

It's agreed, and we leave the woods confident in our plan, which will be implemented on Monday after school. Most of the workmen are down below the vacant lot during the days, hacking away at the foundational rock in where the high-rise parking garages will go beneath the apartments. We will easily be able to get to their cars without being noticed, although Shari suggests we wear clothes that will blend in with the colors of the vacant lot and paint our faces the way people do in the army. Neither Kate nor I feel that's necessary; it might even make us more obvious. We set up a warning system, the kids strategically placed in order to watch for approaching workmen, innocent citizens, or unknowing fathers. At the very first sign of any such person, Shari, Danielle, or Michele will let out a cry resembling a bird, doesn't matter what kind, just as long as Kate and I can hear it.

The Sunday night before our first attack, Danielle wants to know if anyone will be hurt by our actions. I assure her that no one will be harmed, merely inconvenienced, and maybe, hopefully, it will cause them to think about what they are doing.

"If they think about what they are doing does it mean they will stop tearing down the houses and go away?" Danielle asks.

We meet at four o'clock on Monday afternoon, beneath the old oak in front of the Thompsons', which has served as a leaning post many times before. I rest against it, as if this could be the final instant it will be asked to hold me. Looking up into the empty branches, I see so much sky; I wonder if sky is what trees dream of becoming or if they even dream at all? I hope they do. I whisper to the oak. Running my palms against the gnarly bark, I say as many thanks as I can before we begin our dirty work; we don't have a whole lot of time left.

We're all in position. Kate and I slink toward the randomly chosen target cars: two along the periphery of the thirty or so cars that have become permanent fixtures of the vacant lot. Pushing against the nozzles of the inner tubes with small stones, Kate and I easily express the air from the back tires of the two cars and scurry to the safety of our lilac bush scouting blind. All five of us have gathered, panting and flushed with the excitement and fear of subversive activity. Guilt runs smoothly along the inside of my chest as I listen to the heavy breathing of my sisters; I should have stopped this plan. How could I have allowed us to become involved with a plot as devious and mean-spirited as this? Then Kate motions us to be still; she can see the workmen coming up from the cliffs below. Michele lets out a loud screech even though all of us are already back in our safety spot; she's clearly intent on doing a good job of being on watch. "Good job, Michele," Kate whispers.

Everything seems to be happening in slow motion. The workmen are taking way too much time reaching their cars; they are mumbling to one another in a language that sounds foreign; I suppose it's workmen's language. Slow, droopy words are collecting in their mouths and pooling up, spilling out in incoherent gushes. We wait for what seems like years and then the inevitable happens.

The two workmen whose cars have been tampered with finally arrive wearing the relieved end-of-the-day look on their faces. They slump into the drivers seats of their rigs and start up the motors. We hold our breaths. They begin to back out until the flat tires begin to scrape and drag against the ground. The workmen have no choice but to stop their cars. They leap out and rush to the back of their cars where they immediately see just how flat their tires actually are. Very—Kate and I have let out much more air than we'd thought. There is a single moment of anticipation that hangs right there in the air of the vacant lot, when I am sure that our minds meet with the minds of the workmen, for they swing around in our direction as if they know precisely who has done this to their cars and where we, the culprits, are hiding. My sisters and I have just enough time to drop down into the shrubs that separate our property from the Thompsons'. I hiss, "Don't move, kids. Don't even breathe." I am sure the two men are going to pound toward us, discover us lying in the early March muck, grab us by the throats, and strangle all breath from our bodies. But they don't.

We never find out exactly what happened next, because we lie there for probably half an hour before we dared to move. We hear voices, fast voices, then a car motor, car doors slamming, and cars pulling away. Michele whispers, "Can we get up now?"

"Not yet. Quiet."

We wait a few more minutes, and then I carefully raise my head, motioning with my hand for my sisters to stay down until given the okay. What I see surprises the "living daylights" out of me, as Dad might say.

The two cars are sitting right where the workmen have left them, tires still deflated. Stuck into the soil next to one of the cars is the sign that reads: "You call this progress, we call it insanity." Next to the other car is the sign that reads: "Thank you for destroying our home." We slowly extricate ourselves from behind the lilac bushes and stare in silence at the vacant lot. Danielle finally says, "That's not where we put the signs." I look over at the oak, which has witnessed everything. I look at it rising tall and silent against the sky, reminding me to be strong. For another month, my sisters and I continue to plant our signs in the dirt of the vacant lot, but we never let out any more air from the tires of any more workmen's cars.

We are all in desperate need of escape from the battering our hearts have taken ever since we learned of our imminent departure from the cliffs. We get it from friends and extracurricular activities, most of which seem ludicrous and pointless under the circumstances. Dad has been spending more time with his friend Les, who lives just around the corner and whose house is doomed as well. On a weekend night somewhere in the middle of the countdown, Dad and Les meet up at our house, plant themselves in the kitchen, and start singing "God Bless America." Kate and I can't understand why they choose this of all songs, given the fact that it is corporate America that is responsible for tearing our house down; I mean, don't they know that? Adults can be so exasperating. I have to conclude that because they fought in wars, patriotism wins out over everything else, even things like losing your home.

Les and Dad are in the kitchen, raising their fists into the air, emphasizing certain phrases of the song: "From the mountains, to the prairies, to the oceans white with foam." They've been drinking, which Dad only does when he's with Les, as far as we know. They get together regularly, something my sisters and I actually look forward to, especially Shari, who absolutely loves Les. He sways back and forth with such force, I'm always amazed that he doesn't end up on the linoleum or lose his really big nose. We listen from the living room, Kate and I smiling at each other when they really belt out a line. In a little while, they'll go up to Dad's studio and be buddies, continuing to sing songs that are old, from their war days, songs they don't want us to hear.

That night, just before they started singing, I overheard them talking about the state of Old Palisades Road. Their fists hit the table more than once; I've never heard either of them quite this angry. Les's face blows up so red when he's mad, I have to turn away. All the veins in his neck swell; I'm sure blood will soon squirt out all over the walls and floor. Dad tells me Les has high blood pressure but refuses to do anything about it like cutting down on eating high-fat foods or quitting smoking.

Nine months later, Les is dead from a cerebral hemorrhage. His death sends Shari into violent displays of anguish. She throws herself from room to room, wailing and crying out his name. "Why did he have to die? Why?" The rest of us think her grief is way out of proportion—we didn't know him that well—but Shari has been distraught for months, as we all have, and Les's death just seems to bring her that much closer to acknowledging the loss of our home.

Before long, every house except for ours, which is at the very end of the block, is gone. The winds crash into our house without any resistance now; we are all alone on the cliffs. There is emptiness in every direction. I go out into it one cold February night. There's been more than a year of deciphering the currents of our shifting lives, and I am just about worn-out. I go to the open earth, looking for relief. Falling to my knees in the middle of dirt, rock, and splinters from the busted houses, I push my face close to the ground, smelling, tasting, and listening to it. I will it to offer me the kind of peace only earth and stone seem to truly possess. My breathing becomes slow and long as I try to picture all the people who have walked this very spot and quietly pray for an end to the turbulence of these many months. Closing my eyes and nestling deeper into the dirt, I visualize faces spinning into patterns of light and sound: the faces of the people who have gone before us, the ones who moved along these cliffs when there was no Manhattan skyline to admire. I grasp fistfuls of dirt so tightly my hands ache, but I will not let go until I feel the earth and rock of the cliffs entering into my flesh, becoming part of my body; I want to carry something physical from this place within me. I realize that I am bleeding and that blood and earth are in fact merging; I vow not to wash my hands, to let the wounds heal over with the dirt tucked inside so every time I use my hands, make a gesture even, the cliffs will move with me.

Dad remains cheerful despite Les's death, obviously attempting to keep our spirits up for the transition. He spends a lot of time transplanting lilac bushes, bulbs, and trees to our new yard on Main Street; he even remembers to bring along the birdbath that has been a fixture in our family for as long as I've been alive. I can see just how adept he is at maintaining a positive attitude; he's been doing it for so long, becoming a master at it. He appears to remain in this state of buoyancy right up until the final moments. He allows us our grief, even granting us permission to write all over the walls with pencils once everything has been removed. In the stark glow of that last night in our house, my sisters and I scrawl private messages to the only home we have ever known.

Then, it's destruction day. Early in the morning, before school, Shari and I walk over to the house. I can see it rising up as we approach, partially hidden behind fog and smoky river haze. It stands empty and hollow. Overnight it has become gaunt and seems to be breaking open along all of its seams. There is no glass left in any of the windows, so great gusts can scrape away any radiance that might still be lingering there. Our house is unbearably empty the morning Shari and I go to send it off.

We are there to try excavating a few more paintings from the roof. A few days before our house was going to be destroyed, as he was removing windows and usable wood, Dad rediscovered that what lay beneath the shingles of our roof was not the usual tar paper. Many years before, during the Depression, our grandfather had put the practice canvasses of his aspiring artist children, our father, aunts, and uncles, under the shingles instead. Altogether, we were able to retrieve about ten paintings.

On this damp March morning in 1972, Shari and I climb to our rooftop archaeological site to begin working. It has become a crusade, our way of saving the soul of our home. Plucking nails and shingles as rapidly as we can, Shari and I are trying to ignore the approaching bulldozer. A workman steps from the cab of the bulldozer, hands placed aggressively on his hips, inspecting us from the ground.

"You better get down, girls, or you'll get pushed right off the cliff with the house."

Unable to excavate any more paintings, Shari and I climb down very slowly, running our hands along the weathered wood as we say our goodbyes. I watch helplessly and try not to feel anything as the bulldozer effortlessly pushes our wood-and-stone world over the edge of the cliff. The bulldozer man, almost eager in his pursuit of demolition, smashes what is the tender hold of our childhood into a million and a half fragments. I am transfixed, a feeling of anxiety in my chest holding back my breath until, finally, Shari screams out my name. We turn and flee as a surging wind funnels up through cliff and rock, urging us to run faster. I know that our house does not want us to see these final moments and the absolute loneliness of being turned into a hill of rubble.

We run and run until we reach our new home on Main Street. Breathless and silent, we sit in the kitchen, waiting for our strength to return so we can move again. Shari cannot bear the idea of going to school; she wants to be alone so she can write and draw. She allows me to hug her, something that hasn't been easy for her lately, the grief she feels creating a distance between her and everyone else. Shari is uncomfortable with affection and mostly when she really needs it. She rests her head on my shoulder and, for an instant, I am able to offer her comfort. I want to tell her everything will be all right, but I'm not sure it will be, so I don't say anything, holding her gently and breathing in the faint scent of her acne medication. She abruptly pulls away and rushes into her bedroom, slamming the door behind her.

When I get to the high school, I go directly to the art room where I know Kate is having a class. She follows me into the hallway, our art teacher looking on empathetically; they all know what's been happening.

"It's gone," I whisper.

As we embrace, I feel a sense of hope falling away into pieces, disintegrating and quietly disappearing into the cracks and crevices of the old brick school building.

6

~

PEAK EXPERIENCE

The five of us are all leaning in the same direction beneath the snow-and-ice-covered branches this winter afternoon in Pennsylvania, right down the road from Mom and Frank's house, the place I now call home. We lean in toward the lights, refracted colors practically laminating our faces with hundreds of iridescent shapes. The weight of snow and ice sends the branches down around us; we are in a shining tunnel of light, wind spinning pieces of rainbow into ecstatic rhythms.

"It's a peak experience," Shari, breathless and flushed, declares exuberantly. Having recently finished a psychology book by Colin Wilson in which he coined the term "peak experience," I told Shari all about them. I thought it might help her to know that these intense experiences had a name. And as I watch her today I think maybe I'm right; she seems happier, taking in these heightened moments without questioning them. Today we exult in the textures that compose this particular peak experience.

"I'm not thinking, you guys. I'm not thinking at all," Shari's laughter is as bright as this moment, pushing itself into a place where memories are stored, a place where the image of her radiant face can be retrieved again and again.

Mom hardly looks up from her pad of paper, where she is concentrating on the day's list, as we enter the kitchen on our return from the woods. Where does that pad take her? I vow to gaze into that small white world of paper when she's not looking and see for myself if there is a visual spiral descending into a world beyond this one. When I do look, weeks later, I'm not able to discern anything beyond her list, so where my mother goes remains a mystery.

From the doorway, Michele begins to describe the lights and wind, and I watch Mom closely for signs of life. She carefully places her cigarette in an ashtray and strains to pay attention to Michele's animated face. I don't believe Mom ever fully returns from the safety of her pad of paper; her face and body never seem truly occupied.

Kate walks toward her with her hands held out, fists closed. "Pick a hand."

Mom's nail-bitten index finger points at one of Kate's hands.

Kate opens her hand, revealing a small icicle within, which she offers to Mom.

"Boy, is that ever cold," Mom states stiffly with just a hint of jazz longing to ripple the veneer. Mom, c'mon, c'mon, C'MON.

Danielle, Shari, and Michele all present Mom with little icicles and she laughs, letting the cigarette burn itself out in the ashtray and allowing the icicles to melt in her hands, water dripping off onto the floor. She glances over at me expectantly, but I have no icicle for her. I smile self-consciously from the doorway, suddenly aware that bringing back an icicle for her never even occured to me.

Upstairs in my attic bedroom, Shari is back to thinking again and can't help but ask me the same question everyone has asked and continues to ask and to which I have the same rehearsed response. She wants to know why I moved here and attend a boring local community college instead of either staying in New Jersey to attend a fabulous school in Manhattan like Columbia or flying far away to London perhaps, to attend a more exotic university, like Oxford. I reiterate my reasons, ones I've told myself over and over again the last seven months since I made this questionable move to live with Mom and Frank at the clinic and take science courses with a plan to go on to veterinary school. Who am I kidding? All eyes are on me as I explain that I can save lots of money (even though I haven't saved more than fifty dollars yet), that I can get to know Mom all over again (Mom who?), and that I can see them much more often this way, which has, in fact, been the case.

There is silence after I state my three reasons and, as usual, not one of my sisters is convinced by my hundredth limp attempt at a worthy explanation, because the truth is, I was persuaded by Frank's perfectly executed argument that becoming a visual artist, which was my first and most passionately desired life plan, would be a damned waste of time. Kate and Shari look at each other wearily; I know they've discussed my obviously stupid decision, probably during talks on the half-moon couch when Danielle and Michele were in their rooms.

"How can you stand to be with the patients all the time?" Kate asks.

"I've gotten used to it," my voice trails off in this other total deviation from the truth. I haven't gotten used to any of it: not the patients' unintentional dreariness, not Mom and her passive half-state, and not Frank with his oppressively twisted tirades against anything or anyone sweet, pure, and joyful. How did he get like that? Must have been the death of that darned canary. I also haven't gotten used to being away from my sisters; I'm worried about their survival without me and mine without them. In private I ask each of them how it's going at 95 Main Street. Fights, depression, and marijuana pervade. How could I have left them? There's nothing to be done with our first separation except live it out. We all seem to know that it's time for it; we're just not sure how to make it work.

When my sisters visit the clinic, I feel compelled to stay with them at all times, even though I now have my own Pennsylvania friends. Frank totally disapproves; he absolutely hates the people in my new social circle, calling them "the worst excuse of humankind. Potheads, sexual deviants, and idiots are the kind of company you keep. I guess I haven't taught you a damned thing."

I've also become a karate fanatic, all my spare time spent at the dojo where I release every frustration that has formed inside of me over the last eighteen years, particularly the ones brought on by Frank. I stand before the punching/kicking bag, superimposing Frank's face wherever I want my kick or punch to make contact and attack him with the focus of bull's-eye concentration.

My sisters are visiting on a Saturday morning when Frank decides it's time to challenge me to a karate match, even though he doesn't know one karate technique. I am three belts into the Tae Kwon Do progression, putting me at green. I don't tell Frank anything about what green belt means, how much I know, or what kinds of offensives I'm capable of wielding. The only stipulation Frank makes is, "No dirty fighting." I nod my head solemnly and take a fighting stance; Danielle, Kate, Mom, and a few patients are watching from the sidelines in the kitchen where the furniture has been pushed aside to make enough room.

With his unusually long arms Frank throws out punches that initially come very close to my body. I block them and quickly begin to intuit where he'll place the next one. After a couple minutes of vain attempts at making contact, Frank starts to get angry. I have already learned that staying calm is far more effective than getting agitated when fighting someone who doesn't know what he's doing. I am determined not to capitulate to feelings of self-doubt or of sympathy.

I am waiting for an opening, a way into Frank's body that would level him in a decisive blow. I can tell he will give me one soon because he is getting sloppy. In my mind there is the perfect side kick emerging like a beacon; a side kick is what I will use, fast and clean, rising up before Frank can fend it off. I am barely moving now, allowing Frank to look foolish in his frustrated and wild swinging. Part of me wants to stop before this becomes humiliating for him, which I'm positive it will. But the stronger part of me, the one that's been bashing his imagined face in for months, takes aim and side-kicks Frank right to the floor. He lies on his back, stunned and glaring up at me with foaming rage. I close about two inches from his face with a finishing fist, holding it an inch from his nose, wanting more than anything to say something obnoxious, to rub it in, this triumph. But gloating in any form is ugly; I recall students from the dojo who have lorded it over me upon winning sparring matches, and so I don't say a thing nor do I use my fist for anything else except emphasis.

"Kicking isn't allowed," Frank snarls, his thin lips stretched tightly back over his pointy gray teeth, revealing the chipped right front tooth. "This fight doesn't count."

"Are you all right?" I offer my hand.

"Don't touch me." He gets up on his own and faces me, puffing himself up to appear taller. He is mad enough to let me have it, so I prepare myself for a physical attack, tightening my stomach muscles and planning which block to use against a slug.

"You fight dirty, young lady." He resorts to his preferred and now only means of attack, words. "And you look really ugly when you fight."

"She does not," Danielle counters softly.

Frank shakes away our stares and stomps out of the kitchen. Will Mom become the target of his residual anger later? The patients? Someone certainly will, but if I have anything to do with it, never again will it be me or one of my sisters. I am not gloating, I swear. I am feeling pretty free inside, wanting to cry out a series of raucous cheers. And then a realization comes flooding into me as I shift away from my karate posture: I am not afraid of Frank anymore.

My plan for becoming closer to Mom has long since lost any chance of substantiation. I should've known, should've remembered that day on the cliffs years ago when I said goodbye to her, when the dream of our relationship crumbled, fractured arm bones to show for it. She took care of me once, I recall, and hold the image of her bathing my broken arms like a signpost of a time when we were mother and daughter.

～

At four years of age I lived for climbing trees. There were so many trees to climb in our cliff world. Sometimes I knew exactly which one I would go to as soon as I stepped outside. Other days I roamed a while, deciding only after I had touched the bark of all my favorite trees which one to climb.

It was an early July day when I decided to climb the beech tree that hugged a corner of the driveway. Kate and Shari, our newest sister, who had to drink formula because regular

*milk made her sick, were lying with Mom on the lawn. Mom
and Dad never worried about me climbing trees, because they
had seen me climb and knew how careful I was.*

Mom said, "Be careful," and I said, "Okay, Mom."

*The large beech tree had really strong and easy lower branches
to reach, with a big boulder to use as a booster. The tree took
me up. I felt myself going higher than I had ever gone before.
I looked down as I stretched for the next branch, which
turned out to be dead. It could not take the momentum of my
climbing body. Thrown completely off balance and directly
into a state of panic by the sudden noise of the breaking
branch and the sudden disorientation of my newly free arm, I
screamed, lost my grip, and fell backward into empty space.*

*I instinctively flung both arms behind me as I fell, the right
arm hitting the boulder first; both of my arms snapped with
painful cracks. A small cry made its way out of my mouth before I went silent, not to speak, cry, or utter another sound
until after the casts were sawed off six weeks later. With the
sound and feeling of my cracking forearm bones came the
breaking of my four-year-old heart. The tree had let me
down. And since I already knew that when in pain the best
thing to do was keep quiet, that's what I did.*

*I had the casts on during the hottest part of that summer,
during a bout of the measles, and during my fifth birthday
party. Everyone tried to get me to speak, but I simply would
not. I went out to the driveway twice that summer and sat on
the boulder that had broken my fall from the beech tree. I
waited for a message from the tree or the boulder. An explanation or maybe an apology. But no message ever came. I
looked up into the branches, trying to find the place where the*

dead branch used to be. I couldn't find any trace. It was with the utmost sorrow that I decided never to climb trees again.

I don't remember what finally prompted me to say something, but a feeling was being stirred in me, after the casts came off and during those long hot-water soaks when I was methodically tended to by my mother. She had to soak my arms in steaming hot water, morning and night, and follow the soaks with the application of medicated ointment. Mom would tell me stories while my arms sloshed around in the water. She looked gently and coaxingly at my sad face, trying to get me to speak.

Sometime during the hot soaks and ointment rubs with my mother telling stories and talking about all the great times coming soon, I realized that other good things and adventures were indeed heading up the river toward me and that I might even climb a tree again. By the opening day of school, with a burgundy red–lipped Mrs. Fletcher as my teacher and Carol Morgan as my best friend, I was talking, and I was talking a lot. And sometime during that October, I climbed a tree again, but only with my mother watching and only after my father had checked to make sure that there were no dead branches within my reach.

~

The relationship I once had with my mother is now made of vapor, which perhaps could take shape inside some kind of vessel, a vessel that I cannot find and do not have any idea where to look for it. The chance for me and Mom to reconcile is further thwarted by the fact that Kate has just moved to the clinic, too, and whatever time I could've been spending with Mom I am spending with Kate. I have a sister back, even if the relationship is, now, somehow different. Kate is withholding affection and what I assume to be secrets from me while I am withholding the same from her. These are the days of going our separate ways with the coming back together set for late-night talks and motorcycle commuting. I watch Kate climb off my small Honda motorcycle that we drive to and from campus, making her way to the biology room where she works as a lab assistant. She doesn't even look around to say goodbye. Since our year apart, she has become closed off to me in ways I don't understand. I've tried rattling it out of her, but for some reason Kate seems to need the door shut behind her as she finds a path of her own, a path that doesn't include me.

One night we are asked to come together into the ooze of Mom and Frank's relationship slime. Kate and I are studying in our attic bedroom when we hear our mother's tentative footsteps heading up the stairs. We've been aware of a commotion going on in their bedroom for most of the night: groaning and an occasional wail. Neither of us has wanted to investigate. We no longer massage either one of them. We both simply refuse, and when our sisters are visiting we protect them by answering, "No," for them when he pesters for a rubdown. Sometimes I can't help but feel sorry for Frank—maybe the massages help keep the strangulating pain away from his head—but I'm not so sorry for him that I will go back to massaging him again.

Mom is holding a couple of vials of Talwin in her hands. She explains that Frank is trying to stop using it and wants us to hide the bottles of narcotic, not giving it to him under any circumstances. We know he's attempted to quit before and has obviously failed. Reluctantly we agree to help.

Not more than two hours later, having just turned off the lights and ready for sleep, Kate and I hear the attic door open again. From the base of the stairs, Mom asks for the Talwin back.

Kate calls down a firm, "No!" Mom retreats quietly. She's back within minutes, this time asking for the Talwin with an urgency in her voice that neither one of us can ignore.

"Let's give it to him," Kate whispers exasperatedly. "What difference does it make?" She fumbles around in the dark, locating the Talwin, which she has stashed in one of her dresser drawers. We follow Mom to the bedroom. Frank is lying on the bed face-up, on top of blankets and sheets that are a rumpled mess, his entire body spread out in such a way that there is no room for Mom. What has she been doing this whole time? I wonder. Kate and I exchange looks of disgust and pity as Frank turns toward us, growling accusingly, "Why are you doing this to me?" His lips are quivering and spittle is running down his chin. Kate hands him a vial. He sits up slowly, his hands shaking uncontrollably as he reaches for the white paper packet of new syringes. He's so weak, he can't rip the packet open. Throwing it on the floor, he screams, "Someone open it. God damn it!" Kate tears it apart with her teeth and hands him a clean syringe. His attempts to give himself an injection are futile; he either spills the liquid all over the bed or blows up his skin with an air bubble. Finally Kate suggests that we call the resident nurse and get her to administer an intramuscular injection.

Mom agrees and places the late-night call while Frank continues to jab the needle into his arm, which is charged with scar tissue from years of injections. We try to take the needle from him, but he violently shoves us away. I'm thinking maybe he'll kill himself right in front of us tonight, doing everyone, including himself, a huge favor. "Why not be done with it, Frank?" I want to ask him. Frank is not destined to live that much longer. The steroids he ingests will eventually cause his bones to disintegrate into useless mush; his death a slow, excruciating slide out of consciousness. I never wished that on him, although I have to admit my sisters and I did plot Frank's murder more than once. But those were fantasies, never meant to take on any more reality than what the imagination, fueled by repressed anger, will create.

Wendy, one of the clinic nurses, shows up a few minutes later and, wearing a clearly surprised expression, assesses the situation. Embarrassed, Mom briefs Wendy and then tries to explain to Frank why Wendy is here and what she is going to do.

"Is he on anything else?" Wendy asks.

"Just some lithium to help calm him down."

"Lithium?" Wendy, looking puzzled, reaches for another syringe, loads it, and asks Frank to lie facedown so she can inject him in his gluteus maximus muscle. We all help to guide him over. He receives the injection calmly, like a hysterical child finally spent from all the crying. He lies still, gripping his grotesque pillow. The four of us watch him in silence for a few seconds before Wendy dismisses herself, clearly uncomfortable with this scene.

Mom goes back to sitting in the straw chair in the corner, which is where I assume she's been holed up this entire evening, while Kate and I struggle with what to do next. I can see Kate's feeling the same thing I am: turmoil. I see her body surge slightly toward Frank. We both want to comfort him, maybe stroke his brow for a minute, maybe even offer him a massage out of kindness. I'm hoping Kate is capable of a move beyond her repulsion, because I know suddenly and surely that I am not. My body ultimately sinks backward towards the door. I will never be able to offer Frank comfort, ever. Kate sways, pulled between two impulses, then reaches across the bed and lightly touches Frank's shoulder. He opens his eyes and smiles softly at her.

I turn away, unable to view this tenderness and unable to deal with my feelings of rage for both Mom and Frank. I hate their pitiful faces so much I could scream. Before I do, I leave, retreating to our room, where I lie in a seething state of malevolence, which sends my body into spasms of tension. I stuff a pillow case in my mouth, biting it with all the force of my fury. Kate stays behind for awhile, talking with Mom about a plan for Frank's withdrawal from the drugs. Over the years that follow, Kate becomes the undisputed family caregiver, the sister who guides us all toward the right medical choices and the best ways out of an emotional crisis. To this day she is still trying to find the Kate who somehow got sidelined by giving all that care to others.

A couple of days later, back to taking steroids and Talwin (he never got off the steroids and kicked the Talwin years later), Frank is acting like a caring, interested stepfather, engaging Kate and me in discussions about our finances and our science homework as Mom listens on in relief. He seems empty, devils outwitted. On days like this, I almost like him, letting my guard slip below the heart line. In the afternoon, we work on my new car, a 1951 black Chevrolet I bought from an older woman who had only driven it to and from the store. Frank helped me learn how to operate the gear stick, is built into the steering shaft and moves in the shape of an "H." The car has running boards and a visor, and because *Little Lord Fauntleroy* is one of my favorite books from childhood I've named my car Fauntleroy, but without the "Lord." This car carries me and my sisters a few years into the future before I wind up selling it for parts so I could go on a trip to Europe with Kate. I kept the gearshift for many years as an object of remembrance until, during one of my many moves, it got left behind.

Today Frank and I are putting on new brake shoes, crescent-shaped metal disks that are somehow responsible for stopping the car; Frank explains how the brake components work, but I'm never able to repeat back what he has told me. I'm totally intimidated, never having worked on a car before, not believing I'm at all mechanically savvy, and anticipating Frank's impatience. But today he is actually very patient, encouraging me and forgiving my mistakes. We have fun together, Frank and I. When the afternoon is over, I know how to change brake shoes. My hands dirty from the grease and dirt, I proudly walk into the kitchen for the wash up. Mom approaches from her stool, puts her arms around my waist, and tells me how very proud she is of me. I squirm away, repelled by this overt and surprising expression of affecton.

"Did you have fun today?" she asks, obviously trying to connect with me.

"Yeah, Mom. It was great. I love my car." I don't mention the fact that I will always love Cindy With Guts more than any car I'll ever own.

"Can you and I go for a ride in it sometime?" she asks hopefully.

"Sure, Mom."

We go for a brief ride in Fauntleroy the next day with all the windows rolled down so both of us can feel the summer wind blowing against our faces.

"What's the name of your car again, Carol?" Mom shouts the question at me as we ride along a back road in Bucks County, Pennsylvania.

"Fauntleroy!"

"That's a great name!"

Shari calls, her voice sounding ragged. She now feels like she's responsible for the running of 95 Main Street. Shari's the oldest at home now and can't find peace from all the worrying she thinks the role necessitates, even though I suggest she rely more on Dad, Danielle, and Michele. Shari's relationship with Danielle is growing more strained, a passionate tension between the closest kind of sisterhood and jealousy. I ask her where Danielle is tonight and she reluctantly admits that she doesn't know, maybe at a party? Dad just brought home some take-out dinner, and Shari and Michele get ready for another night at home alone with each other.

"Can you go to Nancy and Earl's?" I ask. Shari, Danielle, and Michele had been spending a lot of time with these friends of the family. Nancy and Earl's home has become a refuge, a place where each of my sisters find a stability missing at 95 Main Street.

"I'm sick of going over there. I think Nancy is tired of me. The only one she likes is Danielle."

I'm sure this isn't true, but it's hard to talk Shari out of these lows and I'm not sure how she finally gets lifted out. Danielle's seeming disinterest in Shari's life has been eroding their relationship; Shari invariably ends up hurt, succumbing to feelings of self-loathing. Ironically, it is Danielle who is best at pulling Shari out of these moods.

"Is Danielle doing drugs, Shari?"

"Probably just pot."

"Are you doing any drugs?"

"Are you kidding Carol? Remember what happened when we smoked that hash? I'll never do drugs. I've got enough of my own mind to cope with."

She wants to know if I'm still hanging around with the clinic gang. I suspect she's forming some kind of critical opinion of them and my lifestyle. I wonder if Kate has told her anything about my attraction to women.

"I'm coming to pick you guys up this weekend."

"In Fauntleroy?"

"Yes."

"Great. I'll tell Danielle and Michele. Can I talk to Kate now?"

"I love you, Sha."

"I know. You don't have to say it every time we talk. I mean, I know you love me."

"I like telling you."

"Well, just not every time, okay?"

Kate gets on the phone and she and Shari talk for at least another hour, about what I'm not sure until Kate hangs up the phone and asks me if Shari has ever asked me what sex felt like. I want to say, "Of course she has," but instead tell her the truth. Shari obviously wasn't ready to talk with me about sex. Apparently Shari's been thinking about having sex for the first time with some older guy she met while working at Carvel's. Kate and I are mortified, hoping she doesn't go through with it; Kate tells me that Shari really wants the first time to be with a friend named Peter, but he hasn't returned her shy, hopeful advances.

When I pick my sisters up a few days later, their energy is askew. They come out at me from all different directions as if they don't even live together anymore. There are clear currents of wind separating them. Each one of them is haltingly reluctant to speak about what's been happening at 95; we talk about insignificant drivel like school, TV shows, and favorite rock 'n' roll bands for two-thirds of the ride. We hit the New Jersey/Pennsylvania border, and I'm so sad. Where are my sisters? Where am I? But as we ride on in Fauntleroy, through the thickening layers of a Pennsylvania evening, we start coming back toward one another. The distance from 95 Main Street, the protective red plushness of Fauntleroy's interior, and the softness of the retreating light help bring me and my sisters back toward the center, our original place of love. I have, while focusing on my studies and new relationships at school, been forgetting about the love of my sisters. We are moving away from it as we adjust to growing older. As we drive and I listen to the cadence of my sisters' voices, my mind spins around through phrases and thoughts that will eventually find their way into my journal:

~

Dearest sisters the gone gone gone of it nowhere are you this growing older thing without you this empty light no sound and the curvature of the horizon without the five of us on it so sudden so obvious the goodbye of it as Shari says "I'll die young and tragically" what does she know?

~

"If you die, what's gonna happen to the rest of us?" Michele wants to know.

"No matter what happens, we'll always be connected. I swear, when I die, I'll find a way to communicate with you guys." Shari says as if she knows something about it.

"You promise, Shari?" Michele asks.

"I promise."

"So do I," I say.

Then we all promise as I pull Fauntleroy into the driveway.

Kate is waiting at the back door for us.

"I'm so glad you're here. I miss you too much," Kate says during the hugs and greetings.

The weekend is packed with the kind of concentrated visiting we're forced to have when there is such limited time. Almost as

soon as it starts, the weekend is over, and I'm getting ready to drive
Shari, Danielle, and Michele back to Fort Lee, this time with Kate
along for company. It's going to be a late-night drive and return.

Before we say goodbye, Shari calls me into her room to give me
something. Opening the closet door sheepishly, she pulls a T-shirt
down from a shelf and hands it to me, shirts, pants, and socks
tumbling all over the floor around our feet. She ignores the clothes
that have fallen, closing her eyes as I unfold the shirt. "It didn't
turn out as good as I wanted it to." The words "PEAK EXPERI-
ENCE" are silk-screened in the shape of a mountain peak on the
front of the shirt in blue and red letters.

"I made one for each of us."

"God, I love you."

"Carol, don't forget who you are, okay? Don't try to be so cool.
Just be yourself. I can really understand loving women."

"You can?" I don't attempt to question her about where or how
she found out. Her approval is more important than I'd realized. I
begin to cry and I sputter out the words "I love you" again.

"I know; you said it already. I love you, too, Carol. See ya
later."

Her bedroom door closes behind me as I head into the kitchen
where Michele is sitting, absently drawing right onto the wooden
table with a pen; I kiss the top of her head. Danielle is already on
the phone; I kiss her hand. Kate has gone to visit with Dad in his
studio/living quarters across the yard, and that's where I go next.

"Hey, nothing could be finah than to be with Carolina in the
morning, right, Carolina?" Dad stretches out an arm to take me in,
and I hunker down for one of his hula hugs; he sort of wiggles
himself into the hug like a hula dancer. I raise my shoulders up

near my neck so he won't kiss me there, and he ends up planting one on the top of my right arm. "Hey, can I get you a drink?" he offers energetically, getting us each a soda. Kate and I divulge little about our lives at the clinic when he asks us how things are going. We recite things we know he wants to hear: the made-to-order stories of school achievement and triumph. Kate is currently assisting with a microbiology experiment in the biology lab. "The petri dishes look like miniature moonscapes," she says. I am learning how to make aspirin in the chemistry lab. "You should have seen the crystals raining out of the solution," I report.

Soon it's time for us to leave to drive off into the night. I stop and look into the kitchen window as we cross to Fauntleroy. I can't see the kids, but I know they are in there, warm and safe from the elements. I wonder if Dad ever comes out into the yard and looks toward the window, making sure Shari, Danielle, and Michele are all right. I'm sure he does. I'll wager that he waits until the lights go out behind the kitchen curtains before he closes his big red door for the night.

Kate and I kiss Dad goodbye, climb into Fauntleroy, and drive away, back into our distance.

7

~

PREMONITIONS

I am speeding home from the University of Pennsylvania. I had an interview and found out that I have a 90 percent chance of getting into their veterinary school. Within minutes of my entering Mom and Frank's bedroom, practically leaping out of my skin with the good news, the joy is efficiently extracted and realeased into the air, which is now seething with tension.

And now, here I am standing very still in Mom and Frank's bedroom, listening to Frank's reptilian hiss as he throws ultimatums at me. Besides being stunned by Frank's onslaught, I am very confused; what have I done to bring it on? Frank and I had been getting along so well recently; at least I thought we had.

I continue to smile at first, still caught up in the positive news: I can't really hear Frank, yet. Then, shaking my mind clear of the happiness, I finally comprehend what he's doing: screaming at me.

"I want your room kept clean! I want you to give me a certain amount of money from your veterinarian's assistant salary each week, and I want you to give me regular updates on your academic standing! Do you hear me, young lady?"

"Yes." I say softly.

"I want you to be just like a mosquito under my thumb!" he finishes off, gesticulating wildly, his big right thumb mashing an imaginary object in the air in front of my eyes. I exhale the remnants of my good news and retreat to my room. Kate now living in the attic bedroom, and my room is just beneath the attic stairs; she must go through my room to get to hers. I don't know if she is home or not, and I don't stop to call out for her. I begin packing.

Frank rushes in from behind me and demands, "What the hell do you think you're doing!"

"Leaving, you asshole!" I scream.

Mom is standing in the hallway, tears all over her face. I can see her arm weakly reaching for Frank's shirt. Will she stop him this time?

She backs away as he yells, "Where are you going to go? One of your fucking hippie friends gonna take you in? Then your life will really go to hell!"

"I hope so," I blast back, tempted to fling one of my heaviest textbooks at him.

He turns away and pushes past Mom, who steps into the space he has just held.

"Carol, you don't have to leave. He'll get over it."

"Get over what? What did I do?"

"I don't know, dear. Something set him off is all I can tell."

"It's too late, Ma. I'm sorry."

I find Kate hanging out with some therapist friends in one of the clinic apartments. She takes the news with a mixture of emotions; I can't quite read her. Is she glad I'm leaving? There seem to be some signs of relief on her face and in her posture. But if she's feeling this way, Kate won't say, not wanting to hurt me. My sisters and I hardly ever state painful truths especially to one another; we're simply not schooled in the ways of direct and difficult communication. Shari comes closest to being able to pin truth down and speak it out. Kate is definitely angry at Frank, though.

"What's the matter with him? He sure is being hard on you. What did you do, Carol?"

"I have no idea."

I call my friend Alan, who has a big, wide house over near the community college, and he immediately responds to my plea for help; he'll let me stay until I can make more permanent living arrangements. Thus within hours I find myself living away from family for the first time in my life.

In the end I'll have Frank to thank for the path I strayed onto after I moved out of the clinic house. I never became a veterinarian, dropping out of school a semester later and beginning an era of wandering.

Shari comes to visit for the weekend. It's as though we've been waiting for this chance to be free together our whole lives. She is ecstatic in her uncoiling. With no one around to take care of, compete with, or worry about, she truly relaxes. She loves the house I share with three clinic friends, Shel, Nick, and Peg (my more permanent living arrangement), and begins to imagine a place in New York City where she will live once she graduates from high school in a year. We party with lots of nonalcoholic fruit punch that Shari concocts. She talks about her plans to be an artist and musician and to drive across the country right after graduation. Her passion inspires my own, and we open up the box that contains an old dream: a sister musical group. We write new songs and discuss strategy. We'll meet up in Manhattan after she returns from her cross-country trip and let our talents loose upon the world. On that celebratory Saturday night we go for a drive on the back roads of Bucks County in Kate's car, (while Fauntleroy is being serviced) and crash head-on into a view of the future, and our lives are altered forever.

A huge full moon hangs low, glowing from just over the crest of the hills, as we make our way along a circuitous route from an ice-cream store in New Hope back to the house. It's June and all the windows are open to the green, pungent fragrances emanating from the the pastures surrounding us. Shari comments on what a good driver I am just as we hit an uphill curve going too fast and spinning into loose gravel. Bald tires contribute to the skid as I fight to retain control of the steering wheel. Control is lost. We swerve violently and are propelled directly into a tree on the right side of the road.

When I regain consciousness, my eyes open to a view of the shattered windshield. It takes me a few seconds to understand what has happened and to realize that what shattered the windshield was my head. I reach for my face, pulling my hand away when I feel the warm, slow sensation of blood. Touching my face again, my right pinkie finger pokes into a hole that has been gouged in my chin; when my finger reaches teeth beyond the wound, my mind takes off, exaggerating the injuries I must have incurred. I yank my finger out of the hole, now a gash in my imagination, and turn to find Shari slumped unconscious in the passenger seat. Knowing enough not to shake her, I begin screaming, "Shari. We're dead. We're dead," somehow really believing it even though I am beginning to feel real-live physical pain. Rousing herself, she responds, "No, we're not Carol. Stop it. We're not dead." Her voice is very calm; she is definitely sure that we are not dead.

"Carol, there's blood all over your clothes."

We determine that all this blood is coming from the hole in my chin, which, according to Shari, is not that big. There don't seem to be any other discernible wounds except for where small pieces of windshield glass are embedded in our scalps, which we decide shouldn't be messed with; we leave the bits where they are. All of our extremities are functioning; we climb out of the destroyed car and stare at it. Totally demolished.

"God, do ya think Kate is gonna be mad?" Shari asks.

At the hospital, in between getting stitches, having X rays taken, apologizing to Kate, who has come to get us, a million times, and being told by a young good-looking doctor that we were both suffering from minor concussions and to "please hold still while I remove the glass from your heads," Shari asks me a question:

"Do you feel like we saw something over there?"

I nod.

Neither one of us can sink down to the place where the answers are now stored, but for the next year we would continue to acknowledge this haunting feeling: We had seen something about our future, something really important that remained just out of our conscious reach.

～

I awake to panic, the dream forgotten but not the warning inherent in its fading images. It's the middle of the night, the lost hours of impenetrable blackness. Disorientation controls my body as I reach for familiar objects and feelings by which

I can claim myself back from what feels like the digestive tract of a beast. An involuntary cry flies out of my mouth as I isolate the meaning of the dream's message: Shari is going to die soon. The vision of her slumped body comes to me in crashing brilliance.

∼

Where did we go? I reach for the spot on my chin where the scar now rests. This thin line of hard tissue grounds me, reminding me of the tree that Shari and I flew into as we crashed last June. I see Shari's face framed by those unruly waves of steel-blond hair, her eyes always as direct as the first blue flames of a fire. She comes toward me in the light created by her eyes. Together we see the truth—through the windshield straight into the light. Broken windshield as pathway to a truth.

My hands finally find the edge of my mattress and I remember where I am: my bedroom in the house I share with Shel, Nick, and Peg four months after the car accident with Shari. I am in my room next to Peg's. Bolted into the ceiling above my bed is a huge convoluted piece of driftwood which I dragged back from the lake in Canada where Mom and Frank now live. They bought a one-acre island, built an A-frame house on it, and retired. There are shadows from the driftwood being cast by the light of the moon; the shadows look like dragons and gnarled wizards. I must reorient myself to remember where the phones are. Nick has one in his room; his girlfriend is over tonight, so there is no going in there at this hour. I slide my way down to the hall and dial 95 Main Street. The phone resounds—it rings and rings. An image from the dream makes it imperative that I speak with Shari now; maybe she'll still be in some kind of dream state and be able to remember something important, a message from the car accident perhaps.

Danielle answers the phone, her voice a blend of waking and sleeping currents. She doesn't understand my request to speak with Shari and almost hangs up. I yell her name into the receiver and she puts the phone back up to her ear. "Huh?"

"Get Shari, Danielle, please."

I wait with shaking dread for over five minutes. Shari finally whispers, "Carol? I know you love me, okay?"

"Shari, you have to promise me that you won't die."

"I can't promise you that." Of course she can't; who could?

When I hang up, Shel, my closest friend in the house, is there to comfort me and lead me back to my bedroom, where I spend the rest of the night watching the shadows on the walls and ceiling come in and out of focus.

～

Shari comes towards me in the light of another dream that I remember as soon as I wake up. She's extending her hands out to me, but no matter how hard I try, I can't reach them. I continue to move toward her as she continues to slip backward, just beyond my grasp. Finally I'm able to grab her before she can retreat. As soon as I have a good grip on her, she slumps over, transforming into a cloth doll with a porcelain head. Looking down next to my feet, I discover a hammer-sized bone, which I immediately pick up, somehow knowing what it's to be used for. In a great flashing moment, I raise the bone high over my head and then down, cracking the doll's head open. A fine mist rises out of the crack in the porcelain, and vanishes in the air. When I look down again, the doll is no longer there. I am left alone, holding the bone in my hand.

～

The center will not hold. The blades grow closer. Tornadoes spin all around the windows. Grinning munchkins peer in from the trees. It's almost time.

"C'mon, Shari and Kate," I urge with sly anticipation. It is late March, Kate's birthday, and they're both visiting me at the house I have now shared with Shel, Nick, and Peg for almost a year. I am leading them to a spot by the brook that runs the length of the land where I live. Mud and unfamiliarity slow both of them down on the trail that I have walked many times before. I know that once they find their "cliff feet" ease of motion will carry them lightly to the place I have created for us.

We come around the large oak tree and there it is: this almost perfectly round projection of earth, carved out by the course of the brook, adorned with a blanket, three long-stemmed glasses, and a bottle of wine. Across the expanse of fast-moving spring water is a beautiful stick attached to an empty green bottle, mouth stuffed with a curled letter addressed to Kate. She uncurls it, reads it to herself, and begins to cry. I knew Shari wouldn't ask to see the contents. She probably has a pretty good guess what it says anyway; I'm hoping she doesn't think I say "I love you" a thousand times. She's got to know I'm sometimes more original than that.

We drink toasts to one another and to the kind of spring-drenched potential our young lives are full of.

I'm home from a trip cross-country: living out some of that spring potential. During a month of driving up and down the highways of California, stopping in dozens of coastal towns to gauge each town's prospective livability, two of my housemates, Nick and

Shel, and I tried to decide if California was the right place for us. Along the way we tasted enough drinks, drugs, and people to become sickened and then realized the error of our ways; that was not the life we had envisioned. I can't believe I made it back without more scars to show; there are only the stories carved into bone with indelible ink, to be read by those who can read the bones: the closest of lovers, the ghosts of Christmases past, and perhaps unborn children.

Before I can catch my breath, it's time for the wedding of our favorite cousin, Priscilla, to Kendall, a guy she met at college. Dad carts Shari, Danielle, Michele, and me to Pittsburgh, Pennsylvania, for the festivities, which are being held on June 12, 1976. No Kate on this trip. She is ensconced in Maine with her own clinic buddies, running naked on a beach, getting closer to that playful part of herself that has been dangling just out in front of her line of vision. She doesn't have time for a Methodist wedding.

In the very white church, my sisters and I sit up toward the front, our small line of defense against the event unfolding. Dad has vanished, as usual; he doesn't like to sit down for long periods of time. I turn around and see him standing in the back, arms crossed low in front of his body, sunglasses pushed up over his forehead. Maybe he's taking pictures or memorzing the scene so he can paint it later.

About ten minutes in to the ceremony, Shari starts to cry.

"God, kids, Scilla is getting *married*," she says through her tears. And then, "Childhood is really over now."

Watching Priscilla slip her arm through Kendall's arm, I start crying, too. Sympathetic cousins from behind us pass tissues up, and we gratefully use them. Our crying seems disproportionately grand given the circumstances. Sure, people cry at weddings all the time, but we are sobbing. I glance over at Shari and ask as quietly as I can, "Shari, why are we crying so hard?"

"I don't know," she admits through gagging sobs.

After the ceremony, Shari and I rush outside in desperate escape. Without planning on it, we find ourselves standing in the church graveyard, its stones glistening with moisture from the humidity of this June afternoon. I pull Shari to me, holding her in an embrace that feels extremely important; I must hold onto her at all costs. She lets me, actually putting an arm around my waist as we look out at the gravestones. We stay this way until Danielle and Michele come to find us. They join our embrace, turning it into a huddle. I shudder involuntarily with some kind of unnerving, unsettled agitation that rests in my lower spine. We return to the crowds that are now departing for the reception.

I've just driven Michele and Shari home from Pennsylvania, where the three of us recorded four of our original songs at a friend's recording studio right after the wedding.

"See ya later," I say simply. No "I love yous." No great final words of illumination.

Shari smiles. She doesn't say, "Stay true to yourself," or, "Catch you in another life." She says, "See ya later."

I climb into Fauntleroy and roll home to Pennsylvania, across widening time and intensifying distance. There would be no more of our time together. That was it. That was all.

———

It is the evening of June 17 when I go to see Catherine, a psychic recommended to me by Shel, who has been to see her twice. In her small ranch house at the end of a dead-end street, Catherine and I sit comfortably in the sparsley decorated living room. After herbal tea is offered and served on a plastic tray, she asks me to talk about the most important aspects of my life, and so I begin to say, "My sisters and I—" But before I can say anything else, she waves her hand in a motion that I interpret to mean "Stop." She tells me that my sisters and I have been coming back in various incarnations to help one another learn about all kinds of relationships. She says this is our last life together and one of us is going to die young and tragically to teach the rest of us about pain and loss. "Who?" I want to know. She is not at liberty to say. Then I ask Catherine about our musical career.

She is very still, with her eyes closed for at least a full minute, finally opening them with this response: "Nothing. I see absolutely nothing." She refuses to tell me anything else and insists that this is probably too much difficult information already. "It could be harmful if I go any further." She seems concerned for my well-being and asks me to call her if I run into any trouble. I anxiously walk toward the door when I am stopped abruptly by what looks like a blue flashing light; as big as a dime it is blazing right next to Catherine's composed face. I've never seen anything like this before and thus am compelled to ask her what it is.

"That is a friend of yours who will be helping you from the other side for the rest of your life," she says.

Bewildered and totally unnerved, I try nodding my head calmly; I don't want to appear panicked. Despite my refusal to accept it the first few times that I saw it, the blue flash wouldn't go away, and I have continued to see it at least once every day since the moment it appeared at Catherine's.

After the reading, I drive Fauntleroy to New York City, where I visit a college friend, Suzanne, with plans to see her dance in a modern jazz recital the following evening. I spend the next day creating minor escapades for myself throughout Manhattan: posing for a freelance photographer (set up by Suzanne) in order to make a little extra cash, shopping for jeans at the Canal Street sidewalk market, and watching the roller skaters in Central Park. I didn't know that I was being followed all day by messengers of death. They rattle, chant, and throw garbage can lids at my head, but I pay them no heed.

On my way to Suzanne's dance recital, I stop at a florist to buy her a single red rose. I am carrying it, wrapped in white paper, as I begin my ascent to the second-floor recital hall in a building somewhere near Seventh Avenue and 59th Street. Halfway up the stairs, I see them. Shel, Nick, Cookie, and Wilma, four friends from Pennsylvania, are standing on the second-floor landing, all looking down at me, their faces contorted with anguish. Their expressions are so grim, I suddenly lose my swallowing reflex. I no longer feel my feet touching the steps. "Who is going to tell her?" I hear someone whisper. I know it will be Shel. They surround me. There is no way to escape now. Shel instructs me to sit down. I refuse. They close in. There is a pause, so excruciating in its purpose: This is the last moment I will ever have of not knowing. The last safe moment. The leading to. The almost. Shel looks at me way down beyond my eyes. What would be the worst thing he could say to me?

"Shari was killed in a car accident, Carol. She died early this morning."

The thorns on the stem of the rose take over. They are cutting into my palms with every ounce of my clenched fists. I reach for something to hold onto. I am falling backward. Am I spitting? Something is foaming out of my mouth, down my shirt. Are my eyes closed? Whose voice is that, screaming so loud? There's a face in front of me, twisted. Everything feels wet. Am I being taken away? Someone is trying to suffocate me. I can't breathe. Somebody says, "Don't let her slip!" God, my hands hurt. Someone tries to take the rose away from me and I try to bite him. Soon the rose is gone. The rose is gone. I hear someone screaming, "Shari!" Over and over and over. Blood is coming out of my hands. My fists make contact with a body. I hit it. I hit it. I hit it. I hit it. I feel spit. I feel fangs. Then there are stairs. A street. Shel's car. The backseat. Hands all over me. It feels like my sternum is being smashed. No heart can survive this. The window is open. I am screaming out the window. No words. Someone is driving me. We're in a car. Shari was killed in a car accident. Stop the car. Someone drives. Stop the car. Stop the car. Stop the car. Stop the car!

By the time we reach 95 Main Street, my vision is beginning to clear again. The old world has vanished and been replaced by something distinctly savage. I can't negotiate the driveway or any part of this new world. There is bird shit all over this new world. I see it everywhere. I try to step around it, but it's always right in front of me. Hands try to guide me across the once-familiar yard toward the door. I catch a glimpse of Danielle's panicked face as she sees us approaching. Here I come, the last to find out, full of the freshest grief. My friends let me go at the threshold of the kitchen, and I fall into the arms of my sisters. My entrance opens them back up to that most potent kind of crying. Slowly, as one being, we move toward Shari's room. And that is where Dad finds us, collapsed on Shari's bed, and we begin the agonizing process of acquainting ourselves as a family without her.

THE SHARON E. ORTLIP
FUNERAL AWARDS

(A Break in the Narrative)

The Most Poignant Moment Award: Paul D. Ortlip. For reading a poem that Shari had written to him just a month before she died, titled "To Dad."

The Buffoon Award: The Preacher (can't remember his name). For giving some cockamamy talk about Shari and her ascent into heaven.

The Worst-Dressed Corpse Award: Sharon E. Ortlip. Dressed in her graduation gown (she was supposed to graduate from high school the following week, thus the gown) and a wig (to hide the damage done to her head), she looked like a parody of herself—or, even worse, a real-live corpse.

The Sweetest Moment Award: The Ortlip Sisters. For singing an original song that Shari had helped create, titled "Words."

The Best Art in Funeral Award: Self-portrait of Shari. 1976. Done in oils. Placed right next to the coffin, it looked a hell of a lot better than she did. (Not for sale. Private collection.)

The Thanks for Keeping Your Mouth Shut Award: Frank. For keeping his mouth shut.

The Heightened Awareness Award (otherwise known as the Peak Experience Award): It's a tie. First: Everyone. The heightened state of awareness in that room at Hunt's Funeral Home could have ignited a giant-sized pile of brush into flames or brought a large apartment complex down into bits. Second: Sharon E. Ortlip. We can only hope that as she hovered over us all her awareness was not only heightened; it was at its peak.

III
~

Wandering the World: 1976–81

Carol, Kate, Danielle, Michele
A few days after Shari's death, 1976.

FOR TOO LONG

Are you up there laughing
    with your earnest eyes—
Yeah, I remember them,
    playful and blue and so mockingly wise.

You're watching me stick
    to my own cherished fears—
Yeah, they're a gift from you,
    plentiful and hard and delivered through the
years.

Well, you must be happy
    'cause they've come to good use—
Yeah, I know how you want me,
    frozen and guilty and afraid to break loose.

But does your mind ever wander
    to those nights in the cold?
Well, I can remember,
    We were sisters with a bond
    That was heart-felt and age-old.

And you're still in my blood
    after all of this time—
Yeah, it's been five fast years,
    choppy and desperate and so much out of
rhyme.

Now stop your sarcasm
    and your bratty vengeful game—

No, I'm not gonna listen,
    I broke down and got hurt
    and I still ache from the pain.

So please go to sleep,
    sleep well, my soul mate—
Yeah, you've been with me for too long,
    like an angel and a curse
    and a golden prison gate.

DANIELLE ORTLIP

8

~

PORTRAITS OF THE LOST

M y sisters and I are sitting in lawn chairs talking about it again. How could this have happened? We want to know everything, but just a few details are currently available. Here they are:

~

Shari is asleep in the back of a van being driven by her friend Brian. They are on their way home from a concert at around eleven o'clock. A stolen car driven at a particularly high speed by a drunk man smashes into the back of the van. The van turns over and over on itself. Shari is tossed around inside and then flung out onto the roadside grass. A passerby who stops says she tries to move. Brian sustains minor face lacerations and his glasses break. The driver of the car suffers minor injuries as well. Ambulance to Nyack. A team of doctors and nurses works through the night attempting to save Shari. Her heart stops. They revive her. Her heart stops again. They revive her again. But there's way too much damage. When her heart stops again, they do not revive her. The nurses mention that there is a radiance about her as she dies at 10:10 A.M. on the eighteenth of June 1976.

∼

When we're through talking about the facts, we throw ourselves into the battering heat of trying to blame someone. What else can we do with our grief? And then, after the endless regurgitation of feelings, we swallow the stinking contents down again. So putrid this rehashing, lacking any kind of sustenance, yet so necessary in its function: Feel it. Feel it. Feel it. There's nothing else to do but feel it in all its forms.

We're doing all of this at a friend's house on the Jersey shore. It is here, away from the familiar, that Kate, Danielle, Michele, and I stretch ourselves into a reinterpretation of the sibling structure. It isn't working. Any kind of reconfiguration will have to take place later and, obviously, over time. I look at my sisters and, for the first moments in my life, do not know how to let them be my sisters. Even Kate, my eternal companion, is not as familiar somehow. We need Shari. She was the sister who created philosophical explanations and theories about all of life's situations, whether simple or complex. We need her explanation for this. She was our spiritual leader, our center, the middle child whom the rest of us revolved around. Who is to be the center now?

The four of us are also floundering with the strange feeling that Shari is still moving among us; like ghost flesh, we continue to feel her physical presence. But then we see that Shari is not here, not anywhere. During these excruciating moments the four of us look around at one another in panicked desperation. All we can do then is rant against the forces that killed her and cry out into the space Shari used to occupy. It is through dreams, travel, alcohol, headaches, work, school, injury, and sex that we subsequently seek ways to assimilate Shari's death into our lives.

PORTRAIT OF MYSELF

I'm lying on my wet mattress on the floor in the basement of Wilma's house in Bucks County, Pennsylvania, crazy in my grief over Shari. Wilma, my former psychotherapist and one of the friends who was there on the landing of the dance recital space, has agreed to let me stay with her and her family until I figure out where I'm going and what I'm doing. Good luck. The home I had shared with my clinic friends is no longer an option; the lease was up and we had already begun to move off in different directions before Shari died. Here in the basement of Wilma's home, filled with the kind of junk many basements become dumpsters for, I sleep, write, scream, and get really damp. The summer condensation on a cold water pipe is creating moisture in the already-clammy basement; it's almost ridiculous in its appropriateness, given how I feel: wet, inside and out. There is one small window ten feet above me, offering a fist's worth of light and facing a dense and fetid swamp.

Crude and bloody paintings that I created during a round of psychotherapy prior to Shari's death (I started going to see Wilma during my stay with Mom and Frank, hoping to resolve some of the issues with them while I lived there; the year and a half I spent working on those issues barely made a dent) form a half wall around my mattress. They're propped up against broken chairs and partially unpacked boxes. One of the paintings is a self-portrait: me, ghoul-like, with a large head wound sliced into my forehead.

This image of my face is staring out from beneath stringy globs of blood, wearing an expression of total calm.

At first, no one questions my basement existence. Maybe because I continue to rise up out of this pit long enough to call a sister, drink a glass of water, use the bathroom, and occasionally eat something, which tastes like nothing. Even though Kate is back in Pennsylvania, living in an apartment just a few miles away from me, she doesn't come to visit. We see each other maybe once a month, and when we do get together everything we talk about seems trivial and pointless. We're past the rehashing stage, and so the only subjects we are comfortable discussing are the emotional states of Danielle and Michele. Danielle is almost ready to move with her boyfriend to California, where they each plan on working in restaurants while going to school. Michele is still in Fort Lee with no plans to move; she is the one who gets left behind, eventually moving in with Earl and Nancy, the other caregivers, besides Dad, of the Ortlip five. I mean four.

On July 4, I'm alone. Invitations to Fourth of July celebrations are wasted on me. The thoughts of hot dogs, fireworks, and crowds of people spiral me back down into my basement hole. I crave the wet mold of my mattress. Unbeknownst to Wilma and her family, my mattress is beginning to grow some frightening-looking things, the likes of which I have never encountered before. In fact, when I move out a few days later I have to throw the mattress away. Besides talking with the paintings, I am now also speaking with the mold, whispering all sorts of dark wishes and emotions that I'm positive only mold could totally understand.

And when it appears a couple of times a day, I try to talk with the blue flash, too, which has grown brighter and bigger over time; it's about as big as a quarter now. Ever since that night at Catherine's, I've seen it. It lasts a few seconds and then vanishes altogether.

I've tried communicating with it (though I haven't mentioned it to anyone yet) to assess whether or not it might be Shari. Two nights ago I said out loud, "If you don't appear in ten minutes, I'm going to kill myself." I thought for sure if it was Shari beaming in as a blue flash, she wouldn't want me to die, not this soon anyway. She probably wants a little time on her own, time to figure things out on the other side. But the blue flash did not appear. I got mad, accusing the blue flash of being a fraud. But then I had to agree with myself (or was it the mold?) that if it was Shari, she would not believe that I would really kill myself, especially since I had just told her recently that I wouldn't kill myself even if a sister died, and she would certainly not be so easily manipulated. I had to admit that the blue flash might, in fact, be Shari; at least I should stay open to the possibility. What do I know about psychic phenomena?

So here I am, talking with the mold, the blue flash, and a demented portrait of myself when it hits me: Shari and I must have seen her death during our blackout right after the car accident of a year ago. Why did I paint a portrait of myself with head wounds just months before her death? Shari died of head wounds. Why did I call her and beg her to promise me that she wouldn't die? She couldn't promise me that because she knew she was going to die soon. Why did Catherine say that one of us would die young and tragically? She was talking about Shari. I'm beginning to shake, heading further and further out into a state of alarm, when I hear Wilma calling me from the top of the stairs, "Carol, are you all right? Can we talk?" Saved. Sort of.

Wilma wants me to move out because the arrangement is not working for her. Can't imagine why. She's only harboring a human mold experiment in her basement; she could probably get arrested for it. As she speaks, I realize just how shut down I've become, at least to real-live people. I've been spending so much time with myself, with mold, paintings, and cardboard boxes, that human contact just doesn't appeal to me the way it once did. I simply nod in agreement. God, this feels familiar. It seems like I've been nodding in agreement my entire life.

As I'm listening to Wilma, a huge blue flash appears next to her head. I'm longing to believe that it's Shari's psychic presence, urging me to be strong, witty, and polite; I know she'd want me to be all of those things under these circumstances. I begin to cry. Wilma apologizes for having to throw me out, but I assure her that it's really fine and that I'm crying for other reasons. "I'll leave in the morning." Wilma insists that I stay a few more days. "Okay." I retreat to the mattress, lying as still as possible, willing the blue flash to come back and stay with me. It doesn't, and I stop asking the blue flash or anyone else for help.

Once I leave Wilma's for good, I bum around for weeks, crashing on other mattresses, on other floors, in other friends' homes until I've run out of friends whose homes seem comfortable and welcoming. Lugging the bloody image of myself wherever I go, I finally land back at 95 Main Street. I set up another mattress on the floor and settle in for the autumn.

It comes down to breaking each hour into fragments, fragments to get through, to struggle through. The days go by, and I don't know how we all get through them. I don't go anywhere. I'm not involved with anyone or -thing, only Shari, total involvement with the memories—the nows of sorrow, the nows of anger, the nows of joy. She fills up every hour. So much to absorb. Staring into the sun hoping I'll see her hair reflected there. Dreaming of the child: two fingers in her mouth, the child of mischief. Wisteria arbor where the bees used to hum all day. We sat underneath to smell the light, to stare into a purple sky, to dance together as five, now four. She goes off alone, leaving me alone to be twenty-two years old, knowing she'll never share this life with me again. Knowing there is no end or middle or beginning. Only death. I will never truly rest again. Spider on my leg. I have no fear of spider poison. I'm too stuffed with poison of my own.

Where do I go?

CAROL, JOURNAL ENTRY, JULY 1976

PORTRAIT OF KATE

Kate has her eyes closed. She is waiting for the wind to blow against her face in a certain way, as if it had consciousness. In this wooded glade, visited by the five of us many years ago on a winter's day, the vortex of spirit must be as strong as Kate's desire for a sign from Shari, or any soul who might be passing by. All around Kate, leaves are fluttering like little wind socks. The wind blows from out of the northwest, carrying a chill but no message, at least not one that she can decipher.

Sunlight accentuates the blond highlights of Kate's hair as she finally opens her eyes, hoping to see rainbows everywhere, something, anything, that could be construed as spiritual. All she can see is the sun going down over the tree line. The glade is becoming hushed, falling into the shadows. Kate's eyes rise up, taking in the crown of gold lingering in the treetops.

"Shari, where are you?" The wind, so delicate just a few minutes ago, suddenly gusts out, forcing Kate to squint against it. "Is that you? Is that you?"

As she makes her way back down the road to the mental health

clinic where she still works and which Mom and Frank have retired and moved away from, the sky begins to lose its blue cast.
Only Kate's eyes are blue now, and filled with tears of disappointment. Upon reaching the clinic, her sunken form practically indis-
tinguishable from the surroundings, she turns around and looks
back the way she came. She can see only shadows where once there
were thousands of rainbows.

> Your golden hair is in the sunset;
> I see your eyes in the blue of the sky.
> The questions I ask, but there are no answers,
> And I'm hoping that time will help me to understand.
>
> Oh, Shari, where are you now?
> I just want to see your face again
> And hear your soft voice singing a song.
> Oh, why did you have to leave us so soon?
>
> I know that I feel your spirit within me
> Giving me strength to laugh and sing.
> But the loss I feel is tearing inside of me
> And I cannot keep my mind from looking for you.
>
> Oh, Shari, where are you now?
> I just want to see your face again
> And hear your soft voice singing a song.
>
> Oh, why did you have to leave us so soon?

KATE ORTLIP, SONG, JULY 1976

PORTRAIT OF DANIELLE

Danielle stands at the head of a trail that leads down to what has already become, in the short time she has been in Southern California, her favorite beach. She scans the rocky expanse for people, trying to decide whether or not she should go any farther. If it is too crowded, she'll go back to the apartment, lock the door, and draw the curtains in tightly. Maybe she'll even turn on the shower and pretend that it's raining. The only time she has to relate to strangers is when she works, waitressing at Houlihan's Old Place. When she waitresses, Danielle is capable of faking it, of forgetting about Shari's death, and of shaking off the headaches, the week-long, torturous bone mashers that spin her closer and closer to a bona fide depression.

She attempts to take in a really deep breath, one that could clear away some of tension in her body, but the air will not go in far enough. It stops in her throat, practically clogging her windpipe with the pressure of its intention. She lights a cigarette, the smoke entering her lungs easily, somehow making her feel more alive.

Danielle's eyes, more French blue than the blue-green mix of Kate's eyes, reflect back ocean, sky, and the thin white horizon line that just barely distinguishes the two. She peers hard toward the edge of the ocean, unsure of what she is hoping to see but still looking for something.

"Shari, are you there?" she cries out into that thin white line. There's a blip, a break in the contour of the line. It looks like something is rising up, white itself; the form moves up, up, up, and then disappears into the faint wisp of a cloud that is so transparent, Danielle isn't sure it was actually there at all. She strains to find it again. She can't.

"It's not you, Shari. It's not you. It will never be you."

Danielle hasn't spotted any people, but she turns away from the beach anyway, getting into her Volkswagen Beetle and driving home to the safety of familiar things and the sound of the shower.

Shari—you died.

It's over for you. Idealistic beauty, confusing creature—I envied you. I touched you—then you disappeared. Why couldn't you be touched? Warm and then so cold.

You had conflicts. You loved yourself immensely and hated yourself bitterly. How could you have envied me? Why did you fight to be me? You were so superior. A graceful yet clumsy woman. A tall, thick energy.

You were right. You worked on yourself. Did you give up? You got so distant.

Shari—you died. You were stopped. Is that what you wanted? No. You loved yourself. Did you think that you had only yourself?

I didn't desert you. I never left. You were still the only one. The only one and now you're gone. Now you've deserted me. Now I only have myself.

Shari—I need you!

PLEASE HELP ME!

DANIELLE, JOURNAL ENTRY, AUGUST 1976

PORTRAIT OF MICHELE

Michele is leaning against the trunk of the old white pine tree, which is one of the only life-forms still standing at the edge of our former property, on the cliffs. She rubs her eyes, trying to clear away the nearsightedness that has developed since living at 95 Main Street, a house without a view. She searches the vacant lot for signs of the old life she once knew, when we lived together on the cliffs.

The wind is picking up, scuffling up bits of fine dust from the remaining piles of dirt and rock. Because the conditions are optimal, a whirligig of swirling wind and debris sprouts up from behind the high-rise apartment building that stands, empty, on the exact spot where our house once stood. Michele braces for it; she's sure it will envelop her, maybe even carry her away from this life of being left behind.

The small tornado does come toward her, but at the last second it swerves off to the west, in the direction of where practically everyone who is important in her life has gone. As the agitated earth settles back, Michele's eyes fall on a torn piece of newspaper that has been blown up from a pile beyond the vacant lot. She stoops to retrieve it before the wind takes its hold, sending the paper out of reach. There is nothing of significance or meaning on one side, and Michele's hope for a sign from Shari starts to wane. Turning it over, she is startled and almost ready to twirl into cartwheels as she spots an advertisement for tuna fish.

"I don't know whether to become an actress or eat a tuna fish sandwich." The memory of Shari's words and playful expression returns to Michele as she says into the wind, "It's you, Shari. I know it's you."

Holding the piece of paper to her chest, Michele, smiling, her light blue eyes (Shari's shade but a wink darker) watering up with tears, turns her back to the river, the vacant lot, and the old pine tree, heading west toward 95 Main Street, the house without a view.

Rain. Nature can release her sorrow in so many ways. People can't. I find all of my grief held in me so tightly. I sit here, in a cabin on a misty lake watching enviously as the sky sheds its tears over the water. The smell is so fresh. So simple. I wish I could cry as freely with the rain. Just watching it, though, helps me. I feel like it's a part of me. The tree stretches its long branches up to sky. So free. Nature is so free. People are the only animals confined. Chained to our ridiculous rules. We're not a part of the rain and the trees. I want to dance, scream, thunder, rain, but I'm trapped. Nature is comforting to me. I love it. I feel so close to it. I feel like one of the trees, stretching out to the sky, but my roots are buried deep in this earth. I love life so much. Every moment is so important. Everything is so precious.

Now she's part of it. Shari, you laugh with every breeze. You cry with the rain. Your arms stretch out to the sky, but you're not rooted to this earth. You're free to fly, to thunder and rain. You don't feel pain.

MICHELE, JOURNAL ENTRY, JULY 1976

PORTRAIT OF DAD

Dad is looking into the emerging face of Shari. The life-size portrait of his "Shari Belle" is all he can see and his studio the only place he wants to be. With each brush stroke, she is put back together: the head injuries, the jagged slice down the face, the broken bones, the gashed liver are all painted away as the image emerges out of his gesso-coated canvas. If he could, Dad would breathe life into the form before him, defying the laws of life and death. But he does what he can; he paints. The concentration and willpower that go into this painting do not invigorate; they weaken. By the time he is finished with this memorial portrait of Shari, our father has been diminished, never fully returning with the same vitality. His need for distance from us, the daughters who survive, the daughters whose presence reminds him of Shari's absence, deepens. Shari's death becomes "The Tragedy," against which all other events, good and bad, are measured. Nothing ever measures up.

Lying next to him, on a low wooden table that he built years ago, is a white sheet of paper. Reaching for it every hour, maybe every half hour, Dad reads the words over and over again until his eyes, the deepest shade of cerulean blue, go tired and darken as he turns back to his creation and asks:

"Are you all right, Shari Belle?"

TO DAD

Wild colors of an autumn rose
    kiss the canvas by your side,
Somehow the evening flower knows
    you see love you cannot hide.

Painting the beauty with your hand
    and touching it with your mind,
You easily can understand
    what many never find.

For in their search for something free
    they do not realize
That what they want they cannot see
    completely with the eyes.

When we've all at last begun to die,
    When we cannot feel the tears we cry,
And when we feel the need to fly,
    You'll paint your wings and paint your sky.

SHARON ORTLIP, POEM, MAY 1976

9

~

CRETE

Kate and I are quietly standing outside the cucumber factory in Paleohora, Crete. We're in the middle of a large group of Greek women, most of whom are dressed in black mourning garb. We followed this pack of women from the village; the road, sandy and flat, parallels the ocean and was empty of cars this early in the day. The sun's been up for hours, but Kate and I certainly haven't been. I am still—and will be all day—attempting to thwart the remnants of a hangover; I had way too much Metaxa (Greek cognac) and orangeade last night in the closet-sized café by the beach.

It's about the fifth hangover I've ever had in my life; all of them have taken place just in the last few weeks. The first was a result of a night of drinking that almost kept me from making the ferry to Patras, Greece. Kate and I were having dinner in Brindisi, Italy, when a roving band of soccer-playing young men, fresh from a triumph, came into the restaurant to drink. Two of them sat down with us and ordered a huge carafe of wine. Kate and I were charmed by a guy named Sergio. The fact that he had two puncture wounds in his neck from an opponent's cleats made him all the more appealing to me. I kept wanting to touch the holes with my fingertips, which I'm pretty sure I did later on that night.

In the middle of our second carafe, Sergio grabbed my arm, led me outside to his scooter, helped me onto the back, and drove to his uncle's bar, where I proceeded to drink all of the wine that was offered to me. Somewhere in this frenetic wash of alcohol consumption, I lost consciousness: my first blackout but certainly not my last. Pieces of this evening do return: lying in a wet cobblestone alleyway kissing Sergio and his perforated neck, waving farewell to the thicket of Italian men at the uncle's bar as Sergio drove me back to the ferry, and falling off Sergio's scooter at Kate's feet. She was practically crying with frustration when I arrived at the ferry, so besotted I could not walk without assistance. When Kate saw the condition I was in, she no longer felt like crying; I know she felt like letting me have it between the eyes but didn't. Instead, she got me standing and walking long enough to get on board the ferry, which was only a few minutes from departure. I fell onto a line of attached seats, and there I remained, Kate guarding sister and traveling gear as we made the turbulent crossing from Italy to Greece.

On this European journey, I'm discovering the blazing and blinding effects of alcohol. Already I'm smitten with it, feeling the shift taking place in my body as it makes room for my daily consumption of every conceivable kind of alcohol. Already I can't wait until tonight's first drink—that first reckoning swig smashing the back of my throat, all wet interior flesh ignited. The alcohol falls on fire into my stomach, radiating in every direction toward the far reaches of my body. It toasts me, coats me, opens me wide to heat of all kinds, and I am flushed full with a profound sense of oblivion. I float transfixed in this state of forgetfulness, free from all haunting thoughts; I have discovered a place where there is absolutely nothing: "I'm not thinking, you guys. I'm not thinking at all," Shari's declaration comes back to me from the tunnel of ice and snow. There is a small price to pay for this freedom though: hangovers, but I am rapidly learning to deal with them.

So now what? From inside my head, from every windy vantage point, Shari whispers: "I don't approve." I don't care Shari. I didn't approve of your car accident, either, you know. Each time I swallow down a Metaxa and orangeade or beer or retsina I scream at her: "Here's what!"

Through hazy, sticky vision, I see the huge corrugated steel door slide open; Nikkos, the owner of the cucumber factory, lets us in. The dark and musty interior doesn't hold much of a welcome as we trudge inside. The place reeks of rotten, smushed cucumbers. Kate and I watch in fascination as the women follow a well-worn path to a circle of wooden crates that function as seats. Already stacked next to each empty and upside-down sitting crate are stacks of other crates filled with dirty cucumbers. The slight but obviously sturdy women lift the top crates down from their stacks, place them at their feet, take out cucumbers, and begin to clean them with sponges. With knives that seemingly appear from up their sleeves the women cut off the stems and then place the cucumbers in empty crates. Once these crates are full of clean, stem-free cucumbers, the women carry them to the plastic wrapping machine where they will be packaged and sealed, to be stacked into trucks for shipment to Germany or the United States.

Kate and I look at each other in amusement. After what we've been through, cleaning cucumbers is a fitting job somehow. Our travel path has been fraught with experiences sure to cure the most avid admirer of men of their admiration. We were abducted by two Spanish truck drivers and separated for three days as each truck headed off in a different direction, only to be reunited at the tourist office in Cordova on Halloween eve. Then we were exposed to a Greek man who was jerking off on a lovely Greek beach where we had gone to get away from men. (Yes, by this time Kate and I both know what jerking off is, but we didn't find out from Frank.) And finally, we were pinched and hooted at by masses of Italian men, confirming the authenticity of that famous photograph of a very beautiful woman being taunted by men as she attempts to make her way through the streets of an Italian city with a look of terror on her face.

One of the women motions Kate and me over to the pack, gesturing toward two empty crates. What else can we do but begin? I struggle not to laugh. I struggle so hard that a little bit of drool escapes from between my lips and drips onto my blue jeans. Kate gives me a quick kick in the leg as a couple of the women eye me doubtfully. I wipe my mouth and self-consciously continue to slide the sponge along the cucumber.

Soon we're in a rhythm. The women chatter and sing as they work; it passes the time away. After maybe an hour and a half, we stop for a break: salted cucumber slices for snack. A big blue flash spins out in front of me as I reach for my first piece. I watch Kate as she takes her first bite of salted cucumber, but she absolutely will not let her eyes meet mine. Together we chew, the repetitive chomping keeping us both from the urge to gag. We have a few more breaks that day, all resplendent with cucumbers.

As we leave the factory in the early evening, Nikkos hands Kate and me two slightly damaged cucumbers each. We walk down the road with our cucumbers, unable to speak until we are far enough away from the factory to safely begin going over the absurd events of the day. By the time we reach our room in the village, Kate and I are completely exhausted, primarily from the physical strain of laughing while gripping those cucumbers tightly to our chests in a kind of self-protective defensive posture. We do not have cucumbers for dinner that night, nor any other night thereafter; I find lots of different places to pitch them where I hope they won't be discovered.

That one day in the cucumber factory turns out to be Kate's only day of work. She doesn't need the money, being a conscientious attainer and frugal saver of the money she made back in the States. I, on the other hand—the hand that knows not how to save—must continue on at the factory. Kate and I have decided to stay on in Paleohora for at least a month, maybe longer. If I don't work, Kate will be forced to pay for the room we share, the food we eat, and the alcohol we, mainly I, drink. An arrangement like that could put a strain on our delicate traveling relationship.

Kate is now free to roam, but I am not, and thus I lose her to the mysterious and succulent countryside. She loses me to cucumbers and alcohol. We continue to speak over the dinners we take turns cooking. Kate recalls to me the adventures: high in the hills of Crete, she encounters people, animals, flowers, vistas, and visions that open her to a weeping that isn't about Shari's death. Kate's crying has been, like mine, of the dark kind, the violent waves confronted when the rock slices of grief take aim at our lungs with relentless purpose, tearing away all breath. No, the tears Kate has been crying in the small mountaintop village of Anidri, which overlooks the Mediterranean Sea, are clear and sweet, falling lightly as she smiles into the sunny wind. Kate comes down from the hills filled with the scent of wildflowers and orange blossoms, the sight of mist-soaked olive trees catching the dazzle of afternoon light, and the sound of songbirds, which are sharing the winds with her. Kate seems to possess a secret, her eyes set free into the images she has been given and can call forth whenever she wants to. I sit listening and begin to envy her, for all I have are visions of cucumbers that appear relentlessly inside my head. "Why can't I go off wandering?" I ask out loud. Kate doesn't say anything and, of course, we already know the answer to this foolish question: I spend much of my pay on drinking, and then I'm too hungover to go anywhere outside of my room.

But one day I do rouse myself from the syrupy mush of another morning after. This particular day enters our small room creeping on its hands and knees, quietly urging me to open my eyes but to do it very slowly. Kate is already gone, to where I don't know. She is making friends with a couple of Irish women who don't have to work, either, and who know enough to stay away from the cafés at night.

Instead of making myself a cup of coffee (making coffee in Crete takes years of training—the slop I create in my attempts is not fit to lubricate a cucumber-wrapping machine), I dress and shuffle down to Nikkos's café. Yes, besides managing the cucumber factory he also owns and runs the most popular café in town. There I meet a few other scraggly types who look familiar; were they in the café with me the night before? We smile at one another just to be on the safe side of polite tourist protocol.

Three gritty coffees later I am ready for my hike; at least I believe I am. With a headache and dry mouth, my brain still bobbing around in a partial alcohol bath, I decide the moment to leave the café has arrived. It doesn't occur to me to bring water or nourishment. Exiting the café door, I am nipped at by the resident pelican, who nips at almost anyone who gets close enough. I take this as a sign of affection; I probably should have taken it as a warning.

Halfway out of the village, I glance back to see a rainbow cresting the tops of the trees, one end resting in the aquamarine waters of the Mediterranean Sea, the other end reaching up to touch the soft orange-colored cliffs that border the northern edge of Paleohora. Rainbows appear regularly over Paleohora; it's obviously an ancient relationship among sea mist, cliffs, and sun. When I turn back around to continue with the hike, I am totally baffled by what I see. There, moving next to the world I've been hiking in, is another world, which I assume is a mirage or hallucination. People, cars, and buildings that do not belong in Paleohora, much less in Crete, are blocking my view of the sea.

Shaking my head and rubbing my eyes vigorously, I whisper a brief beseeching plea to all Greek gods and goddesses everywhere to clear away this vision. I throw in a quick plea to Shari in her new blue flash form, thinking it can't hurt. But nothing changes. I wave my arms, stamp my feet, and shout, hoping to frighten this escaped reality back to where it has come from even if that means back to the inside of my head; I've begun to fear that I've lost my mind and that I'm the one creating this aberration. I vow to stop drinking, the thought progressing up from the explanation lobe of my brain that maybe my new habit, which I've heard destroys brain cells by the millions, has brought on this attack of the visiting dimensions. And what kind of a silly dimension is this anyway? Cars that look like they're from the 1920s? People in suits, dresses, and bowler hats? City avenues and buildings? It feels suspiciously like a Shari-instigated trick, if I've ever witnessed one. Standing with my hands folded in front of me, I try negotiating with her: "C'mon, Shari. Can we let this one go? I know you don't like my drinking habits. I'll stop. Just make this go away. Please?"

If Shari is listening, she's not about to give up on this trick yet. I take a step forward and flail my arms around, hoping the movement will break a hole through the hallucination. Maybe this is simply an optical illusion brought on by the same conditions that bring on the rainbows. No such luck. It doesn't go away. I decide to walk right into this split reality. Side by side, Paleohora and Chicago, Illinois? in the 1920s? exist as my new world now while I continue hiking toward Anidri. I try relaxing into it, realizing this could actually be a psychic phenomenon that I'm being allowed to participate in. What do I know about psychic phenomena anyway?

I've reached the olive groves, Paleohora and the sea no longer visible. As I come around a corner in the trail, two goats emerge from behind the trees while a car drives in front of a crooked fire hydrant in front of the goats. One of the goats jumps up onto a low branch of an olive tree; I stop to take in this new and startling sight: a goat in a tree. This savvy goat looks me right in the eyes and bleats at me. This intense bleat compels me to ask in all earnestness, "What do you want, little goat?" It bleats once more and honest to Zeus, Chicago, Illinois, in the 1920s vanishes. The goat jumps off the tree and joins its pal, and they both disappear into the grove. Could this altered state of reality possibly be Kate's secret? Has my consciousness been altered because of Shari's death? Or am I really going mad?

I never make it to Anidri that day. I run—as best I can, given the awful physical shape I am in—back into Paleohora, where I go to a café and order a double Metaxa and orangeade. The promise I made to Shari that I would stop drinking is the first of thousands of promises that I would break so quickly and dramatically in the years to follow. The split reality thing never happens to me again, leading me to conclude that I was not necessarily severely mad, maybe just a little mad, with alcohol playing a supporting role.

―――――

If a face can express three or more emotions at once, then Kate's face surely is achieving it as I tell her about my encounter with "another side of reality" that night over dinner. Exasperation, disbelief, and tender concern all show up at once. Ever since the fateful first drinking night in Brindisi, Kate has been looking at me with combinations of expressions, revealing her confusion. She seems to be trying to figure me out in a whole new way, not quite certain what to do with this new older sister who is acting more like a younger sister. I'm positive that she's been writing to Danielle (and maybe Michele, too) about our shifting relationship and my growing weirdness, for I receive a letter from Danielle full of questions and straight talk about the dangers of life as a "cad and a fop." I confront Kate about it, and she admits to writing letters to Danielle about her confusion over my questionable behavior. This prompts a tearful tell-all heart-to-heart where we both spill fears that we haven't dared reveal, not wanting to alienate each other just in case one of us dies suddenly and goes to the grave tortured by thoughts of sister betrayal. We don't want to end up like Danielle, who will probably feel eternally guilty about the state her relationship with Shari was in at the time of Shari's death: tense and hostile.

Danielle tries not to give away too much in her letters, but it's clear from what she doesn't write that things are getting worse for her. Not once does she mention happiness or that she's noticed something lovely recently or that she can't wait to see us, things she would always write about in letters she used to write, before Shari's death. Danielle is one of the most appreciative and effusive people that ever walked this earth, so the fact that she isn't writing about her appreciation makes Kate and me nervous. And this is how it will be from now on. Even when there are just three of us present, talks that occur between two will always include a part where we are compelled to wonder about and discuss the well-being of the one who is not there.

The closing lines of Danielle's most recent letter that send me to the café for my opening drink of the day are: "And God, I miss that girl. Why, Carol? Tell me, do you, with your blue flash, know why she had to die? Because if you do, it would help me enormously if you would tell me. I'm not so sure about this life anymore, Carol." Neither am I, dear Danielle; neither am I.

Soon after our liberating talk, Kate and I take what turns out to be our last hike to Anidri together, all serious discussions shelved as we enter the holy landscape of southwestern Crete. The Mediterranean is particularly shiny when we reach the village. As I look with soft focus at my sister, my first true companion, I think about all the traveling we've been doing together for the last twenty years, over cliffs, along paths, into worlds uncharted by either one of us. Kate and I have been communicating with each other in ways we don't, nor ever will need to, talk about. I know Kate like I will always know the cliffs that move within me. I look at her as she sits, legs dangling off a rock, face held up toward the sky in quiet and reflective appreciation for this sight; I hold onto this picture of her, and I try not to become morbid, imagining what life would be like without her.

~

Kate was just a little baby, spitting up all over herself again while she was trying to speak with me. The spit was slopping right down her chin, but she still smiled at me, especially since I was making a yucky face close to hers. I liked making Kate smile. I'd been making her smile for a long time, ever since she came to live with my father and mother and me.

One of the best things about Kate was her hair, which was very curly and jiggled around on her head whenever she laughed or tried to say words back to me. I stuck my finger into one of her curls. My finger went even farther into another curl and then into another one behind that one. I couldn't do that with my own hair, because it didn't have any curls. Kate reached up and stuck one of her fingers into a curl, too. Her finger had spit covering it, and so some of her hair got sticky before I was able to pull her finger away. "Uh-oh," I said. Kate thought I was trying to do something silly, which I really wasn't, and began to laugh. I couldn't help but laugh, too. Another good thing about Kate, my baby sister, was her name. I really loved her name. Mom and Dad told me that she had a big name, Kathleen Joanne. But they said I could call her Kate, which I was very happy about because it would be a lot harder to say "Kathleen Joanne" all the time. I asked Mom and Dad if I had another big name. "Yes. It's Carol Aileen, but we will call you Carol and Kate will call you Carol, too."

"You're a big, fat mess, Kathleen Joanne," I said to Kate as I poked her lightly on the nose. She reached for my hand with her dirty one. We were both big, fat messes then.

∼

When Kate and I say goodbye a few days later in front of the café and as I watch her ride away on the bus out of Paleohora toward a rendezvous with her boyfriend in Italy, I can't get back to that sweet vision of her on the mountaintop. Her face, behind bus window glass, distorts and disappears into a black reflection of a twisted tree; I grab onto a blue window shutter that has fallen away from its frame. The shutter slips, taking me to the ground with it. Sitting in the dusty road, I mouth out: "Wait, Kate. Don't go." Must every goodbye now be fraught with these premonitions of danger and loss? I shake my head furiously. Stop it. Stop it. Stop it. Stop it. Feeling a pinch on my upper right arm, I swing around to find the pelican biting me. I try to shoo it away, but it won't leave me alone. Finally, I decide to just let it be. As soon as I choose this course of nonaction, the pelican walks around me, shakes its tail feathers in my face, and begins to waddle up the road, soon turning a corner onto a lane that leads to the sea.

After Kate is gone, I have a dream about dying:

～

I am running frantically through a city, as are thousands of other people; a bomb is about to be dropped and so we are searching for a place to hide or for a familiar person to be with. Just as the explosion is upon us, I raise my eyes to see Danielle holding out her hand to me. As we touch, the explosion occurs and I feel myself dying, breaking apart into pieces as my mind lets go into a state of acceptance and exhilaration; all the while I'm aware of Danielle's presence. From my heavenly vantage point, where I am now floating as spirit, I view the world crumbling, buildings pounding into the sea in great swelling chunks. The splashes are enormous, creating tidal waves that surge toward the cities.

～

I wake up in my little room in Crete, looking around for Danielle. As parts of the dream return to me, I can't help but become perplexed by these questions: Why did Danielle come to help me die and not Shari? Aren't people who are on "the other side" supposed to help humans die?

I spend Christmas with my Greek, German, and Belgian drinking friends. We respectfully participate in the village routine of cooking a turkey at the local bakery. Since most of the houses do not have an oven, on major holidays such as Christmas everyone brings the dishes to be baked to the bakeries in town, of which there are two. These ovens are cavernously huge and can fit many turkeys, pies, breads, and casseroles all at once; it's simply a matter of the bakers monitoring the schedule. The resident Greeks get the times of their choice, leaving us tourist types groveling for whatever times we can get.

I bring the turkey that I purchased in Hania, the port city a few hours' drive to the north, to the bakery at 5:00 P.M., putting dinner at around 8:00 P.M. I had to take a bus all the way to Hania to get this turkey, which was alive when I first saw it. Underneath a large dome, I walked through the market until I found the turkeys running around inside a pen, kicking up dirty sawdust into the air. After choosing what looked like a suitable candidate for Christmas dinner, I watched the keeper of the turkeys lop off its head, wrap the entire turkey, including the head, in brown paper, and hand it to me. As per the instructions of the turkey keeper, I spent that evening plucking and burning out with a cigarette lighter what felt like a million feathers.

It's an ugly bird, covered with blue inklike feather plucking holes, that I present to the bakers at 5:00 P.M., but I am proud of it nevertheless. I hope that I've planned the cooking time correctly; otherwise my friends and I are going to end up picking at a half-baked bird. But the Cretan bakers have timed it perfectly, and we eat one of the best turkeys ever, accompanied only by bread and retsina. (I was a little preoccupied with the turkey. It never occurred to me to buy anything else for dinner.) This feast ranks up there with some of the best Christmas dinners Dad, my sisters, and I had at 144 Old Palisades Road. Dad would cook for hours and set a table laden with all our favorite foods, and I got to eat both drumsticks, which my father always set aside for me.

Not long after Christmas and the amazing dinner, I leave Crete on a night ferry after too many nights and days of drinking, playing, and howling at the moon and the rainbow. I leave Crete because I know if I stay I'm going to get hurt or hurt someone or maybe never be able to leave. I leave because I'm growing scared, getting close to admitting that I have a problem with alcohol; I'm not ready to do that yet.

Nikkos doesn't seem surprised when I tell him that I am leaving and won't be working at the cucumber factory anymore. I'm sure he's become used to the comings and goings of wandering and working travelers. He hands me three cucumbers as a parting gift, and we say goodbye.

I walk slowly down the beach road toward my place this last time, not paying much attention to my surroundings. I'm disappointed, feeling that I never allowed myself to fully experience Crete, that my perpetual state of inebriation or recovering from it kept me apart from everything and everyone.

In this state of reflection, I'm not aware of a car that is speeding toward me from behind until I hear its horn. The sound is so close and loud, I am startled enough to leap off the road directly into a ditch that I didn't know was there. My right leg is cut open by a sharp rock and the cucumbers are smashed into my chest. I lie at the bottom of the ditch, looking up at the aquamarine sky, wondering if the cucumbers are going to stain my shirt, one of the four shirts that I brought with me.

Suddenly two heads appear above me, blocking out my view of the sky. Their faces are hard to discern, darkened by shadow, but I can soon see that they are men who seem very agitated. Reaching out their hands to me, I stand up and let them pull me out of the ditch, leaving the mess of cucumbers behind.

They escort me to their car, with the horn that sent me into the ditch in the first place. One of them, speaking in choppy English, says he could not believe it when I vanished from sight. At first he thought that I was a ghost, sent by an evil spirit whose name I would never be able to pronounce or remember.

Back at my room, I assure the men that my leg wound is superficial and send them away. Upon examination, I discover that the cut is fairly deep, but probably not deep enough to warrant stitches. After cleaning my leg and packing my things, I get into bed, avoiding the café scene for the first time since my arrival. I'm scheduled to leave in the morning, and I don't want anything to interfere with my departure. I'm sure that the car horn, the ditch, the gash, and the mutilated cucumbers are warning signs, meant to send me on my way home to 95 Main Street.

Without saying goodbye to anyone, afraid that I might be persuaded to stay despite the risks I would surely take if I did, I board the bus for Hania, with a final peck from the pelican. As I am crossing to Athens that night by ferry, Kate is crossing, too, back to Crete; we literally pass each other in the blackness of a deep January early morning. All Kate finds when she arrives in our little room in Paleohora is a loving note from me. I imagine her turning toward the Mediterranean Sea as she reads it, tears reflecting back the image of the water. I imagine she completely understands the reasons that I had to leave and blows her understanding into the wind that reaches me as I bid farewell to Greece, boarding a train for England.

What I don't imagine is her staying on in Crete for another three months while I return to the States and become employed in another series of jobs that are meaningless and servile, but that's what happens.

It's a sad, pudgy me that walks across the snowy yard at 95 Main Street, back from the airport. No one is there to greet me and, while I didn't really expect there to be, I can't help but feel a desolation that rattles my fragile sense of balance; it doesn't take much these days to do that. I sit at a chair in the kitchen taking in the dreariness of this house, which is still not fit for haunting. I can't feel Shari anywhere.

I suddenly have the overwhelming desire to get to the cliffs. I race out the door and run the three blocks back to the site where our house used to be. The only familiar thing left standing is the large white pine at the end of the long driveway that always served as our guard tree. I lean against it now, looking past the thirty-two-story apartment building that is finished but remains empty due to some kind of legal battle between builders and financiers. I expect to see a rainbow radiating up from the Hudson River, extending toward the spot where Maggie once grew, but of course there are never rainbows this time of year. What could I be thinking? As I stare out into the river view, wondering what to do next, an image of Kate comes to me, her face in the sun, orange tree blossoms framing her gold and wavy hair. A universe away, I hold out my love for her into the river winds, hoping she is safe and still full of the secrets that make her smile and cry sweet tears.

As I turn to walk back to 95 Main Street, a light in the sky above Manhattan catches my attention. It's not the blue flash this time; it's a sun dog, one of those small rainbows that, under the right conditions, can appear high in the clouds. I whisper, "Thank you," like I have many times before, and practically from this very spot spin away from the cliffs and slowly return to the gray house on Main Street, where I must begin to find my way home.

10

~

THE HAUNTED

I have planted myself directly in front of the door to Danielle's apartment, in Santa Barbara, California, attempting to command my psychic resources to allow me either to see through the wood (I want to listen in on the discussion my sisters are having about me; of course, they can only be talking about me) or to go up in smoke, never to be glimpsed or listened to again. I simply cannot create a smooth entrance right now. I'm so self-conscious and unhinged that I am convinced any classically patent phrase from one of my siblings will cause me to collapse in disappointment. I don't want this Christmas reunion at Danielle's beautiful apartment, the first full reunion of the four of us since Shari's death, to be stale or polite or nauseatingly sweet. But what else can it be? We haven't figured anything else out yet. Trite and stupid words and phrases flicker on and off inside my mind; I catch the tail ends of them before they darken and slip back into the inner recesses of my brain. I mean, what can we say to one another that would make everything better?

To make this whole disaster-in-waiting even worse, I have this rusty taste smearing the inside of my mouth, probably because I've been sucking on the paper clip that was holding my plane tickets and flight schedule together. Maybe we should have put this reunion off for another year—we need more time to adjust—but, for God's sake, when will it be the "right" time?

I focus and refocus on the door handle, hoping the door will open itself, so I won't have to. How can this be? How can I possibly be afraid of seeing my sisters all together again? Just go in. Just go in. What's the most awful thing that could happen? They will all be dead, lying on the floor newly murdered, and I'll have to deal with the pain and torment of multiple deaths. That's not going to happen, especially since I can see them moving around inside. They'll all notice how bloated and misshapen I've become and reject me. No. No. No. That won't happen, either. C'mon. Just go in. . . . I can't.

As I start to turn around toward Victoria Street, the only route of escape, thinking that perhaps I should walk into town for a drink, a pickup truck slides in next to the curb. A friendly face bugs up at me and says, "Hey. You must be Carol. I'm Joe." Oh, great. It's Kate's new sunny love. There's no escape now. "Hi," is all I can come up with.

He, skinny, tall thing, jumps out of the rig and hugs me. He's wearing all sorts of necklaces and dark turquoise rings, and he smells like pot or maybe patchouli oil. I try deflating myself down in size by sucking in my stomach and whatever else can be sucked in along with my stomach. I can't imagine Joe would be so cruel as to make a comment about my weight, but I try shrinking anyway. I really do want to make a good first impression.

"Goin' in, are ya?" He smiles. This throws me off-kilter. I'm not centered enough to declare my intentions to flee, and so I follow

Joe inside. Kate, Danielle, Michele, and Michele's high school friend Fran, who flew all the way out to California with Michele from New Jersey, are scattered throughout the apartment engaged in various pre-Christmas tasks, most of which get quickly covered up or put away into bags and boxes. Nice save, kids. For crying out loud, maybe they really weren't talking about me after all.

As soon as Kate sees Joe, she levitates into his arms. I've never seen such a thing except in the movies. They kiss for an inordinate amount of time given the circumstances, and I cough uncomfortably. Danielle, Michele, and Fran have begun to swarm around me, blocking out my view of the newly beloveds. I have to admit, their hugs feel safe and real and right, and I am able to take the first truly relaxed breath in what may be years. We lapse into benign recitations of the safe utterings, and I must reevaluate my expectations for our reunion.

But before I can even begin my reevaluations, Danielle grabs me. With soft blue precision, she gets through to me, the look of penetrating compassion arresting all expectations in a wink. Sometimes Danielle is so strikingly gorgeous I can't look at her. At this moment, though, standing in the living room of Danielle's apartment, all I want to do is look at her or into her, absorbing her wisdom and loveliness through all of my senses, which are suddenly open and very receptive. She looks beyond my alcoholic bloat, my self-derision, and scorn. Her eyes make me want to confess everything: I want to tell her all about the two women I've had sex with and Richard, the guy I'm thinking about traveling cross-country with, and the way cocaine focuses my attention and the way I've been crying myself to sleep each night even though I'm really, really happy now, especially since I'm working at a cool restaurant called O.G.'s Dining Rooms on Thompson Street, where people line up at the door waiting for a table so they can eat the sour cream pancakes I flip on the soapstone grill on Sunday mornings.

Danielle moves closer to me and says quietly, "I miss you so much," then rests her head on my shoulder, her wavy hair against my mouth. I stroke her head, not saying a word, trite, confessional, or otherwise. She begins to rub one of her temples, which makes me suspect that she's in the thick of a headache but doesn't want to burden me or anyone else with it. This is how it will always be: even when she's sick, Danielle will try with all of her resolve not to burden us.

～

Mom had fallen asleep in her chair, still holding Danielle and still holding a cigarette. Kate took the burnt butt from Mom's fingertips and placed it in the ashtray. I extracted Danielle from Mom's arms and carried her to the couch where Shari, Kate, and I had been sitting and watching TV. The four of us spread into one another beneath a blanket that Kate retrieved from one of our beds. Danielle, half in and half out of sleep and lying with arms and legs across the three of us, absently stroked each of our faces with her small hand before falling back to sleep.

Later, somewhere in the night, I felt Dad lifting me from the couch, putting me in my own bed in the room I shared with my sisters. Before I fell asleep, I looked over at each of the beds where my sisters were already nestled in their blankets. Danielle's eyes popped open then. She sat up, looking around at each of us, too, doing her own little safety check. With a final smile, she rested her head on the pillow. "Good night," I whispered. "Good night," she replied.

～

The four of us are facing a large mirror in Danielle's bedroom attempting to determine which parent each of us resembles the most, something we've done many times before. We've always agreed that I look the most like Dad, even though I try pointing out my high cheekbones and deep-set eyes, which are characteristics that Mom has, not Dad. Kate's definitely a combination of Mom and Dad, and even if she does look more like Mom, we're all reluctant to declare it. After all these years of coming to grips with our feelings about Mom, none of us want to look more like her than like Dad, because if we don't resemble Mom, then maybe she won't turn out to be our mother after all, even though we have to admit, she has always been very attractive. We're clearly still punishing her, and sometimes I hate myself and my sisters for doing it. We will probably always be punishing her and we will always be compelled to leave the door open to other possibilities, for example: the Julie Andrews possibility.

When we were little, Julie Andrews was our number-one candidate for "real" mother. Once we saw *The Sound of Music* (we saw it nine times at the Rivoli Theater in Manhattan) Julie Andrews photos went up all over our walls and we would hold Julie Andrews sing- and look-alike contests (which I always won), and I would kiss each photo good night before going to sleep. There were never any real-live mother candidates because, quite understandably, no one else could possibly measure up to our (mostly my) mother fantasies of Julie Andrews.

We move on to look at Danielle in the mirror. Tough call. She looks more like Dad, but hints of Mom run through her, in the high cheekbones and almond-shaped eyes. Michele? Toss-up there, too, although she falls more into the Dad category as well.

The inevitable questions arise: Whom did Shari look the most like? Do we get out photographs or go by memory? None of us want to admit that we don't remember exactly. It's only been two and a half years; shouldn't we be able to recall instantly? Isn't her face memorized in the bones? I stop and take a closer look at Kate's, Danielle's, and Michele's features. God, do I really know them? Would I be able to identify them if I went blind?

We conclude that Shari, too, was a true combination of both parents. Of course, aren't we all? Shari's features, as I remember them, were finer than Dad's. I'm ready to say, "I think Shari looked more like Mom, you guys," but I can't. Somehow it would be a betrayal. Shari just has to look more like Dad, for his sake, even though he isn't here. Maybe someday we'll be able to look at a photo of Shari and not only see the resemblance to Mom but maybe even honor her for it.

It's Danielle who says she wants the four of us to sing, which is actually somewhat of a surprise, since she was one of the least enthusiastic participants in our sister singing group. Maybe it was all that posturing and mugging in front of the mirror that triggered an ancient, deeply embedded urge to sing. Suddenly we've erupted into loud gargles and hiccups also known as "vocal exercises." They always preceded the songs at singing lessons with Lela Holiday on Saturdays, and they precede the songs now. Then we are ready for our "special" songs, the ones chosen specifically for each sister by Lela Holiday, who explained, "Because each of you has a unique personality."

"What was your song, Michele?"

" *'I wanna be loved by you, just you and nobody else but you. I wanna be loved by you, alone. Boo boo pee do.'* I hate that song."

"What was your song, Danielle?"

" *'That perfect boyoyoyoy, some perfect boyoyoyoy, is sure to happen along, come along one wonderful day.'* I hate that song. Why did it have to be mine, you guys?"

"Kate?"

" *'Clang, clang, clang went the trolley. Ding, ding, ding went the bell. Zing, zing, zing went my heartstrings. From the moment I saw you I fell.'* "

"No. That was Shari's, wasn't it? Yours was 'Feelin' Groovy.' "

"You're right."

No one can remember my song, and it's just as well, because Danielle gets out a borrowed guitar from the living room closet and hands it to me so we can sing songs that we wrote. We haven't sung together in years, since before Shari's death. At first our voices are filled with tentative hushes. By the time we're finished with "Words," our voices are at full strength and we can't stop singing. Here, in our songs, are the cliffs, the river, Maggie, the rock slide, Fauntleroy, lilacs, Mom, Dad, wisteria, the rope swing. Here, in our songs, is Shari, living through the sound of our voices as they rise up into the end of the light on this day in December in Santa Barbara, California.

The next afternoon, we head downtown to a tattoo parlor. As one of her Christmas presents to us, Kate dared: "Get a tattoo and I'll pay for it—I dare you." It's plain from the minute we walk into the place that the tattoo artist is enamored of Danielle. This happens often. She frequently turns the heads of most human beings, men predominantly. Sometimes it's a drag, especially when the rest of us aren't feeling great about our looks. Currently I'm definitely fat, so it's not a shock when no one gives me a second look. Michele isn't exactly flirting yet, at least not in front of us. Kate isn't the least bit interested in flirting with other people now that she's found Joe. So when it's clear that Danielle will be the focus of someone's lusty attention, Kate, Michele, and I fade into nonchalant silence. We are watching the interaction from a distance as we start looking over the tattoo choices displayed in large notebooks.

Kate volunteers to go first since she's the one who came up with this idea. She gets through the hour-long procedure with little more than a series of winces when the artist is injecting the color into a tattoo of a star and a moon above her left breast.

I decide to go next. I have drawn the design for my tattoo, not liking any of the standard offerings. It's not as painful as I thought it would be; it feels like a delirious mosquito, obsessed with drilling its proboscis into my flesh over and over again, not at all interested in finding the blood beneath the surface. I can't tell whether it's turned out well after the artist finishes because there is too much drying blood to see through to the tattoo. Over the tattoo an impressive scab forms, which lasts for a week. When it falls away, revealed is the image, in sharp color and vivid detail, of a ball of burning fire heading across my right breast. Danielle and Michele both choose tattoos of roses in two different phases of development. Danielle has her rose inked onto her upper right butt, and Michele chooses a spot just below her right front hipbone.

My sisters and I are very pleased with our tattoos. Having them somehow makes us feel even more connected. We are more than blood sisters now, and we are each carrying a secret that only the four of us (six of us, including Fran and the tattoo artist) share and know about. This is one of the best Christmas presents ever, and when I get back to New York City and climb up the short ladder to my loft bed I look at my tattoo and decide that perhaps it's time to stop crying myself to sleep. I decide it's time to stop drinking and it's time to stop doing cocaine also.

Two of the "decide tos" last all of one week and then my will topples over a bottle of beer some innocent offers me at a party. After I write in my journal the following morning, it's back to headaches and sunglasses as I flip pancakes at O.G.'s Dining Rooms.

I am twenty-six years old and last night I cried hysterically. I couldn't sleep in my apartment. As I crawled into my loft bed, rising ten feet into the air, I knocked a mug of grapefruit juice down onto the floor. Screams from the couple next door. I couldn't tell if they were loving screams or fighting screams. It didn't matter.

I cried. I wanted to cry louder, but I felt inhibited. Someone among these 1980 apartments would hear me and conclude that I was a sad soul. A tormented woman with no lover to soothe her aches and longings. A loser.

After cleaning up the grapefruited mess, kicking the dirt off the rug, and blowing my nose, I lay down to try and reach sleep. I could smell the fresh Sunday *New York Times*. I didn't care. I could think only of my torment. I tried to imagine others who were going through the same thing. I mean surely this wasn't a unique state to be immersed in. Damn. That thought just made it even more depressing. I'm the only one to feel this, at least from my angle.

I heard the couple scream again and I longed for Richard. I wanted out. I wanted to travel. I wanted an explanation.

What is this?

Twenty-six and talented.

Wondering and not doing anything about the wondering. Getting drunk, shrugging aching shoulders, and falling asleep. Food slopping it out to hungry Soho'ers. Once skinny, now developing a beer belly. Crying late at night in absorbed frustration. 1980 and Reagan is Father America.

Do I pursue my artistic rantings in such an America?

I am a woman who is ready for everything, yet I'm so tired of it I could consider leaping from this sixth-floor walk-up.

What is this?

Why can't I make up my mind?

It's cold. It's winter. It's windy. It's twenty-six years into the life of a woman who seeks to find. Find what?

I'm twenty-six and I'm frantically living.

CAROL, JOURNAL ENTRY, 1980

I'm working three jobs now: pancake flipper at O.G.'s Dining Rooms, assistant to a landscape architect, and bagel baker at an Upper East Side bagel shop. My Greenwich Village existence is accelerating the pace of my footsteps, my mind beat, and my heartbeat. In order to keep up with myself, I participate in practically everything that draws me in: feminist guerrilla theater as an actress, jazz clubs as a flute-playing jazz musician, and painting workshops as an artist's daughter. To maintain my energy and allow enough time for jobs, extracurricular activities, and a social life, I hardly ever sleep (it's a waste of time), hardly eat (nothing tastes good except for falafel pockets from the Armenian guy on Bleecker Street), and increase my alcohol intake. Alcohol has become a medication, taken in large doses in order to overcome creeping life fright and early-morning insomnia. Now, if I don't drink, I'm truly incapable of functioning in the world. Social events must include alcoholic beverages; otherwise, I don't attend. Beginning just about when I wake up, I consciously plan my drinking schedule: when and where I'll have my first drink of the day, which routes I'll take to work so I'm assured a dose before and after, and which neighborhood bar to end up in so it won't be a long walk home alone.

Years later when I finally check myself into the halls of Alcoholics Anonymous, I calculate how much time I actually spent, not only in the physical act of drinking but also in planning for the drinking: approximately ten years of the serious kind of drinking and conniving, which means at least three hours spent each day conniving and probably four hours (conservatively, averaged and rounded out) of actual drinking, and I come up with 25,550 hours of drinking and conniving. That's 1,062 days or just about three entire years spent in an obsessive relationship (definition of "relationship": in direct contact with a container of an alcoholic substance) with a liquid.

One day, on my way to a party in the lower, lower East Village, I find myself standing in front of two bums who are making out on the sidewalk. Shari comes at me suddenly in a late, already-inebriated afternoon vision. I hear her tell me to reevaluate this tenuous existence, to take a look around and see the dirty puddle I'm swimming in—the festering snarl of it. I'm staring at the bums, lured and repulsed by these filthy people who are getting closer and closer to an all-out sexual encounter. One of them is practically naked; I can't really tell if either one of them is male or female because both their exteriors are so disguised by grime, distortion, and weathering. "Look. Look closely at them, Carol," what I assume to be Shari's voice says.

"I don't understand what they have to do with me," I say out loud.

"Well then, look again," comes the answer.

I look hard into the shaking flesh of the intertwined bums and without warning see myself twisted and contorted, mushing around with some slimy stranger. I suddenly feel like I'm in my own private version of Dickens's *A Christmas Carol,* viewing a possible future that might come true if I don't stop my self-destructive ways.

The bums must sense my presence, because they both stop what they are doing, turn around, and, with startling vehemence, tell me to go away. One of them shouts, "Why don't you take a picture? It'll last longer!" I haven't heard that phrase since elementary school. Embarrassed and dizzy, I walk around the corner and find a stoop to sit on. My head is burning up with hopeless visions; I can't get rid of a sweaty dread. I begin to feel extremely sick, and the street is the only place available: I vomit until there is nothing left inside of me. As I lift my head up from the pavement, my eyes meet the gaze of one of the bums, who is up and moving on. He smiles grotesquely and continues on his way, leaving me to a graphically clear view of my own swill.

A few days after my experience with the bums, Michele finally reaches me by phone. Calling from Earl and Nancy's, where she's been living for months after being invited by them to move in, she sounds breathless and strained, as if she's been running. She's got pent-up news, news that's been building up like acid reflux in her belly. She just about gags out the words: "I've been kicked out of Earl and Nancy's."

"With no warning?" I ask quizzically.

"No. Nancy just told me that I had to leave."

"Any explanation?"

"She told me it wasn't working and that she wanted me to move out within the next two weeks."

Michele's going to live back at 95 Main Street, where Dad is an infrequent visitor. He finished his portrait of Shari long ago; it remains enshrined in his studio. Dad sleeps at the studio, works there sporadically, and goes to be with Mary, his acknowledged lady love, which we all feel supportive of, even if the relationship does take him further away from us. We honestly do want him to be happy, and it appears that he is as happy as he could be, despite his broken heart from the loss of Shari.

Michele is clearly feeling distraught about living, practically alone, back at 95 Main Street; too much abandonment for one seventeen-year-old life.

"Should I come and speak with Earl and Nancy?"

"No. No."

"With Dad then?"

"No. No. NO." Michele doesn't go into great detail, but she intimates that her friend Josh is taking up some of the abandonment slack by becoming a loyal, responsible, and consistent companion. I guess it's time to let this one go; there's nothing I can do. She's obviously old enough to take care of herself. Michele is going to graduate soon. She'll be fine.

When she asks how I'm doing I say, "Fine," not wanting to tell her anything substantive about my life in the city; it would only scare her. It makes me realize just how disconnected our lives are becoming. Before we get off the phone, I ask for news about Kate and Danielle; we've all become less and less forthcoming with the others about one another. We just can't stand knowing certain things about one another; we'd rather remain in states of naïveté for now, still trying to hold onto what once was our sibling land-scape. I do learn a shell of the truth from Michele, that Kate is still seeing Joe, although there seem to be some clouds moving into their relationship, and I learn that Danielle has gone even further into a depression-filled fog. She's in therapy and on some medication named Elavil. She's actually talked about moving back to Jersey. For what? Go back to the source of the pain for a round of original atmospheric insight? Jersey as gateway to healing? Gotta call her immediately.

But first I call Kate. Home for the afternoon from nursing school classes (when did she start nursing school? I have to wonder), she's got some time to level with me. It's true. Kate suspects Joe of fooling around with other women, and she is quickly losing trust in him while growing increasingly jealous.

"What about Danielle?" I ask. It's bad. She's crossed over into a darker kind of self-blame and a crumbling of her ego; she doesn't believe that she deserves to be alive and constantly asks herself why she didn't die instead of Shari. This self-punishment gnashes her central nervous system, biting its way through to her senses, which go into overload and begin to break down. She gets dizzy spells; she can hardly speak to customers at Houlihan's, where she wait-resses; she wants nothing to do with Jeff, her boyfriend of three years, but then sometimes insists that she can't live without him. He might be sneaking around, too, just like Joe. She wants to come home and find a semblance of the Danielle who once knew what life meant—before Shari's death. Is New Jersey the place to regain a sense of self? I wouldn't have thought so, but just maybe . . . to be near cliff rock, to feel familiar river wind . . . maybe.

When I call Danielle, she simply reiterates what Kate and Michele have told me, in even less descriptive tones. She says, in a flat voice, one I hardly recognize, that coming back east to Jersey might renew her sense of vitality. California is just way too sunny for her now, and I encourage her return.

Three months later Danielle does make her way back to New Jersey and 95 Main Street. So does Kate, and so do I, for short amounts of time. Michele has already come back, first alone and now with Josh. They move into 95 Main Street before moving into their own apartment farther upriver. It's the moving back that allows each of us to move away again, once and for all. We come back to take a last deep breath in the one place we all lived together. We come back to look at the Time-Life encyclopedias that are still lodged on those white shelves in the living room; we come back to run our hands along the kitchen table where many discussions took place; we come back to rest our feet on the old log bench Dad crafted years ago. We come back to slip into our strength, to get realigned with the past so we can go on into our futures.

While at 95 Main Street, after taking acting classes in Manhattan and interning at regional theaters in New England, Michele heads toward a career as an actress/director/casting director and embarks on a lifelong relationship with all things and people involved with plays and movies.

While at 95 Main Street, Danielle figures out that she wants to go on to college. She ends up going to Rutgers in Newark and lives for a while in Hoboken with her boyfriend, Jeff. Somewhere in the middle of her studies, an observant professor suggests that Danielle go to law school, encouraging her with other students' and his own eyewitness accounts of her analytical mind at work in the classroom. After finishing two years of her undergraduate studies, Danielle goes to law school in San Francisco and eventually, upon witnessing how women are treated in the working world, specializes in sex discrimination law at a prestigious law office in Santa Barbara, California.

While at 95 Main Street, Kate figures out that she wants to be something other than a nurse, eventually moving to Albany, where she gets her master's in social work. Through Michele, she meets her future husband, Michael, an actor, with whom she eventually makes a marriage, babies, and a home, living out her own wild version of domestication.

While at 95 Main Street, Dad finally admits to himself and family that he is in love with Mary. They marry and Dad extricates himself from the corner of Main Street and Bigler, moving to live with Mary in the heart of Bergen County. The house without a view goes up for sale much to everyone's relief. 95 Main Street served out its purpose, and we are all ready to let it go.

While at 95 Main Street, I decide that I've got a few more adventures left in me before turning in my traveling pass. Richard, the last great male lover of my life and the one guy I ever considered marrying, drives with me across the country to the deserts of Arizona, where he has a house. We attempt to live together for a little over two months. Richard rearranges the house and patio so I have my own space. He patiently shows me all over Tucson: the college campus just in case I feel the desire to start up my college studies again, the best places to buy health food, and the most convenient, sanitary Laundromat. We climb Mount Lemon along a hidden back trail; we go to the movies, plan and cook meals together. We help each other try to adopt effective ways of dealing with grief, his over the suicide of his only sister and mine over Shari. We do all the stuff couples are supposed to do when becoming serious about their relationship.

One boiling day, we make love on the flatbed of his truck, in the middle of one of his favorite desert spots. The air, still and dry, vacuums all moisture from our bodies, and we scrape against each other like two long rasps. Richard is tender, his face kindly urging me to trust and become vulnerable to him, and I almost, almost do, but not quite; I just can't. For a few weeks I actually feel that I could love Richard, for years maybe, but an undercurrent of tension holds me back and I know viscerally, instinctively, that this can never be.

My sisters had encouraged the relationship with Richard; they wanted to see me settle down so they could stop agonizing about my potential demise. Ever since Danielle visited me in New York City and watched me crash onto Sixth Avenue into oncoming traffic after I'd had four gin and tonics on an empty stomach, she, Kate, and Michele had been begging me to stop drinking and straighten up.

It is partly because of my sisters' fervent wishes for my safety and happiness that I head north with Richard, hoping for a shift in my view of him along the way, one where I would be able to see him as my lifelong mate. Halfway to a Rainbow Gathering in Montana, which is an annual weeklong celebration where crowds of hippies dance, sing, do drugs, and commune with nature, Richard pulls the pickup truck over to the side of the road. We haven't spoken at all these last two hundred miles. His face gives away the bewilderment I'm sure he's experiencing. I reach for his cheek with my fingertips, but just before I touch him he moves back, his head pushing against the window.

"You're not going with me, are you?"

"No, Richard. I'm so sorry. I really wish I could go with you, but I just can't."

"Where would you like me to take you?"

"Eugene, Oregon. I have some friends there who told me that I could show up anytime."

———

I saw Richard once more, many years later, after I had moved to Vermont. He stayed with me for one night in the home I was sharing with my female lover, who happened to be gone for a week. He asked if we could make love again, for old times' sake, and I actually wanted to but simply felt it would be wrong. "Could we just sleep together once then?" his sun-baked brown eyes forever hopeful. "I can't, Richard." The next morning he handed me a hawk feather that he had found on his way to Vermont and then left to hitchhike back to the desert. I watched him vanish into a blue Toyota station wagon, pulling his mangy red backpack in after him, waving until the car rounded a curve in the road.

I stay in Eugene for a couple of days before I leave for Seattle to go on one of the last risky adventures I would ever take. The friends who took me in, having done it themselves and made lots of money in the process, advise me to go king crab fishing in the Aleutian Islands. It's a journey that brings me the closest to death, subsequently turning me around long enough so I can see the way back to my sisters and to myself. Without communicating it, without needing to, Kate, Danielle, and Michele are simultaneously coming toward and moving away from one another as we assimilate changes into our sibling structure.

But I am not finished with my wandering yet; I must do my assimilating from hundreds of miles away from my sisters, at least for a little while. I go to Unalaska in the Aleutian Islands, where madness and the sea both stake their claims on my life.

———————

"Come back," I hear Shari's voice from inside my head once more as I step on board the *Kona*, a king crab fishing boat that is ready to head north across the Gulf of Alaska.

I will. I promise.

11

~

SHARK'S BLOOD

I am walking as confidently as I can along the deck of this fish-processing plant in Akutan, Alaska, where my friends told me to come to look for work, toward Rick, a bulky red-haired man of Scandinavian descent. He is the young skipper of the *Polar Queen*, a ninety-foot king crab fishing boat. I have just heard from one of the fish packers that Rick is looking for crew, green or experienced, to assist with the autumn harvest of crab. If I don't nab him now and get him to take me on as crew, I could wind up processing fish right here on this flat hulk of a plant with hundreds of other processors—wayfarers like me and native Inuits all making minimum wage—I have not come all this way to be on an assembly line, scooping mashed fish into cans.

I am lucky that there is a boat that still needs crew members. I just barely jumped off the *Kona*, a gigantic oil tanker converted into a crab boat, the vessel I hitched a ride on from Seattle. The *Kona* already has enough crew and the skipper, Sam, would have kept me on as his live-in-for-the-season sex partner, but I refused.

He made this proposal over glasses of the oldest cognac I had ever tasted. I was flattered for about two minutes but then got over it, certain that he had tried negotiating this kind of deal with young women such as myself before. I am on this adventure to go king crab fishing, make a lot of money, and return to the East Coast, where I plan to enroll in school, hopefully to finally get my bachelor's degree in art.

Rick has big, rosy cheeks. He seems to be thinking seriously about my request for a job and says, "Yes," within seconds, even though there is already a woman on board named Denise, designated cook and on-deck backup crew. According to Rick, no boat in the history of king crab fishing has ever had two women on board as crew. It seems he likes the idea even though there is an old wives' tale that women aboard sea vessels bring bad luck. Rick turns out to be the kind of guy who is usually up for a challenge, especially if it defies wives' tales and superstitions. He'll use me for backup cook, main baiter, and part-time crew. I'll be paid $100 a day for a season that will last a couple of months, and if the season is really good, he might be able to pay me even more. The only rules are no drugs, no alcohol, and no sex while fishing. (I find out later that we can ignore all three rules on the two days it takes to reach the fishing grounds and on the two days it takes to come back in. As a matter of fact, Rick provides both the cocaine and the beer on our first trip out, but not the sex, as he is a devoted married man.)

After his quick scrutiny, even faster consideration, and subsequent nod of approval, Rick picks up my duffel bag and escorts me to the *Polar Queen*, where I'm introduced to the crew, a motley-looking bunch of hippie types: Luke winks at me, Ted barely acknowledges me, Ralph grins like a coyote, Chris grins like a woodchuck, and Denise smiles at me suspiciously, leading me to believe one of these guys is her boyfriend. It turns out to be Ted, but I have no romantic interest in him or anyone else onboard the *Polar Queen*, believe me.

The seasickness that began a day into our trip from Seattle has abated for now. This short hundred-mile ride from Akutan to the port of Dutch Harbor on the island of Unalaska is relatively smooth. As far as rides go, my passage on the *Kona* across the Gulf of Alaska was very uneventful, except for my queasiness. During the entire ride, I spent as much time as possible on deck breathing in real salt air, ate the saltines that I kept in a small plastic bag, tried to stay away from the greasy boat food, and never read in bed. These steps worked extremely well when the sea was calm. But out on the Bering Sea, all four steps are useless.

A chewed-up looking stretch of green land is the first glimpse any sailor receives of the island of Unalaska when approaching from the east. This introductory view somehow intimidates me; like a saw blade or a set of monster teeth, this jagged peninsula seems ready to disembowel or fatally wound any seafaring traveler who gets close enough. Fog plays around the higher peaks as winds swirl, almost freeing the island of its shroud. I feel a distinct skip in the beat of my heart, a strange gap in between one beat and the next, and twisting within that momentary lapse in rhythmic connection lies a troubling surge of doubt and terror. This island, this raw, treeless, forsaken-looking spit, is about to digest me whole, claiming my life for its own. I feel it grab me—extending its talons directly into that crevice between heartbeats, taking its hold. In all my life so far, I have never seen a landscape so ominous or so breathtakingly gorgeous.

Grasses, buoyant and lush, reveal themselves as we draw closer to shore. Every green hue imaginable sings up from within these grasses; ignited by bursts of sunlight, it's as though the hills are carved from animated jade. Barely perceptible crosswinds shift the grasses so they appear to be changing color: emerald turns to jade turns to pine turns to a green that hasn't yet been named in English. My mouth drops open in disbelieving paralysis; I can do nothing but stare.

In Dutch Harbor, we dock near the Unisea Corporation buildings that house a restaurant, store, bar, hotel, and entertainment center. It is here that much of the emotional and physical unwinding takes place before, during, and after the fishing season. There is another bar on the Unalaska side of the harbor called the Elbow Room, which I quickly learn to stay away from unless accompanied a friend. Curiosity (or is it imbecility?) and a woman whom I befriend named Laura compel me to enter the Elbow Room on numerous occasions. The Elbow Room has been described by its patrons as a "cauldron of depravity," and rightly so. The same alcohol is served there as is served anywhere else on earth, but I swear, Elbow Room alcohol must be spiked with voodoo brew. Start drinking in the Elbow Room and be prepared to leave the planet, waking up to stories about yourself and your friends that are best forgotten.

The process of stacking the *Polar Queen*'s deck with the king crab fishing pots and mending the fishing mesh that is twined around the square metal frames, each weighing 750 pounds, takes approximately two days and one full night of work. During this time, the crew members take turns playing, sleeping, and procuring supplies at the Unisea, the only place in Dutch Harbor to get anything, including some of the recreational drugs. But there are other, less expensive places to buy certain drugs, where gun-bearing Inuits, hidden behind doors and walls, determine who gets the drugs and who doesn't. These drug-dealing natives don't take kindly to strangers; only experienced buyers dare to make the walk into the village, on the Dutch Harbor side of the island. Ted and I go to buy some cocaine a few hours before the *Polar Queen* is scheduled for departure. I'm already sore from stacking pots, my forearms practically unable to do anything else but hang idly at my sides as we trudge through the muddy streets to the inconspicuous hut in the center of Dutch Harbor village.

Ted knocks three times on the door at the run-down gray shack. A knock comes back at us from inside; Ted knocks again, this time twice, and the door opens slowly, revealing a smoky, gloomy dining room with two Inuit women sitting at a table. I'm wondering who opened the door for us; I can't discern any other human forms in the room. The women say nothing and express nothing as they study Ted and me, observing my face longer than Ted's. After ample time for studying and approving, and presumably concluding we were safe bets, the women push a clear plastic envelope filled with cocaine across the table to Ted, who slides a wad of bills to them. He waits as they count the cash, and when they give him a nod we are allowed to depart.

A month later, I go back to this shack alone, with the intention of buying more cocaine to give the crew as a gift. I knock on the door three times, the same way I believe Ted knocked. At first, no one comes to the door, nor is there a knock from the inside as there was a month ago. I knock again, this time a little higher up on the door. Ted is taller than I am by a couple of inches; maybe they are not responding because I'm too short to reach the spot they use as a signal of recognition. Still, there is no response. A cold north wind is rustling around the shacks, pulling at my thin coat, and sending chills through my body. Something doesn't feel right, but I decide to try one more time; I know the crew would appreciate this offering, and I'll likely score some points with Rick, especially since I am the newest crew member. Finally, the door is opened, tentatively, like whoever is opening the door just learned how to do it.

Glaring at me from behind the flimsy door are the two women I "met" a month ago, hostility clearly showing on their faces. The women act as if they have never seen me—or sold anything to me—in their lives. When I try to tell them that all I want is a little cocaine for Ted, the guy I came with last time, a strong, hairy hand from behind the door reaches out and grabs my right arm, pulling me into the darkness of the curtained dining room. Before I have a chance to explain myself, I feel something cold pushing against my temple; with side-glances I discern that the object is the barrel of a small handgun. There is no need for words of warning; the message is obvious: we don't sell drugs to people we don't know and trust. Later Ted tells me that they probably thought I was an informant for the police.

"I'm sorry. I'll never come here again," I stutter. Whoever is wielding the gun shoves me back outside, where it has begun to snow. I stumble down the rutted dirt road back to the boat.

That gun against the temple sets the tone for the rest of my stay in Unalaska: a bullet pointed at my brain, lying in wait for trigger release. What will it be: life, death, or insanity?

———

By nightfall, we'll be ready to head out into the Bering Sea. Since we'll be on the water for over two weeks, now is the time to do any last-minute land errands. I run to one of the phone booths to call 95 Main Street, where Michele might be. When she doesn't answer, I try Santa Barbara, where Danielle might be, packing up her belongings, getting ready to make the move back to New Jersey. She answers the phone.

"Oh my God, Carol. You're doing what? Why did you have to go all the way to Alaska to make some money? Don't try anything stupid, okay? Hey, Carol, I think I saw the blue flash. What do you think it means?"

"Well, I do think it might be Shari. What do you think, Dan?"

"I'm not so sure it's Shari. Maybe. I don't know if I really believe that it could be Shari or not. Please be careful, Carol. I'm gonna look on a map of the Aleutians so I can picture where you are."

I don't speak to any of my sisters again until almost three months later.

We're out on the Bering Sea and the sky is in my face, with stars and surrounding darkness all that exist. The *Polar Queen* plows through the waves, which, after two days, have grown from five- to at least ten-feet large. Each climb over the crest of a swell takes my face even farther into the heavens. I'm on deck, fighting with my stomach; it won't calm down no matter which tactics I attempt. Saltines: futile. Fresh air: Band-Aid. It's the worst kind of nausea, the kind that refuses to go away even after the periodic emptying of all contents. Add the cocaine dregs and alcohol remnants and color me wretched. I try inhaling great gulps of air in the desperate hope that a strong whiff of Bering Sea mist will help. I've been having imaginary conversations with Michele, the sister who keeps turning up in my dreams and thoughts. I've begun to worry about her; maybe she's in some kind of trouble and is trying to send me messages. I have sent her a couple of postcards at 95 Main Street, just to make sure that she knows I'm still alive. All this worry is only adding to my nausea. I'm loathe to go back down inside the boat, especially if it means to my bunk, which is in the apex of the bow, top bunk no less, which is the worst bunk of all; continuously thrown from side to side, I never get any satisfying sleep. That's what I get for being the greenest greenhorn: no choices.

Every so often Luke sticks his head out the deck door; as my buddy, he keeps tabs on my whereabouts, and I do the same for him. Everyone on board has a buddy, it's fishing boat protocol. It's Luke's dedication to responsibility that saves me about a week later, during a particularly long stretch of dropping strings of baited pots into the Bering Sea.

Exhausted, cranky, and soaked through to the muscle, all of my clothes hanging off my body in drooping folds, and after twenty-four hours of straight work (fifteen-minute breaks for coffee and a nibble of something that resembles toast), with alcohol and drugs long since washed out of my system, I go to the bait locker to begin another round of preparing the bait. With an ax, I chop out boxes of frozen herring, which will be thawed and then stuffed in small knife-perforated plastic jugs. The jugs are then hung from metal hooks in the pots in order to lure the crabs inside. Long pieces of extremely ripe cod are also hung inside the pots, so the crabs have something to chew on, keeping them occupied so they won't even consider crawling back out through the narrow openings. The bait locker is kept at below freezing temperatures, with a round metal safety release attached to the inside lock mechanism so that if the door slams shut, whoever happens to be inside can hit the release and get out.

I go inside the locker to get the bait ready under the assumption that the release is functioning; I do not know that it has become frozen stuck. A big swell hits the boat broadside and the door shuts decisively. In a flash, I am thrown onto one of the huge stacks of frozen boxes of herring, which slides backward as I land on it. It's pitch-black and for a second I'm totally confused, not at all certain what to do. I sit for a moment, dazed and aching from the fall. Then, I remember the safety release. I stand up and jam my palm against it. Nothing moves. I jam my hand against it again. Nothing. Panic, which has been resting somewhere near the base of my spine since I boarded the *Polar Queen*, careens through me. All I can do with the adrenaline rush is scream and pound the door.

I scream and pound until my adrenaline is diluted—then weakness sets in. I crash back onto the boxes and begin to cry, imagining myself ending up dead in a bait locker, like so much frozen, stiff herring. This is no way to go. It can't be. The smell of fish overpowers all other senses; maybe I will turn into a herring. Finally I start to laugh. I can't believe this is how I'm going to die: freezing to death in a bait locker, on board a king crab fishing boat, on the Bering Sea, alone in the deepest kind of darkness.

Of course, it takes a good while to freeze to death, and after maybe fifteen minutes of being trapped in the bait locker, crying until I can't anymore, the door opens. At the door stands Luke; he's been looking for me and upon his routine and mandatory buddy check he realized I was nowhere to be found.

"Needed some quiet time, didja?"

I never get trapped in the bait locker again, always making sure the door is hooked from the outside.

The tenth morning out at sea I wake up with my hands curled into what look and feel like dead bird claws. It even feels like rigor mortis has already settled in; I can hardly pry my hands open. Denise assists by running my hands under warm water as she massages them.

"Most greenhorns go through this, Carol, unless they work with their hands for a living. It'll pass," Denise reassures me.

"How long will it take?" I ask tentatively.

"A few days, maybe."

With Ace-bandaged wrists, I'm relegated to solo cooking duties, which I abhor. Creating food while being rocked back and forth and then side to side is not an appealing process, especially when seasick. Although I've pretty much gotten over that by now, thank Poseidon, god of the seas.

I try my best to enjoy life in the linoleum-and-formica-plastered galley, listening to music and watching lots of close-ups of Clint Eastwood's face in the only video we have, *The Outlaw Josey Wales*. (I never did and still don't like Clint Eastwood, particularly less so now that I associate his face with undulating, almost-curdled chipped beef.) Mostly I gaze longingly out at the deck through the small galley window, wishing with all my sore ligaments that my hands would relax back into hands again. Eventually they do relax adequately, and I can put in some hours back on deck as master baiter and deckhand. Denise and I continue to split the cooking so at least I don't have to cook all the time, spending only a few hours a day with pots, pans, freeze-dried beef, and Clint.

Do we ever get to eat any of the king crab we harvest? As it turns out, yes, but only once, due to the fact that it is not a good season. We're not catching enough crabs to fill the holding tanks, and many of the crabs are showing up burned or mutated from the effects of underwater nuclear tests conducted a few years ago by the U.S. government on a nearby island; we have to throw a lot of these crabs back into the water. I ask Rick for more details about this testing, but he doesn't want to discuss it, and neither does anyone else. Like stories about capsizing boats or crew being swept out to sea, stories about nuclear tests are not shared during the season. It could bring bad luck. This is an area where Rick will not try to defy nautical tradition.

Approximately 10 percent of the so-called healthy crabs that we do keep die on their way to Dutch Harbor for reasons that can't be explained, with "dead loss" practically equaling the live catch. We all stop talking about the promise of "big money"; this is not going to be a lucrative season.

Maybe that's what Rick is thinking about on the afternoon we almost capsize.

We've collected all the pots—the deck is stacked to capacity; the pots, like pieces in a great puzzle, fit together to form towers three or four pots high. The holding tanks are as full as they're going to get, and this helps balance the *Polar Queen* for a lower, smoother ride into port. The Bering Sea has been running high—waves at ten to fifteen feet, with an occasional renegade twenty-to-thirty-footer rolling off in the distance. The cold undercurrents from the Pacific help create the incredible turbulence for which the Bering Sea is notorious. The Bering's shallow waters are the perfect feeding grounds for bottom feeders like crabs; for years they have proliferated here, drawing large numbers of fishermen. But crab fishing is risky business, with many catastrophes occurring every season; already this year a powerful wave blew out the wheelhouse window on one of the boats, killing the captain and two of his crew. Rick occasionally mentions an accident he has heard about over the radio, once more trying to defy existing superstition. When we hear the bad news, it silences us, each one of the crew praying for some kind of protection. I pray to Clint Eastwood, even though I don't really like him, figuring he just might be the *Polar Queen*'s guardian angel. I also pray to Shari, who, as the possible source of the blue flash, has appeared to me here on the *Polar Queen* more than anywhere else thus far, even more than in the East Village of New York City. I suppose it's because I need all the blessings and divine support I can get on the Bering Sea.

It's after lunch. Denise is in the galley cleaning up the lunch dishes; the rest of the crew is resting—we're on our way in to the docks, no work to be done now, just the anticipation of some fun to be had in town. I'm in the wheelhouse, sitting in the leeward-side chair as Rick navigates from the starboard captain's chair. I'm still amazed that we get anywhere at all, the waves like huge mounds we must overcome, slowing us down enormously. Wave upon wave rise and vanish, rise and vanish, the horizon in endless motion.

Rick is staring straight ahead and occasionally at the underwater radar, the CC2. Through red-colored ultraviolet imaging it indicates the many objects, like sunken logs and hulks of ships, that lie beneath the waters—large things that could potentially sheer the keel. On the mandatory two-hour wheel watches, I have seen forms that I couldn't identify, long serpentlike shapes that appear for a few seconds and sink away again. Huge sticks? Sea monsters? Capsized ships? Rick never tells me what he thinks the shapes are, smiling slightly as I continue to ask him what they are.

It's in a brief swivel to the starboard side, sensing the presence of something dark and large, that I see the wave. Rick, in his current state of preoccupation with this disappointing season, has not seen it. It might be twenty feet or maybe more like thirty; I don't know exactly. All I do know is that it's huge and it's going to hit us. I scream, "Rick!" He looks at me, not at the wave.

"Jesus Christ!" he involuntarily screams once he sees the giant wall of water approaching quickly from perhaps half a mile away from us.

Swinging the boat around now would be pointless. If Rick had had the time he could have turned the boat directly into the wave, but now we simply must brace for it. The slam is powerful enough to tip us over leeward. The window is open next to my face and water gushes in, soaking me instantly. There are screams from the galley and bunks below and the sound of crashing plates and cups. "Rick!" Denise's panicked voice rises up at us, the loudest voice; the rest are muffled.

There is a tentative moment as the *Polar Queen* hangs in between an ocean floor grave and the continued forward motion toward Dutch Harbor. She seems to be deciding, the pots on board certainly contributing to the pull of the ocean floor. I am looking smack into the face of the sea, almost in a kind of stare-down, as the *Polar Queen* makes her choice.

Slowly, achingly, she straightens up, assisted by a leeward-side fifteen-foot wave. We're up. I stumble awkwardly across the wheelhouse to give Rick a slap on the back.

"Jesus Christ," Rick repeats in a great exhalation, his face the color of ocean foam. "She almost got us that time."

After helping Denise clean up the galley, I sit stupidly watching *The Outlaw Josey Wales* again and again along with the rest of the crew, all six of us jammed into the available seats. Somehow I find it reassuring after what we've just been through, and it appears everyone else finds it comforting as well. The familiar plot, faces, and scenes from the movie bring us back to a state of ocean-bound reality.

Stepping onto the protected land in Dutch Harbor after fourteen days at sea is a disorienting experience. The ground seems to heave, and my legs must try to compensate. I stumble around for at least an hour while my body acclimates to terra firma.

We have one day and one night before we head out for our second round of fishing. There will be at least another three rounds before Rick will store his crab pots and head south for his home in Seattle. I've already decided to go back out for another fourteen days of fishing; I have to make at least enough money to get home to the East Coast.

There isn't enough time onshore to do much but find intoxication. Our pay comes from Unisea Corporation and the money goes right back to them as we spend it in their bar; a lot of fishermen refuse to do this. Instead they choose to spend their money at the Elbow Room. I wander over myself, with Denise and Ted, for our one night of carousing.

As we approach the ordinary-looking turquoise-painted shack I see the name, "The Elbow Room," scrawled in black haphazard letters across the top of the door. Blaring out at us from the open windows of the bar is the loud and raucous sound of many voices, and for an instant I stop, ready to flee back to the Unisea. "Oh, c'mon, no one is going to attack you. You're with us," Ted tries to assuage my growing fear.

The smell that emanates from inside is an overwhelming combination of sweat, fish, blood, smoke, vomit, and alcohol. If the smell isn't bad enough, the sight is worse. The place is packed with slobbering men in various stages of drunken stupors. The square room, barely large enough to hold five long tables with accompanying chairs, is a mess, with garbage, bottles, and other forms of refuse strewn everywhere. There are a few native women sitting around in provocative postures, surrounded by leering gangs of men, and I can sadly imagine what the women are offering. The craziest sight by far is the freshly hacked off shark's head that is lying right in the middle of the old linoleum floor. One of its eyeballs is hanging from a thin string of shiny flesh, and no matter where I go in the room, this eye finds me. Blood is running out from under it, creating a slick and sticky stream to navigate, which is what we try to do.

It is while we are carefully crossing the room, trying to avoid the head and blood as best we can, that I slip and fall down into the bloody slime. There is an immediate surge of laughter from the crowd, as a couple of guys reach to help me up. They grab me and begin circling around the shark's head, singing in incoherent monosyllables; maybe they're singing in a foreign language? My backside and hands are now covered with shark's blood and all I want to do is get out of there, but the two guys will not let me go. Ted hands me a beer as the guys continue to lead me around the head in a ritualistic march. A few more circles around the shark's head and the dancers let me go; I slide away toward the back of the bar where I hope I can hide. The guys instantly grab another woman who seems more than willing to join them in their ceremony. I stand in the corner, drinking beer upon beer until the scene in front of me softens and becomes celebratory, losing its sinister quality.

Sometime during the evening, I go to the rest room, which is literally a stall with a chipped porcelain toilet and rusted-out sink, both ready for the junk heap. When I return, Denise and Ted are gone. The blood on my pants has dried by now, I'm pleasantly buzzed, and so I decide to stay on. When I am midway into another beer, paid for by one of the shark's blood guys, a small dark-haired woman slips out of the shadow next to the jukebox and sits down next to me.

Looking at her from out of the corners of my eyes, I shudder with the realization that she bears a slight resemblance to Shari. Her hair—full of loose, loopy curls—is very different from Shari's. And she's small, much smaller than Shari. This woman's figure, tight and erect, reminds me of a Midge doll I played with when I was a kid, which had extremely good posture.

She turns to me and smiles, a thin silver scar rippling the skin above her upper lip. I want to turn away, but I'm fascinated by the motion of the scar, which she can't seem to control, and then by the opaque blue of her eyes. Her face is all dug up, like someone did some excavating with a tiny pickax or shovel.

And then she says with an accent I cannot discern, "Hi. My name is Laura. Do ya need a place to stay tonight?"

I watch her mouth as it twitches just a few more seconds before I respond with a, "Sure." It's late and crawling back on board the *Polar Queen* could prove to be dangerous (many a drunken fisherman has fallen in between the boat and the dock when trying to board ship).

The Elbow Room never really closes. Many drinkers wind up sleeping there and then start up with their drinking as soon as they wake up the next day. But Laura and I don't fall asleep here tonight. We walk slowly and silently (so far Laura hasn't shown much interest in conversation) up into the hills behind the Unalaska side of the harbor until the village, the harbor, and the lights have disappeared over a ridge. Laura lives in a squat brown hut, away from the rest of the world and facing south toward the Pacific Ocean. Once inside her place, she directs me to a generous pile of cushions where I collapse, exhausted. I have no idea where she goes to sleep, as I hear her rustling around in what I assume to be a loft area above me.

I wake to the smell of coffee, but no woman. She has left me a note that reads: "Gone to work. See you later. Laura." I get up, drink a fast cup of coffee that Laura has left for me on the counter in the tiny kitchen, and race back down to the *Polar Queen*; they won't wait all day for me, the greenest greenhorn.

In the two months that follow our initial meeting, I spend practically every minute when I'm not fishing and when she's not working with Laura. She works for the Alaska Department of Transportation, which, up here, means maintaining the integrity of the dirt roads and plowing when it snows. We drink, we eat, we talk (rarely), but mostly we roam the hills. Through Laura, I truly find my way into this unforgiving, raw landscape.

Laura is extending her small, muscular arm to me as we climb the steep hill behind Unalaska. So thick with water, light, and wind, the grasses respond to our weight as if they are sponge. In some spots, the grasses thin out and our feet sink down into the exposed earth. Laura, resembling a bobcat as she aptly climbs and used to this bouncy terrain, sprints on ahead as I struggle to keep up.

I don't know why I agreed to this late-afternoon hike, with darkness only an hour away, at best; with winter coming on, the days are growing shorter. Laura, with her seductive whispering voice and inviting descriptions, has been convincing me to try a lot of things in the last few weeks. There are days when Laura actually calls me by foreign names, names that I not only respond to but which also somehow sound familiar. They are Swedish names mostly; at least I believe they are, given her Swedish background. Her parents are Swedish immigrants, who spoke Swedish as she was growing up and probably still do.

When I reach Laura at the peak of the hill, she is staring intently out across the Bering Sea, northward. The sky is chalky white, going pink with the streaming last rays of light. Laura's face, like the grasses beneath our feet, is shifting from the light and wind, as it does constantly. The odd color of the light reflects off of the small scar above her lip, like a slice of pink lightning, breaking across the night sky of her face.

We say nothing to each other as the darkness grabs hold of everything it touches. Even with Laura standing right next to me on this ridge, I feel more alone than I ever have. I suddenly cannot sense my place on this earth; all connections seem to be gone. There is no blue flash. I haven't spoken to Kate, Danielle, or Michele in weeks, nor have I received any letters from them; they feel millions of miles away from me. I close my eyes and push my feet down into the grasses, willing a sensation. Something is trying to get closer to my brain. A force. An idea. A message. I can't see it yet. I can't distinguish it. But I know it would answer the question: What have I come here to find?

I open my eyes, ready to ask this question of Laura, but she is gone. I hold up my arms to the sky and scream, knowing full well that, unless Laura is hiding close by, no one will hear me and that no one will respond, especially Laura, even if she does hear me. She likes playing hide-and-seek. I scream until the sound of it sounds foolish, until I am filled with self-consciousness. Then I lie straight down on the grasses and, totally exhausted, pass out.

———

I wake to the darkness of death, or so it seems. So close and filled with a physical presence is this darkness that it feels like I could smash my fists against it. I lie still, until the memory of where I am and how I got here returns to me. Slowly, my body starts coming back to life, as if I've really been dead and am rising back into form. Everything is soft, even the darkness, and I feel no sense of panic or fear. I am floating on a cool cloud of grass, which seems to have absorbed all discomfort and pain. I will never move again. I will stay this way until the grasses take my breath. I will die sinking into this deep softness.

I am just beginning to fall asleep again when an animal cry breaks through the silence, charging my blood with electricity. I sit up, looking around futilely. I can't see anything in this blackness. It takes a few minutes, but my eyes finally adjust to their dimension-less surroundings and I catch the faint brush of a light below. I have some idea of its direction and I know that I must go toward it. I know that I must not stay in this place any longer. I must not fall asleep again. I must not die here.

I begin to climb down the hill. It doesn't take long for me to trip and land on my face, my eyes unable to discern anything in front of them. The light I come upon, after what seems like hours of walking, turns out to be from Laura's kerosene lamp, the one that sits on her kitchen table. She has kept it burning in a window for me, a light to help me find my way back.

I tiptoe into the house, peek up into the loft, and find Laura asleep in her bed, a deep sleep by the looks of her. She doesn't move at all. I search the cabin for paper and a pen, suddenly want-ing to write letters to Kate, Danielle, and Michele, letters that would explain everything, letters of apology for my passage to a world that excluded them. Maybe I'll even write a letter to Dad; he hasn't heard from me in almost six months, our relationship growing more and more nebulous. But I can't find anything to write with, and so I simply sit in the dark, waiting for morning and for Laura to get up.

A mysterious breed of people move to and stay in the Aleutians. The native Inuits are mysterious, too, but for different reasons; they keep to themselves, watching the rest of us with what appears to be suspicion and derision. The immigrants are people who have come here to get as far away from the world of order and rules as possible, people who seek a land without laws and reason. Here, on this island of grand isolation and winds, people ride the ripples of dementia. Maybe they are people in touch with a sense of the holy; maybe they are simply in touch with their own outer boundaries, exploring with realms of consciousness others are too afraid to even consider.

I find through bits and pieces of conversation with Laura that she has been living here for over two years after escaping a volatile life at home in Michigan with abusive parents. Here, at age thirty, she has found a refuge, where no one asks any questions or asks for something she cannot give, intimacy. She has no plans of ever going back to live in the lower forty-eight; anywhere below the borders of Alaska and Washington State is too close to her parents. I almost end up becoming an immigrant, too, for after three rounds at sea I move into Laura's cabin and settle in for what I think will be a long winter.

Laura and I are alone together on yet another windy evening. I'm sitting at the picture window, drinking scotch and looking at the stars in the seemingly endless dark sky. I offer her a drink, which she refuses. As soon as she sits down in the dilapidated armchair, the silence deepens, becoming more pronounced than when I was alone.

We remain like this for half an hour, until Laura clears her throat and says, "Carol, I need to tell you something."

"Sure."

"You have to go away from here. If you don't leave, I swear, you're going to die. I saw it in a dream."

"That's ridiculous, Laura. I thought you wanted me to stay."

"I do. You're a great friend, but I wouldn't be able to live with myself if I let you stay and then something happened to you. Carol, for real. You have to go."

She gets up and walks out the door. I continue to sit at the window, drinking until the bottle is empty.

It's closing in on December, with the winter advancing like a stalker of all things green. The grasses have long since turned the color of dirty metal, snow filling in and covering everything with wind-driven ferocity. From the hut window, through a six-by-four-feet plate of double-paned glass, I watch storms eat the sky—raging horizontal blasts that blow holes through the skin, ripping open the flesh to an arctic siege.

Fishing is over. Rick and the crew of the *Polar Queen* have all gone back to the States with their earnings. Luke advised me not to stay on in Unalaska, warning of the mental treacheries that come with a more permanent habitation, and now Laura has told me to leave as well, but I ignore them both. Two nights after Laura's words of warning, she and I go to the Elbow Room for another night of what I think will be our usual routine: drink, drink, and go home to sleep it off.

There's a puffy, almost tropical crosswind blowing as we step into the air of early morning after being in the Elbow Room for hours, with stars so bright and numerous, they practically illuminate our way. We're halfway up the hill when Laura stops in front of me, focusing her gaze straight into my eyes. I have never seen such a sad and penetrating look.

"Carol. I'm going to tell you one last time. Leave." With that, she shoves me so hard I start to fall backward. I recover my balance and shove her back.

"Leave!" Her strong hands knock me off balance again.

"Stop it!" I command, holding a fist up in front of her face.

"Leave. I tell you. Now!" There are tears in her eyes as she hits me in the chest one more time.

"Stop it. Stop it. Stop!" Suddenly released from the world of control, given permission by some aberrant wind that is blowing up from a primeval jungle south of here, I feel my fist pull back into a center punch position. In a final glimpse of Laura's face, my eyes poised and ready to close, it is Shari that I see.

Closing my eyes, with the force of an anguish that has been waiting for this moment, I feel my fist burst out and into Shari's face, connecting with cartilage, flesh, blood, and bone. "Why did you have to die?" I scream. "WHY?"

Then there is silence. Hesitantly I open my eyes, and find a form lying on the ground at my feet. With a gasp that wrenches all the muscles in my throat, I realize what I have done. I reach to pick Laura up, but she pushes my hand away.

The wind is still blowing from the south; I can almost smell the scent of warm rain falling through trees. Laura finally stands up and looks me in the eyes again. Her nose is bleeding and she's beginning to get a red welt on her right cheek. How many times did I punch her?

"Are you ready to leave now?" She touches my cheek with her fingertips, turns, and runs into what remains of the darkness.

How did this happen? Who in the world am I? I have to speak with a sister. Something is wrong. I am gone. Long, long, long, long gone. I race back down the hill and across the bridge to the Unisea, where there are pay phones. I don't remember whom I speak with; I think it's Michele. No, Danielle. I think I call 95 Main Street. No, California. I'm not aware of the time or what I say or how I dial the number or where I find the money for the call. I'm looking down at my fist as I speak. It's unrecognizable. I am talking fast and loud. I am asking forgiveness. I am asking for Shari. I am asking for Shari's forgiveness. I am asking for Laura's forgiveness. I am asking if I can come home now. I am going mad now. I am squeezing the trigger. I am dying now. No. No. NO. NO. I am living. I am living now. One of my sisters says, "HELLO? . . . Carol? . . . Yes. Come home. You need to come home now." I am dropping the receiver. I am going home now.

I get to Laura's hut somehow, pack my things in a blur, leave a goodbye and apology note for her, and stumble to the docks, where I hunt down the next boat heading back to Seattle. A mastless fishing boat is leaving in little over an hour. With the captain's permission, I board ship and nestle into an available bunk for the five-day journey southeast.

I bring a few things back from the Aleutians: lithographic prints for each of my sisters, a meager amount of cash, dreams of green grasses, an absolute aversion to chipped beef and *The Outlaw Josey Wales*, a goodbye letter from Laura, which she stuffed into my bag without me knowing it, and an awareness of the razor that lives in the mind, ready to slice an opening into the world of madness if given half the chance.

In the first few weeks back, in California, on my way home to New Jersey, Danielle loses all patience during an afternoon of listening to me ramble on about my harrowing escapades and talk endlessly about Laura. Danielle, her face a few inches from mine, standing on her toes, yells, "Stop it. Stop talking. I can't stand listening to you talk about yourself anymore or about your precious Laura, whoever she is. You can't see anyone else or anything else but yourself and your needs and your drama. Did it ever occur to you that all this running around and flirting with death could be hurting us? We're all feeling pain, too, you know. Grow up, Carol."

She leaves me sitting in a chair in her living room, holding the crumpled letter from Laura, which I had already read at least one hundred times, five times to Danielle this morning. Danielle's words are like the winds that rise up first thing in the morning. Cool and bracing, they make it clear that time and my sisters don't want to wait while I search for the meaning of Shari's death in states of chemically induced oblivion. My sisters want me alive and accounted for. And I know that Shari would want that, too.

After speaking with each one of them upon my return from Alaska, I discover that my sisters have already begun their way back to the land of the fully present. Just like it was when we heard of Shari's death, I am the last one to find my way back, and not because my pain is any greater than Kate's, Danielle's, or Michele's. But as oldest and translator, I am having a particularly difficult time defining my new role. And so I come back from the Aleutians, determined to find out who in the world I must now try to become, for myself and for my sisters.

IV
~

Recovery and Return: 1982–91

Kate, Michele (holding Paul), Danielle, Carol
At Kate and Michael's wedding party, 1990.

I am twenty-seven years old today. I feel excited, strong, and so, so hopeful about my life. It's a clear, windy, invigorating day. The mountains so bold and clear, mirroring my mind. *Swan Lake (Sleeping Beauty?)* is playing on the radio. I feel such surges. I feel so young and so old. I am wise, and as each year goes on I feel freer and freer from the warped things that bind me up—fear, insecurity, memories. I am slowly peeling away all the layers and achieving freedom, acceptance, and love. I am in love with so many, it makes me cry.

KATE, JOURNAL ENTRY, 1983

12

~

STATES OF

RECONSTRUCTION

NEW JERSEY

Michele is lighting up the room with her incredulous expression. She is holding the photographs I took in the Aleutian Islands as if they are explosives about to go off in some spectacular fashion. These small three-by-five images are like windows directly into the dreams Michele had while I was in Unalaska. Can scenes be sent through the airwaves into someone's dreaming mind? Michele and I have to think so, given this remarkable case in point, this coincidence or mind synchronization.

Before I showed the photographs to Michele, I asked her to describe the dream images to me. Some of her descriptions were, detail for detail, so precise it was as if she had actually been there, standing either next to me or inside me, directly taking in the scenes.

As she goes through the photographs, I have to worry: was Michele privy to all the images transmitted from the Aleutians? I can't help but think about the shark's head, the gun barrel, the cocaine lines on the back of the toilet, and Laura's bloodied face.

"Are landscapes all that came through, Michele?" I try to sound as casual as possible.

"Mostly. I did see a few small huts, but that's all."

What a relief. This must be a case of selective telepathic communication. Did I know unconsciously that Michele would be like a TV set, receptive to the vistas I saw all around me? Did I shut down or cap the lens when scenes became sordid or bizarre? Why did this only happen when I was in the Aleutians? Why not when I was in Crete? There must be something about the place of transmission, the latitude and longitude and the atmospheric conditions, that made this possible.

As I'm watching Michele look through the pictures, I wonder when she became so poised and confident? She's very animated and adult now. Have I been away that long? Her newfound stage presence is even evident here in the kitchen at 95 Main Street; she's obviously becoming a star at the regional theater where she works. The woman before me doesn't fit inside the child I've been holding onto for years. I realize as I take in this more sophisticated, mature Michele that I don't feel much like the oldest sister anymore. Whenever we were together in the past, at sister gatherings, at family reunions, or on those rare occasions when she and I went to the movies or theater together, I naturally possessed the qualities of wisdom, worldliness, and authority. But with visions provided by the stories of my frenetically risky antics and the judgmental concern of Kate and Danielle, it would seem that I have tumbled from my height as older, cooler sister and Michele has ascended.

～

Michele, rubbery and red, was kicking her white blanket off in a big fit. The blanket was getting twisted around her tiny legs. Kate went over to smooth it out and noticed that she needed changing. Kate and I were learning how to change Michele's diapers and even enjoyed it, too; we liked feeling responsible and grown-up. Shari and Danielle were too young to help take care of Michele, according to Dad and Mary Octer, our new housekeeper. Mom didn't have much to say about Michele, so we didn't ask her.

Mary Octer, who had been making dinner while Mom and Dad went into Manhattan for another one of Mom's doctor visits, grumbled a bit as she came over to change Michele; she is the one who does most of the diaper changing. Kate and I watched carefully because we really wanted to know how to do it right, and then maybe Mary Octer would let us change Michele's diaper more often. Taking off the diaper sure seemed easy, but I wasn't ready to ask Mary Octer if I could try it by myself. Michele kicked and kicked, smiling the whole time. While Kate and I held onto Michele, Mary Octer went to get a fresh diaper. Mary Octer began to tickle Michele with small pecks, which made Michele giggle.

Without warning, when Kate, Mary Octer, and I were not expecting it, Michele stopped kicking and peed straight up into Mary Octer's face. Mary Octer sputtered out a word in a language Kate and I didn't understand. (Later we found out it was German, because Germany was where Mary Octer was born.) Kate and I looked at each other in a burst of terror. Would Mary Octer get mad and hit Michele or one of us? But Mary Octer didn't hit anyone. She grabbed the fresh diaper, *wiped her face, shouted out, "She pees like a boy!" and began to laugh even harder. Kate and I were thus released to laugh, too, which we did. Shari and Danielle, who had been playing with their dolls in the playroom that Dad had recently built for us, came running at the sound of all the laughter. They couldn't help but laugh along with us, even though they had no idea what had happened.*

Kate tells Dad and Mom the news of the day when they got home later. Mary Octer watched patiently as Kate explained what happened; I was watching and listening, too, making sure she didn't leave anything out, and she didn't. Dad smiled right away. Mom's face twitched for a moment and went no further, so Kate told the story again, this time aimed more directly at Mom. Dad's face held his smile as we all turned to look at Mom, who was finally and genuinely smiling with us.

～

Michele is eyeing me warily now. as I speak of my Aleutian adventures—the censored version. I imagine that she is thinking about the dozens of other times she has heard similar tales. Those downward glances and slow-burning exhalations give her away.

Behind her expression of growing impatience I can sense a longing for my focused attention and approval of the things she's been doing, and I finally give her both. The youngest of five sisters certainly deserves praise that belongs to her alone, not the diluted praise and interest from those who have given praise four, three, or even two times before, the kind doled out by parents, teachers, and older sisters.

After she tells me about her work in the theater, a tense silence fills up the kitchen until I ask Michele about her relationship with

Josh. She's squirmy as she speaks but begins to divulge some of the intimate details nevertheless, and then it's me who becomes squirmy. I'm definitely not ready to hear about Michele's sexual relationship with Josh, if, in fact, that's where she's taking her train of thought. I nod, smile, and change the subject to something more benign: the kitten she's just gotten. It will take years for us to venture into conversations about our intimate relationships; it's too weird.

As I say goodbye to Michele, heading home to my new apartment in the city, I am struck by the way she waves. It's a commanding farewell, arm raised in a single gesture with her head tilted up, receiving the last light of the afternoon. In her eyes is that grief that will always be there. Kate and Danielle have that sadness in their eyes as well, as I'm sure I do. But I also see hope in Michele's eyes, as big and colorful as those rainbows that I remember rising over the orange-colored cliffs in Paleohora, Crete. There it is and there it will grow, propelling Michele, strong and as sure of herself as I've ever seen her, standing front and center on the stage of her unfolding life.

NEW YORK

It took Danielle longer to get back to the East Coast than she anticipated. Every time she got close to getting in the car and driving away, some power of resistance made her jump right out again. With the ocean in the front yard, avocados in the backyard, her boyfriend, Jeff, and a newly arrived Kate tugging at her heart, I'm sure Danielle was torn about her move back to New Jersey.

We meet in Greenwich Village again, a few days after her arrival. This time I am not drunk or high in any way. I've shaved my drinking down to the cocktail hour and after, just into the early-evening hours, becoming an alcoholic in miniature, the giant-that-had-been replaced by a little sipping Lilliputian. Memories of those close encounters with my ravenous desire for forgetfulness provide plenty of motivation to keep things under control. Danielle's look of resignation and disappointment simply adds to my determination to keep my drinking in check.

Danielle doesn't want to talk about her depression, exasperation, and impatience brought on by too many therapy sessions. If I even begin to broach the subject, she uncharacteristically snaps at me. I decide we need to do something physical—it always helps me—so we get on borrowed bicycles and head uptown to a midtown office where I have a part-time job taking care of the plants. I'm what is known as a landscape architect's assistant; my boss is in the middle of creating a terrace garden for a famous musician in Soho, so I've been relegated to watering, clipping, fertilizing, and dusting the plants she has planted and arranged all over Manhattan.

Danielle has no problem keeping me in her sights as we maneuver through the dense human and automobile congestion. Each time I turn around to make sure Danielle is okay and close behind me, I find her smiling. She must be having a good time or remembering other good times. Either way, it's a sight so welcomed, I have to smile myself. When Danielle catches up to me, out of breath and still grinning, she hugs me with all the force of someone born again. (*"I'm not thinking, you guys. I'm not thinking at all."*)

At the midtown office while I water and prune, Danielle uncovers her dormant charm, engaging the employees in Dan-O's Flirting Game of Hide-and-Seek. It's only a matter of minutes before I am besieged by people telling me what an amazing sister I have. They don't care what kind of experience she's had; they'll hire her on the spot—they simply must have her come to work with them. We leave a couple of hours later with a crowd of Danielle's fans—feverish with the zeal of awakened devotion—waving effusively from behind the big glass windows in front of the building.

On the way downtown, we stop at the Swedish Institute of Massage, where I'm enrolled and about to receive a certification so that I have a trade while I continue my studio painting courses. I've got to do something in order to make more money than the meager amount I'm being paid as an architect's assistant, and everyone knows that I'm good at massage; all those years of cracking Frank's big toe paid off at long last. Although Kate, Danielle, and Michele have supported my pursuit of a massage license and career, each one has expressed doubts about its viability. They wonder how I can work at an activity that previously caused me such anxiety and disgust. Won't it just conjure up those horrid moments of being forced to give Frank rubdowns?

Despite everyone's misgivings, I get my massage license and certification and stick with massage therapy long enough to establish a sizable clientele in New York City. With practice, I am able to breathe through my aversion to giving massages. But every so often, I have to admit, Frank's face, body, and ugly big toe come floating up over the table, hovering like holograms in front of my line of vision, momentarily arresting the massage already in progress. In those moments, I pause, take a deep breath, look intently at the person lying on the table (usually a skinny bearded guy, who bears a slight resemblance to Frank), and massage through to a place of compassionate deliverance.

Danielle and I are talking about massage as we make our way to my apartment, riding side by side along the "quiet" lower end of Fifth Avenue, when I see her expression and bearing plunge back into the underworld. By the time we pull up on Thompson Street, that excited, ebullient goddess is gone. She looks so tired, whispering dejectedly about a headache coming on, that I don't even attempt to revive the vibrant woman who was with me just minutes ago as she turns to go. Hers is not a commanding farewell as I stand on the sidewalk watching her fade away behind the corner of a building, heading home to 95 Main Street. At best, her goodbye is a disillusioned half-gesture. I can't stand it. Leaving the bicycles where they are, sprawled carelessly on the pavement, I run after her. She is within shouting distance when I round the corner, and I yell out her name. When she turns to look at me, Danielle gets what I'm feeling, like she always has, ever since she was a child with the ability to read other people's emotions. "It's okay," her eyes say, taking care of my feelings with a look of reassurance. We smile, wave once more, and move away from each other.

Slowly, Danielle. We make our way.

COAST TO COAST

When Kate phones a few days later for a full report on my perception of Danielle's emotional condition, we try to find our way back to our familiar positions. It's as though the half-moon couch rises from out of a garbage dump in northern New Jersey somewhere, allowing us to commiserate once more from our older-sister summit. The air is chilly and crisp and illuminating from this vantage point; we can still see Danielle and Michele clearly enough so great insights and judgments can be handed down.

From our imagined peak and from inside our wishful thinking, Danielle would be back to full strength, her passion and great appreciation for life filling the world. She would be working as a tour guide or a counselor, where her mind and emotions, in a fine state of balance, would come together without protest from that internal place of insecurity. There would be no more headaches, and the freedom from them would allow her to get back her deep sense of joy.

From the half-moon couch, Kate and I can imagine Michele as queen of all she surveys in the land of theater. She would be out from under the shadow of her sisters, holding her own with clever finesse. She would be learning how to deliberate in the world of casting, retaining her sweetness as she struck deals with cutthroat agents, directors, and egotistical actors. At the end of each day, she would sit back and relish the sunset with Josh, who will continue to deliver solid, unwavering support.

From up here, Kate and I are having a hard time viewing our own relationship. She remains guarded and I've become awkward in practically everything I say and do around her. I know she's not divulging anything about her life that I haven't already heard from Danielle or Michele. Danielle is now Kate's confidante. Ever since our European trip, Kate and I have not been able to connect with each other, trying to be respectful as we look for the heart of our once-close relationship. Some kind of trust was broken on that trip as we went in totally different directions.

I finally say something that makes her laugh, and just for a moment I relax, knowing I can still reach her through humor; this rift is not irrevocable even as our alliances shift back and forth among sisters. In the depth of Kate's laughter lies the key to our healing, and we're bound to use it again and again.

NEW JERSEY

I visit Dad at his studio, where he is sorting through paintings, sketches, and art supplies getting ready to finally move everything to Mary's house. He is effervescent, making high-pitched cartoon animal noises the way he used to years ago. His two-year marriage to Mary has revitalized his sense of imagination and luster. He's almost singing as he speaks of her believing that their relationship is an act of providence; he's all destiny and kismet and appreciation and romance. I realize just how much I've missed the playful side of him. For a few minutes I join him, and side by side we become jesters. I try telling a joke that I heard recently, but I fail miserably at it, the way I always do; I've never been able to tell jokes. The punch line comes out backward, but Dad seems to get it anyway and he laughs, looking at me with another zany face.

～

I used to get lost in the faces Dad made as he painted portraits of me. I would hold as still as I could. When I started to move, he made a face. Dad never said, "Hold still"; he just made faces. For one of my favorite silly faces, his lips got very big and then they vibrated quickly so I could hardly see them anymore; he looked like and sounded like a duck. Sometimes his glasses fell off his nose and onto the floor, but they never broke.

Dad painted lots of other people besides me. Everybody in Fort Lee wanted Dad to paint them or someone in their family. Most of the time they came right to our house and sat in his studio. But sometimes Dad took his paint box, canvas, and smock and went out to them so they could sit still and keep quiet in their own homes. Dad took me with him once in a while, especially when there was a kid for me to play with while he painted.

Once when I was four years old, he took me to the crumbly house of a really old man who had a long beard which went way down his chest. I thought, at first, that he was Santa Claus, but it turned out he wasn't; he was Old Man Yoman. He was kind, making sure I had a bowl of jelly beans, probably the way the real Santa Claus would be if he were having his portrait painted by my father. There were no kids to play with at Old Man Yoman's house. That was okay. I didn't mind. I watched my father paint, and I drew pictures of people with my special pencils.

∼

Dad slows down long enough to tell me the traveling and painting plans he and Mary have made. "Nothin' could be finah than to be with Carolina." He pushes his glasses up over his bushy eyebrows and makes the Donald Duck/Jimmy Durante face, to which I make my predictable response: the smile of the lovingly amused. Then he offers me something to drink, which I gladly accept.

"What's the good word, Carolina?"

NORTH OF THE BORDER: CANADA

Soon after my celebratory meeting with Dad, I travel northwest with my friend Judy to spend some time with Mom and Frank on their small island on a lake in Southern Ontario. The distance between visits had yawned open and stretched out into years; I haven't seen them in at least three. I'm not enthusiastic about the trip and try thinking of reasons not to go even though Mom has been inviting more often than usual lately, and I'm not sure why. But she is my mother and she seems desperate to see me, so I decide that I've got to visit her.

At first we're all into the charm of it. It's best behavior day on the island, Frank charismatic and almost gallant in the tone he is using with us. He's trying to impress, and when he's trying to impress he's impressive. Like a great professor, Frank can lead his imagined charges toward the inspiring exploration of ideas. Then he starts talking about his courtship of Mom and how he was intimidated by her beauty and intelligence. Frank, intimidated? He never stops surprising me. Because of his display of tenderness, I let my guard slip, foolishly thinking that perhaps he's mellowed since leaving the clinic.

A day of civility and drinking passes without incident, but by evening Frank's deteriorating inebriated mind renders what little self-control he possesses useless. He has returned to saying whatever he feels like saying to whomever is in his path, including my friend Judy, who doesn't know what to do as she struggles against a desire to flee. What was I thinking? Sometime during the early evening, he says something that will always be embedded in a place of disbelief. In the middle of watching TV, Frank turns down the volume and says, "So, why do you like sucking pussy better than you like sucking cock, Carol?"

I look incredulously at Frank for a second and then raise my hand up in front of his face so I don't have to look at the expression of indecent delight. Were the people on TV talking about anything that could have led to such a question? How in the world is his mind wired up?

Judy looks at me beseechingly, with a "Can we go now?" In the silence that follows, everyone is looking from face to face as we try to gauge reactions. After catching a definitive glare from Judy, I turn to look at Mom, who has sunk into a mortified stare out the plate-glass window. Mom, say something. Say something. Anything.

She begins to utter his name, "Frank . . . ," but he cuts her off with, "I think it's a fair question, don't you?"

God damn it, Frank. Were you calculating this attack all day? And what's fair about any of this? That you were subjected to the harshest kind of scrutiny and restriction as a child? The way you punish everyone in sight for your anguish? The annihilation by your doubts and fears of the gentle man you might have become? The way you have to ruin every loving relationship? Is any of that fair?

I look straight through the alcoholic froth hooding Frank's eyes, trying to find a way into his heart. This is it, Frank. I am making a last attempt to get through to you. This is it. This is it.

But it's way too late. Frank is now all gloat, and everything is closed off and sabotaged. He can't see me. He never will. I turn away, my own heart beating fiercely with the awareness of what this moment really means.

It means goodbye, Frank. Goodbye.

Judy and I leave that night. I am now determined never to subject myself to his brutality again. I do not return to the island until after Frank has died seven years later and been cremated and Mom has called to tell me that she has buried his ashes on the island next to his beloved cat, Basil.

VERMONT

There is a piercing tension scorching the back of my head at all times now. Brittle and dry, the skin pulls my muscles into spasms as the manic energy of Manhattan lunges and bites at my ankles, trying to bring me down. I've got to get out of here. After two years of living in New York City and with the urging and help of a friend, I head north once more, this time to Vermont.

It's a hot day in July 1982 when I slowly climb out of my friend's car and set foot on the dirt of a back road in southern Vermont. My senses are immediately fortified by the steam-poached fields and powerful scent of cow manure. I take the deepest of breaths as I look around. There are trees having close relationships with other trees here, the forests going on and on into hills that seem to roll out in a great welcome. There are rocks being nestled by the darkest soil, soil I instantly want to sink my body into. A small orchard decorates a slope nearby, the trees dotted with young apples. And there are the birds, dashing small birds that seem to be everywhere and nowhere at once. Because I don't know birds very well yet, I identify them all as sparrows. And indeed, there were sparrows among the flocks, but also finches, chickadees, phoebes, juncos, vireos, brown creepers, and cardinals, to name just a few. I have since come to know most of these birds.

Everything that seems worthy of discovering is right here before me. I take in a realization with a growing sense of excitement. As the feeling rises into my chest, I begin to recognize it. Do I dare let it through? I don't have a choice: I feel like I've come home.

There's a holy moment a few years into my life in Vermont when an advertisement in the local newspaper grabs my attention. I am working at the local food co-op and doing some massage and storytelling on the side and not really looking for a new job. I have to admit, though: I'm getting bored of all three, and lately all I want to do is be with children. As my eyes scan the want ads, a virtual thumb-through, there it is, the letters practically elevating up into three dimensions:

A small alternative elementary school needs a teacher's assistant for a kindergarten through second grade program.

Without a good reason not to, I call them the next day and schedule an interview.

When I open the big red door and walk into the Neighborhood Schoolhouse on a cold January afternoon, I know that I've just passed through a portal of destiny. It is here, in the little schoolhouse on the hill, that I discover my affinity for working with children, and subsequently, find my way back to one of the sources of my greatest joy.

On an unusually warm March morning, we're climbing the small mountain that overlooks the Connecticut River on the New Hampshire side during our annual early spring trek. The entire school population is hiking up the mountain, children talking with all kinds of energetic enthusiasm and glee. At home the night before I had had one too many beers, and so now I'm viciously aware of the volume of two things: their jabber and my headache.

Then a five-year-old boy steps up and asks me if I would please tie his shoe. I kneel down in sweet compliance; his face, open and trusting, is all I can see, his eyes blazing a trail through my growing sense of rupturing guilt. I become momentarily paralyzed. Years' worth of images from the depths of intoxication rush up behind my throbbing eyeballs as I finish tying his sneaker. All I can think is that I am being completely dishonest with this trusting boy. He believes I'm present, full of the zest someone who is tying a shoe on a mountain should naturally possess. Forming within the sweat that is beading up all over my skin on this March morning are rivulets of self-disgust, followed by an awakening couplet of promises: no more looking into the eyes of a child while alcoholically compromised. No more looking into anyone's eyes, head clanging with a poisoned sense of reason.

I stand up, lurching sideways, visibly enough for this youngster to offer his hand, which I gladly take. Tears begin to clear away the years of guilt from behind my eyes as we continue up the mountain hand in hand until one of the boy's friends makes him a better offer: "Come here, quick!" He accepts, leaving me to a solitary walk, for which I am more than grateful.

I stop drinking that day, but only for the remainder of the school year. In June, on a vacation in Maine with friends, I lift a glass of wine interminably close to my lips and, unable to resist the anticipation of its results, drink it down in a flashing gulp. I drink for two more months, haunted all the while by the face of that five-year-old boy and my subsequent stumble on the mountain.

On August 25, 1989, the time arrives. I wake to an energy cell mutiny—they refuse to provide me with any energy. I lie on a mattress on the floor, in my small apartment next to the fire station, once again unable to move, blood pooled up like it does in a corpse that has been left in one position for too long.

It is while I'm lying in this muddled state that my heart rate slows down and a blue flash quietly slips into view above my head. This kind of entrance is different, almost like it's tentative, questioning its right to appear. It hangs in the air just a little bit longer than usual. During the few seconds that the blue flash lingers, my entire body softens; I am all fluid. It is clear, so clear, that in this form I am a useless slob, a slug, practically antimatter. The blue flash fades as a kick of adrenaline commands my bones and connective tissue to take action. I jump off the mattress and reach for the phone. A real-live nice person on the other end of the line says,

"Hi. How ya doing?" and then automatically recites the times of all AA meetings for the day in southern Vermont. There is ample time for me to make the "Nooner," the meeting at noon.

If the Hallelujah Chorus could have been playing as I drove into town, it should have been, for all channels are optimal for my moment of acceptance into the Alcoholics Anonymous fray. Every word the AA attendees speak on that day sounds intimately true, like they are talking directly and purposefully to me. I feel as if my brain is taking in everything at once, like those fireflies in South America that gather in the trees and blink on and off all together.

This day in late August is my point of entry into the land of sobriety and into the next decade. My arms are open and out-stretched toward the promise of a forward-moving passion.

I call each of my sisters that afternoon with the news of my commitment to a sober life. Kate, Danielle, and Michele are elated to join me in the light of that promise, their arms outstretched toward dreams of their own.

13

~

EXUBERANCE IN FOUR

MOVEMENTS

KATE, 1990—THE GRATEFUL DEAD, "UNCLE JOHN'S BAND"

I hear Kate calling out to me in my dreams. Her voice is urgent, a strong-enough force to wake me again and again throughout the night. At 5:30 in the morning the phone rings and Michael, Kate's husband of one year, says, "Ya better come quick." Driving as quickly as the Green Mountains of southern Vermont will allow, I reach Albany Medical Center by 8:30. There is no other place in the world I'd rather be than with Kate as she gives birth to her first child.

Kate already looks like she's given birth when I show up in her room.

"You look exhausted. When did labor start?"

"Last night. My lower back is killing me. I'm going to ask for an epidural."

Michael is sleeping on a cot at the base of the bed, mouth

open, sucking in the air of the weary. Impulsively I balance a small teddy bear on his forehead, legs dangling down over his cheeks, without waking him up, and snap a photo. I brought the bear with me to give to Kate for support, but I think Michael needs it more than Kate does, and she agrees. He thanks me for the teddy bear and the photograph later.

For the moment the contractions have subsided, and Kate takes this time to beg for strength from any saint or angel who might happen to be passing through the area. She's got a thing for Mother Teresa, so of course I suggest she pray to her, even though she is still alive (not quite saint material yet) and living in India. Meanwhile I pray to Julie Andrews, since she is kind of a saint (even though she, too, is still alive), and when I get tired of her face I pray to Alice from *The Brady Bunch*. (I have always had a fascination with Alice. She's still alive, too, I know.) It can't hurt.

In about an hour, active labor begins. I shake Michael, who sputters, as he wakes up to a faceful of stuffed bear. Kate is wheeled on her bed into the delivery room as Michael and I follow her, along with the doctor and two nurses. It's a blank slate of a room—all blues, grays, and cold steel. With Michael on her left and me on her right, Kate bears down. With the lower back pain becoming unbearable, she finally begs for an epidural. About twenty minutes after she receives it, Kate's legs become like sandbags; as Kate pushes down, Michael and I must heave her legs up toward her head, and soon we're all in a sweat. Michael looks especially disoriented, his face ashen and his lips quivering, as Kate's next wave of grunting begins, a blue puffy hospital hat slipping down over his forehead, almost over his eyes. Both Michael and I are wearing gowns, hats, masks, and booties; this is not New-Age birthing room garb or procedure by any stretch of both our imaginations. We're talking traditional hospital rules and regs here, and we must comply or we'll be given the boot.

In between contractions, I give Michael all the reassurance I can rally, occasionally telling him how fabulous he looks in blue. I've worked with actors, Michele's worked with actors, and Michael is an actor, so I feel safe saying that most actors like being told and retold how fabulous they look, no matter what the circumstances are. Michael doesn't say anything, which is astonishing, because he is clever and swift and has never before been at a loss for words, as far as I know. I think that helping and watching Kate give birth is scaring the bejesus out of him and, as he is a Catholic, I'm betting he's praying to the pope or, maybe more appropriately, to Mother Mary.

I stroke Kate's face when I'm not encouraging Michael; she is either staring straight ahead or closing her eyes; every inch of her (except for her numbed legs, which Michael and I continue to hoist) is focused on the release of her son, Paul Michael.

It's while I'm stroking Kate's forehead that I have the visions: little poplets of light, like bubbles, bringing Kate's childhood face into view. Neither one of us is dying (I check the heart monitor just to be absolutely sure), but nonetheless, pieces of Kate's life are flashing before me:

Kate in a yellow sunsuit, lower lip and belly protruding in a stance of disappointed sorrow.

Kate crying as she lay on the ground at my feet next to the wisteria arbor after one of our weekly wrestling matches in which she lost to me again.

Kate with blood oozing out of a gash on her foot after she'd accidentally stepped on a tin can. She almost lost a toe to that calamity.

Kate on a winter's day, light radiantly streaking through her hair, standing in awe of the sunrise over Manhattan and the Hudson River.

And now: Kate in these final moments of pushing out the head to its crowning and . . . .

. . . . he's out.

It's his ears that I'm smitten with first, "What beautiful ears!"

Michael, the pale new father, stands completely still for a couple of seconds before transitioning into the role of responsible dad. Then he struts to the table where Paul is being cleaned, weighed, and measured, watching with an expression of regal pomp. While Michael offers his son some sound and early advice, I take more photos. It almost looks as though Paul is attempting to take in all of Michael's wise words as he squints and twists toward the voice of his father in this newfound environment of air, light, and sound.

While father and son are bonding, I make sure Kate is all right as the nurses take care of the finishing details: stitches and Betadine. She's eager to hold Paul, and already her face is relaxing into the softness of an adoring mother. I can practically feel Kate's body in its aching need to hold him. Wow. I never knew it would be like this. And then they are together, these two beings cut from the same flesh.

Who starts it? Probably Michael now that he's retrieved his voice and his mind. As we follow Kate and Paul, being wheeled through the halls en route to their room, we're compelled to let fly with a song appropriate to the event. Grateful Dead's, "Uncle John's Band":

"Well, the first days are the hardest days
Don't you worry anymore."

By now, and after much discussion, Michael and I have concluded that there is a song for every occasion, maybe even more
than one song, which leads me to believe that life just might turn
out to be an opera after all.

And so it is that Paul ends up being musically gifted, even having
what musical experts call perfect pitch. Michael and I are sure that
besides genetics, it was those first few minutes of exposure to our
mellifluous voices that stirred the sense of song and pitch within him.

CAROL, 1991 — GLORIA GAYNOR, "I WILL SURVIVE"

I'm at a Valentine's Day dance with friends when she comes toward
me from the side, dancing sleek, with undercurrents of a passionate turbulence. This woman can dance—she and her partner are a
fused wave of rhythm that is drawing all eyes to them.

At first this woman is like a parallel thought, moving around
the periphery of my vision as I flail, big and dramatic arm slashes
that must be taking up too much room. But I need these larger
motions—they alleviate the tension, the sort that used to get eased
only through drinking.

She dances back and away from her partner. Soon I am dancing with her and another woman, Diane from the co-op, our bodies creating a triangle of respectful distance. We don't touch, but
there are those uncertain curious glances—attempts to read each
other's body language and intentions, if there are any at all.

Diane spins off toward another group of dancers, and I am left alone with the sleek and passionately turbulent one. She comes to me beneath a white overhead light. She smiles, suddenly and fleetingly, and I return it gladly. This face-to-face meeting probably lasts all of thirty seconds, but I have plenty of time to view her features, realizing that they are exactly what my features are not: fine, small, and dark. I also realize, with joy, that she is maybe just an inch or two shorter than me, not three or four or five, which many of my romantic interests (including a few men) have been.

Soon we are back to three, and Diane looks just as interested in this new woman as I am. Where did she come from? I've never seen her before in this red-bricked town beneath the mountain. I can't tell if she's spending more time looking at me or at Diane. With as much apathy as I can fake, I dance away from them, hoping she will follow. But she doesn't, and the woman she was originally dancing with slides back toward her. The high hopes and fantasies which I had been entertaining are dashed. She's way too beautiful for me anyway: I'm all gawk and splatter; she's maraschino cherries and cuff links.

I go back to flailing in my corner of the dance floor where others join me. We dice it up. We push the bounds. We pant and sweat and I almost forget all about the sleek dark one in the amber shirt tucked into low black pants.

The next morning she and I come face-to-face again, this time in full daylight in the bulk department at the food co-op. I'm making grocery money while taking elementary teaching classes at a nearby liberal arts college. I'm talking to a mutual friend of ours in front of the bins filled with flour, not knowing that they are friends until she comes around a corner and they say, "Hey," to each other. I'm fumbling around for the key to where I've seen her before, and then it hits me, but she says it first: "You're a wild dancer."

Her smile arrests my ability to come up with anything other than: "You, too."

Couldn't I have thought of something more provocative or engaging? In that silly second when all thoughts seem like they could be both clever and inane I become horribly conscious of my red apron; it must look so stupid. I have the overriding urge to rip it off. She is watching me as I nod, fidget, and lick my lips, which are beginning to feel as dry as rice cakes. Before I have the chance to demonstrate how witty and captivating I can be, she is gone, walking out of the co-op without the hint of a backward look. I stand twisting the material of my dreaded red apron, watching the fluid way this beautiful woman practically floats across the parking lot.

I find out from the mutual friend, after interrogating her the next time she comes into the co-op, that the beautiful woman's name is Gemma: part French, part Italian. She's the administrator of a statewide grant that provides support services for the elderly and also, I find out later, a visual artist. I get her phone number and call her a few nights later. We go on a date. It's the romantic kind where the waiter, Claude, trips around and blushes because he can feel the energy between me and her.

For the last ten years I have been dancing with Gemma, first at a respectful distance, then in increasingly closer rotations, passing the barriers into that place of trust, abandon, and comfort. All kinds of love are possible when the dance is close, considerate, and filled with a wondrously tantalizing, passionately turbulent wind.

MICHELE, 1991—THE RIGHTEOUS BROTHERS, "UNCHAINED MELODY"

Michele is posed before the full-length mirror with Danielle by her side. The preparations for Michele and Josh's wedding are under way in this cottage on Martha's Vineyard. The cottage is overflowing with women of all ages and sizes, shapes, and relationships to the bride. A cousin, friends, a mother-in-law, and sisters. Only months into our new relationship, Gemma and I have decided that we are both not ready for her attendance at this event, but I call her with periodic updates.

The main job of dressing the bride has been relegated to Danielle. Kate, preoccupied with a toddling Paul, moves in and out as second dresser. The rest of us serve as the oglers; we "ooh" and "ah," occasionally shouting out a grand holler of praise. Michele is becoming more and more stunning as dress, jewelry, and makeup are applied. As our collective appreciation and encouragement pour over Michele, she seems to be taking it in, absorbing the energy through her skin; her eyes are bluer, her cheeks are flushed pink, and her stature is taller and more regal. By the time she is ready to take Dad's arm for the walk across the lawn to where Josh, equally gorgeous, is waiting, Michele has become a woman whom we recognize but don't fully know.

Josh and Michele meet on a hill that rises above the sea. The sky is scratched by only a few wispy clouds as they face each other. I can't hear what they say because it is too windy, but I imagine it comes down to something like this: "We've come this far together; let's go even further."

From the sidelines of the dance floor after dinner, with newly sober older-sister eyes, I watch as my sisters dance, and when they reach for me I join them, celebrating with a clarity I haven't known before. In this brief state of rapture, our hands and hearts linked together, Kate, Danielle, Michele, and I dance beyond all grief, entering a land of exquisite liberation.

DANIELLE, 1991—LEON GIBSON, "FROM A WINDOW"

At Kate and Michael's house in Albany on Christmas Day, Danielle is talking on the phone to her new boyfriend, Eric, her hands, face, and legs swinging all over the place as she takes in his unleashed adoration. Kate, Michele, and I haven't seen her this excited about a man in years. Who is this guy capable of stirring such passion in her? All she's divulged about Eric so far is that he's a doctor and a professor and he's a great kisser. Sounds good to us. Please, please let this be the man who will appreciate her the way she bloody well deserves.

Because Danielle's moods have such an impact on the climate of all family functions, this particular Christmas celebration is practically off the charts with jubilation. Her happiness is our happiness—we take it in with great gulps. More. More. More. More.

Michael is basting the turkey, the scent of which is filling the house as Kate slips one of our favorite Christmas tapes into the tape deck. Mostly we listen to Julie Andrews's Christmas tapes, of which there seem to be a plethora to choose and which really are the best Christmas tapes ever made, we all agree. But no Christmas would feel like an authentic one without playing "From a Window" by Leon Gibson, one of our musically talented cousins who happened to write and record this original Christmas song. All of our relatives received a copy of "From a Window" by Leon Gibson a few seasons back.

As soon as Danielle hears the fast-paced melody, she whispers a romantic goodbye to her new, hot boyfriend and joins Kate, Michele, Paul, and me in the kitchen for a mini–dance party. We take turns dancing with one-and-a-half-year-old Paul as "From a Window" carries us to greater Yuletide heights.

Danielle, as free from doubts and ghosts as I've ever seen her, laughs and sings with all the force of pure, recently ignited ardor.

In the kitchen and to "Through a Window" we dance, again and again, into the light of exuberance.

"From a window
From way up high
There is a light burning into the night
For you and I."

V

~

A Quiet Sunrise: 1992 to Present

Kate, Carol, Michele
At Carol's 40th birthday party, 1994.

Hey, my loved ones—and you *know* who you are:
if I should die young, like Shari,
Please know that we're together and that it's not a horrible
    scary place. And that I'll see you all again, too.
And that *I really, honestly* did achieve quite a bit of
    happiness on Earth so my life wasn't in vain. And
    that if there's *any* possible way of contacting *any* of
    you—I *will.*

Don't be scared.

We love each other.

It's ridiculously beyond words.

DANIELLE, JOURNAL ENTRY, 1978

14

~

A SPECK OF GOLD DUST

Gemma and I are watching a movie in our rented house in Underhill, Vermont, as close to Mount Mansfield as we can get without being right on it. It's some movie with the word "Paradise" in the title, I think; that's all I remember of it now, except that Don Johnson and Melanie Griffith were in it. Watching a movie on this cold November afternoon is meant to distract us, and today it's even more important than usual that it does. We are doing our best to stay focused on the movie; it's not easy. On the thirteen-inch TV screen there is a porch door swinging back and forth. I realize suddenly that I have no idea why a porch door is swinging back and forth in a scene from the movie. Where was I? Did someone just go through the door? When I ask Gemma about the porch door, she doesn't know, either. Where was she? Obviously, this movie isn't working as a distraction, but I'm not sure any movie would work under the circumstances—not even *The Sound of Music*, my favorite movie of all time. I take Gemma's hand, always warm, and ask her what she's been thinking about, as if I didn't know: Danielle.

Ever since the beginning of October, Danielle has been bruising frequently and easily—the mere squeezing of her arm during a playful romp with Eric, her boyfriend, leaves lasting finger marks, and subsequently she has undergone extensive blood tests. And now the days are underlined with that surreal sense of foreboding and anticipation. Phone calls make us jump, and imagined words of the coming diagnosis swirl around in the autumn air. Safety walls are going up, and the search for protective gear has begun. But of course, there is no such thing as a safety wall or protective gear. We all know that if the news is bad, there will be no going down beneath it, up and over it, or round about it—there will only be the going through it.

Then the phone call comes. Gemma and I exchange looks of the hunted as I reach for the receiver.

What I hear is Kate's voice, sounding tight and dense, like compact rock, granite maybe—all hard against her throat, like blockage, like cliffs that can be pounded against, like anything but the mild, curly sweetness of welcomed news. I don't want her to say anything with this voice. Hold on. Back off. Call again. Carol's not home, at least not the Carol who was breathing here just moments ago on a Sunday afternoon, full of mountain and forest, full of November, full of a porch door swinging back and forth.

Danielle's got myelodysplasia. What in the world is that? It's a bone marrow disorder. She's got the best kind. Best kind? She'll probably live for at least ten more years, maybe longer. Maybe longer? She's going to call later. She needs the day to be with Eric. Myelodysplasia?

Then Kate says she has to take care of Anna, her crawling eight-month-old daughter, but wants to speak briefly with Gemma before she hangs up. The shaking in my body has already begun—the rekindled pit of no turning around. The petulant zone of disbelief. The cauldron.

I run outside toward the mountain and into the November day, incapable of listening to the phone conversation between Gemma and Kate without becoming a dervish of spinning arms and legs. All I feel like doing is ripping up the upholstery in the house, which doesn't belong to us. So I head up, to be received by the mountain—always this running, this accelerated heartbeat so my breath is pushed, so my lungs are filled, so my mind can be stopped. Go. Go. Go. Go. Go.

"Mountain," I say. *"What do you think? You in your sloping calm breathing toward the sky. What do you think? What do you think?"*

I run against the mountain, hurtling rocks and sticks at its silent face. Okay. Okay, Carol. Slow down long enough to get ready for Danielle's voice when she calls tonight. There's an afternoon to angle it just right: the response. Take out the panic. Do the voice over. Practice. Get ready for the response.

The mountain listens to a rehearsal of the benign words and phrases that I imagine I'll say to Danielle when she calls and then, back inside, Gemma listens as I try it again. But I falter. I crack. There is no way I can pull this off; when Danielle calls I'll fall apart. I've got to go outside again. When I race up the mountain it helps to slow me down. I'm halfway up the mountain and back down before dark, when Danielle calls.

"Carol. I have some good news and some bad news. The good news first: Eric and I are going to get married on January twenty-ninth. Can you believe it?"

I'm sure I asked questions and supplied all manner of enthusiastic support, but my recollection of our conversation is dimmed by the twitching expectation of the coming bad news. I picture Danielle's face as she speaks, as if she is right here with us. Gemma holds my hand.

And then:

"The bad news is: I have myelodysplasia." She explains it, and I don't interrupt. I let her explain it in words she has probably been rehearsing, too. Her explanation is so casual; she is forever trying to make life smoother and more palatable for all of us.

"I just need you to be my big sister right now, Carol."

Danielle, I will not come undone. I will be like a mountain. I know a mountain is big, but it doesn't show emotions. I will offer strength and resilience. Mountain, Danielle. There is only mountain.

Remember when you were here in the summer with Eric, Danielle? We climbed half a mile up the mountain and stretched our gaze far out over the southern hills of Vermont. Eric, you, and I were quiet for almost five minutes as the winds hollowed out the air, scooping up any haze that hindered the view. It was clear then, warm and just slightly moist. A perfect summer moment. Eric and I dropped you back at the house because you were tired and he and I wanted to hike up to the peak of the mountain. When we reached the top an hour later, we looked down into Pleasant Valley, where you and Gemma were probably talking, which you always did so naturally. It was like the two of you had always been talking, sisters in a past life, kindred spirits in this one. I think Eric and I even spotted the house, back porch and all. We waved, knowing the two of you couldn't possibly see us, up this far, but we wanted to wave to you both just the same. It was important that we wave, connecting the four of us together. That night, the four of us watched fireflies, sitting on the couch in the living room, our arms all over the backs of one another and the couch. Remember the fireflies, Danielle, and the way the mountain was strong before us, even as we sat in the darkened house all together? I didn't know which hand was touching me, and it didn't matter. There were fireflies and the mountain and your breathing, close to me.

So there's this mountain now, Danielle, and it's in me. I will be the mountain, Danielle. Okay?

Gemma is still holding my hand as I hang up the phone, and then she and I begin the next phase of our relationship, deep and consistent selfless support for each other. Just a year and a half into our relationship and it's into the monsoon.

Transfusions and perpetual blood tests are what follow for Danielle in the next month. She moves from the "best" kind of myelodysplasia to the "worst" kind, with a bone marrow transplant her only chance for survival. Kate, Michele, and I get tested as possible bone marrow donors, but none of us match. I pray every day to the mountain for help with the assimilation process as the information comes through in installments—incremental measuring cups—a bit-by-bit drip feed. And then it hits—the full-blown gale-force wind against our bodies.

On December 19, Danielle is admitted to the small municipal hospital in Santa Barbara, California, because the myelodysplasia has, in its relentless reproducing and gnawing through Danielle's system, turned into acute leukemia. If she doesn't get chemotherapy immediately, Danielle might have a stroke and perish. Leukemia. Stroke. Are there clear, layperson explanations for all of this? Can someone please help me understand?

Kate tries. As a nurse and hospice practitioner, she searches in books, on the computer, and in medical journals for information about myelodysplasia and phones me and Michele with it. But having the information doesn't seem to help.

How do you get someone ready for her first round of chemotherapy? How do we prepare ourselves for Danielle's first round of chemotherapy? Gemma and I have the flight out to California to try to get ourselves ready, but we find out soon enough that getting ready for what's to come is an impossibility.

On December 20, in sunny California, as Gemma and I enter her hospital room, Danielle tells me she loves my sneakers. How can she find it within her to notice and comment so cheerfully? She is pale, with an expression of subtle panic creeping in from her shoulders, which are hunched in anticipation. The flimsy white hospital gown, replete with precious blue flowers, tents up around Danielle's body, concealing everything between her neck and thighs. Her thin lower legs—they have always been thin—stick out from beneath the gown, and I take both her feet in my hands, holding them gently as she continues to brace herself for the arrival of the nurse. There are small bruises on her right arm where the doctors have drawn blood and given transfusions.

Eric, as Danielle's protector and medical advocate, moves in all directions at once, making sure she has the best of everything. The room is decorated with a few of Danielle's personal belongings that

Eric brought for her: photographs, crystals of all shapes and colors, and some of her favorite books are set up on the windowsill and on top of the small white bedside table. One of Dad's paintings of the Hudson River is hanging on the wall that faces the bed, where she can see it at all times.

Gemma, Eric, and I position ourselves in three corners of the room as an overly chipper nurse wipes Danielle's arm with alcohol for the insertion of the needle that will administer the red, viscous liquid from inside the heavy plastic bag with a DANGEROUS warning label on it. The nurse is wearing the kind of leaded apron that one is forced to wear when being x-rayed. Gloves and goggles finish off her nurse's ensemble of doom.

"It burns." Danielle grimaces. This will be one of the only times during Danielle's brief struggle with the disease that we see her wince. When I see Danielle pull back, all I want to do is strike at the nurse, to make her quit smiling. I have an even stronger urge to rip away the bag of chemo, needle, and tube. I look at Gemma who is watching Danielle's face, too, and whose calm presence subdues my fury, and I remember: I am to be a mountain. I am not to let Danielle experience my big emotions. Okay. Okay. I remember now.

As politely as she can, Danielle asks Gemma and me to leave: "Can you come back later? Is that all right?" her clenched teeth seconds away from a wail or a shriek. Will she wail or shriek? Not with us here, and probably not with us gone, either.

Gemma and I leave to go occupy our time, along with Josh and Michele, who arrive in the afternoon from New Jersey. How are we supposed to occupy our time, exactly? Are we in time? Do we use time? Why does time move more slowly when we are making a conscious effort to occupy it?

Time seems to be speeding up and slowing down all at once,

and we shake our scraggly heads in disbelief at how quickly and slowly it's moving. This is a phenomenon I have never experienced before. With excruciating lethargy, time slugs along as we reach for hope and as we endlessly wait for answers, none of which tell us anything. And then, just as convincingly, time zooms by without any regard for the poignancy of these final days. It seems that as soon as I get to the hospital for a visit with Danielle, it's already time for me to leave again.

Michele, Josh, Gemma, and I all fly up to Kate's house in Oregon and, after a half-baked attempt at Christmas, return to our lives, miles and miles from one another, with daily phone calls to one or all sisters. Invariably, Danielle can't come to the phone, leaving the rest of us to speculate about what she's doing with all that time, alone in her hospital room. Later, after she's gone, we decide she must've been communicating with the spirit world, getting herself ready for the transition.

I do three things in January that are intended to assist Danielle in using her time alone optimally and are intended to alleviate my sense of helplessness.

In the living room of our house in Vermont, I construct an altar underneath the picture window that faces the mountain. Candles, stones, objects that Danielle gave to me, photographs, and letters from her cover the small table. As I place each item, I urge the mountain to observe, asking for its full attention. *This is for Danielle. Please help keep her here. Okay?*

I visit a shaman named Susan. Recommended by friends, she might be able to persuade Danielle's soul to stay. The session takes an hour, during which time I'm asked to lie still on a massage table while Susan, beating rhythmically on a drum, enters an altered state of consciousness. All I can hear the entire hour are the sounds of rhythmic drumming and an occasional moan from Susan. When I open my eyes, cued by her gentle touch on my shoulder, I find Susan standing next to the massage table, crying. All she will say is, "I did what I could."

And I send Danielle my only copy of a favorite childhood book, *David and the Phoenix*. I'm hoping this simple story about a 500-year-old phoenix that builds itself a pyre where it dies, only to be reborn as a new bird, will give her strength as she moves closer to having a bone marrow transplant. I believe, in my naïveté, that the book will encourage her to rise from the wreckage of a ravaged body after the transplant and take her place back with us as a warrior and eventual conqueror.

Michele, dropping everything in New Jersey to go to California and be with Danielle, begins to read *David and the Phoenix* aloud to Danielle in the evenings. One night, as Michele tells it, a third of the way into the story, Danielle turns to Michele and in a calm, assured tone says, "You don't need to read any more of the book to me. I already know how it ends."

On January 22, Danielle is allowed to go home to the house she shares with Eric. We'll never know whether the doctors let her go home because they thought she was on the mend or whether they knew she was soon going to die. Eric drives her up to the mountain spot where they were to be married at the end of January, she walks along her favorite beaches, she tries to eat her favorite foods, she sleeps in her own bed and spends time with Michele and Eric, while the rest of us wait and maintain what we can of our normal lives, still clinging to the belief that she would mend. Her body, stripped bare of an immune system, is wide open to infection: aspergillus in the left lung settles in and begins to spread. Within two weeks, she's back in the hospital, the lung teeming with the infection. Kate flies back down with Anna, to join Michele and Eric as a supporter.

Kate, Michele, and Eric don't call me as often as I'd like, and I become a pacer, walking the rooms in our house beneath the mountain with all the energy of a contained bolt of lightning. Gemma provides supportive bedrock for my pacing, stopping me on occasion to give hugs and nourishment. I become practically useless at the college where I've gotten a job as assistant admissions director, spending most of my time staring at a card Danielle sent me for my college graduation, which I carry with me wherever I go. Underneath a drawing of a rising star, Danielle wrote: *"To me you are a star."*

One day Gemma takes out seed catalogs and begins to cut. Images of flowers fall onto the living room floor as I pace around Gemma and her creation. She asks for an expendable photograph of Danielle, one she can cut up and use in the collage she is making. Placing a smiling Danielle in the center of a piece of cardboard, Gemma layers the flowers in cascading waves around it. Soon Danielle is floating within a veritable three-dimensional garden, complete with birds, butterflies, and a welcoming sun. Gemma sends the collage to Danielle, who, after receiving it, takes everything else down from her hospital room walls, replacing all of the images with that single one:

Danielle, alive, in spring, in a garden.

———

I phone Mom and Dad on a regular basis; they've both been asking for more frequent updates, and I have volunteered to be the liaison between them and Danielle. Relationships with both Mom and Dad have become low-maintenance over the last few years, with sporadic visits, bimonthly phone calls, and occasional letters. Dad's better at the written correspondence, with Mom more at ease on the phone. The increased communication that Danielle's illness necessitates revitalizes the separate relationships I have with each of them, stirring their need to be closer. As much as I wish it weren't true, I am still resistant to a closer relationship with Mom. But despite my resistance and my judgment of her behavior during this time, Mom and I do get closer, as she confides in me about the guilt she still has over leaving us years ago.

Dad wants to know if it's time for him and Mary to go out to California again. He was out once in early January, and he asks if I think Danielle would want him there now. "Let's wait," I offer. Let's wait for what? Mom, still awkward and unsure of her relationships with us, doesn't ask about going out to California. She doesn't know how to go to California and be there for Danielle. Not going (choosing to stay on her island rather than leave it in winter and claiming that as her reason for not going) will become one of her greatest regrets.

Then Kate does call me, again with that raspy voice, and says: "You'd better come now, Carol. Danielle has to have a lung removed."

As Danielle is being hooked up to the intravenous apparatus that will administer the anesthesia, I am boarding a plane for California. As Danielle is being cut open for the very last surgical procedure of her thirty-four-year-old life, I am somewhere above the United States, asking for another ginger ale but really wanting to order a beer. (Thanks to AA and angels, I never do drink during this ordeal.) As Danielle's left lung is being removed from her tired body, I am still high above the earth and perhaps closer than I normally am to some kind of compassionate god. I pray with as much belief as I have left in me. It doesn't take long for me to stop praying because I just can't get this question out of my head: How can any god be letting this happen to Danielle? There isn't a god. There isn't even a mountain.

My breathing diminishes, becoming shallow. I can't breathe in here. It's too close and hot. This kind older woman sitting next to me asks if I'm all right, and I have to answer, "No." With that, I begin to cry as we start our descent into Los Angeles, where it is raining with torrential determination. The monsoon. The woman sitting next to me holds my hand for the landing.

"Is someone picking you up, dear?" the older woman wants to know.

"Yes." And there is Tina, the office administrator from Danielle's law firm, who has come to get me in the rain. They must love Danielle. Who wouldn't? Tina reports that Danielle has successfully made it through the surgery. The doctors believe they were able to remove all of the infected lung tissue; she should be able to rally long enough to make it to the transplant, a month away. Our ride to Santa Barbara is filled with talk about the wonders of Danielle. Can this much adoration become a force that keeps her here? Can't this much love kill that confounded disease?

At Eric and Danielle's house later that night, Kate, Michele, and I have our first real-live meeting as three, while Eric stays at the hospital with Danielle. I ask them for every detail, hoping that recounting the ordeal will renew their hope. Soon they have lifted themselves and me to a place of enthusiastic conviction that Danielle is over the worst and will make it to the bone marrow transplant. She's come this far. She will endure. We stay up half the night, taking ourselves on into the future: old ladies on a porch, sipping tea, and eating large quantities of cake and cream-filled pastries, with no worry of getting too fat.

In a few hours, I will see Danielle, an image of her as a beautiful old lady with a cup of tea in her hand providing the strength I need to walk through the door of Cottage Hospital.

Mountain. Carol. Mountain.

A cold anxious silence floods my body and mind as I am once more faced with a brutal truth. I have experienced this silence only once before: upon seeing Shari's body laying in the white satin-lined coffin. I look through the glass window that separates me from Danielle in an ICU hospital bed, and I am filled with that silence again. It stops me. I am momentarily unable to move forward.

This then is what my mind and heart cannot take in but must pretend to within seconds or else lose all sense of being a mountain for my sister: Danielle is in the Intensive Care Unit with half-inch blond spikes of hair bristling from her white scalp. A breathing tube is clamped over her mouth and down into her throat, pushed through to the good right lung, and it is preventing her from being able to speak. Her stomach, which is usually as flat and smooth as the bark of a birch tree, bloats up from beneath her gown. Hands swollen, her puffed right index finger is attached to an oxygen meter. And last, but almost the most disconcerting, are her eyes: wide dark pupils trimmed by fading blue irises, they seem hounded.

Her eyelashes are partially stuck together with Vaseline, the way they get when recovering from conjunctivitis or when coming out of the water after swimming out too far or too deep.

In her drugged, bewildered state, Danielle's eyes dart back and forth slowly. She hasn't seen me yet, and now would be a good time to make an escape back to the lobby or outside, to where I could see sky, earth, trees—anything but this old, worn-out Danielle. How could Danielle have aged this much in just over one month?

The silence inside of me is now flooding over with screaming voices. Every bone, tissue, and organ is ruptured. Salty liquids are pumping chaotically against my fragile frame of flesh. I am being pummeled from within; gigantic fire hoses have taken aim.

Michele and Kate are already standing next to Danielle's bed in the Intensive Care Unit, smiling and talking in soothing tones. How long did it take them to become used to this? They warned me over the phone that she would look different. Different? She is practically unrecognizable. I find myself asking the same question I asked upon witnessing Shari's body for the first time: Am I in the right place?

As Kate, Michele, and Danielle turn to look at me standing behind the glass window, the answer is obvious: Yes. I am definitely in the right place, and I have been announced, as I had waited too long to make my escape. A retreat would certainly raise Danielle's level of fear and suspicion. She is looking at me with such eager tenderness. Her left hand rises up and waves me in, and before I reach her bed (all of ten steps away) I have become mountain.

The next seven days are filled with the creation of routines and schedules that assure Danielle round-the-clock care. Everyone believes that she has rallied and will move on into the next phase of recovery: the transplant. Gemma and Josh arrive to join the "celebration." Paul remains at home with Michael. We are like an army of support and encouragement.

We take shifts: I am on the morning shift; Kate, who must bring Anna, leaving her with a nurse, one of us, or in the hospital nursery, is on afternoons; Michele is doing evenings and sleepovers at the hospital with Eric. Whenever Danielle feels up to visiting with people who are not immediate family, Gemma comes over. To everyone's surprise, Danielle even asks to visit alone with Gemma on two occasions. But one morning as Danielle sleeps, I am witness to what all of us have been denying and dreading. I glimpse what can only be described as Danielle's withdrawal from her body; I sense the coming departure of her life force.

She is propped against three pillows, the position that seems to enable her to breath more easily. A long, gargling snore is erupting from her throat; Danielle never used to snore. I place my hand as gently as I can on her right arm, not wanting to wake her, just wanting to make contact with her. Her skin is the color and consistency of week-old meringue. She is twitching, as if she's in a dream, running maybe, flying, away from the confines of her damaged body. I feel her try to come toward me and feel close to me. But she can't. Instead I feel her absence. Her arm is cold and a film of sweat coats her skin. I push my hand a little deeper into her flesh, seeking the connection I am so used to feeling with my sister. I want to race after her, to run forward into her body until I find what is left of Danielle's essence.

The weight of my hand with its desperate intention must have gotten through to her consciousness, for she opens her eyes and looks directly at me, confusion dimming her understanding of where she is or whom she is with.

"I don't want to take my clothes off," she insists, attempting to push herself up and away from the pillows. "Why are they making me take them off?" she asks me without recognizing who I am. She reaches for the button that calls the nurses, and within seconds one of them has responded.

"They were making me take off my clothes, weren't they?" Danielle is even more agitated, her voice rising as she tells the nurse what she believes has happened while looking over at me for affirmation of the accusation.

I nod my head and say, "Yes. They were making you take off your clothes."

"I didn't want to take my clothes off."

"I know you didn't. It's Okay. You don't have to." The nurse, obviously used to these kinds of hallucinations, goes along with Danielle, too, and with both of us comforting her, she is soothed. I offer her some ice chips, placing one in her mouth, sighing in relief as the ice meets her tongue.

I reach for her hand again. So cold, it sends ice running through my blood.

As unbelievable as it seems now, everyone who loved Danielle was convinced, until just twenty-four short hours before she died, that she had made it, that she had rallied and would make it through to the preparation stage for a bone marrow transplant in Los Angeles; a donor has finally been located. Michele even decided to go back to the East Coast for a brief respite, to get a little work done at her casting agency and to recuperate some of the strength she had spent caring for Danielle this past month.

I'm on the morning shift once again and Danielle needs ice chips. With ice bucket in hand, I am coming out of Danielle's room en route to the ice dispenser down at the nurses' station when Dr. Walker asks if he can speak to me. Apparently he has just gotten back the results of the latest routine morning blood tests. It is clear from the moment I see his gruesome expression that the days of rallying are over. This is not the expression of someone who has hope. Dr. Walker leads me away from the door to Danielle's room and farther down the hall. In a very quiet voice he tells me that Danielle's other lung is now severely infected with aspergillus and recovery is no longer possible. This final statement to me is so narrow, its purpose so clearly meant to cut away any room for hope, that I almost laugh; this is absurd. My reaction compels him to say even more strongly, "There is no hope, Carol."

I suppose my look of incredulity justifies the repetition of those words, for he says it again.

"There is no hope, Carol."

I have just enough reason left in my mind to ask him how long she has.

"Twenty-four, maybe forty-eight hours, at best. I am so sorry."

I get up with the ice bucket and begin walking back toward Danielle's room. Three steps from the door to her room, my legs begin to go numb as if they are no longer connected to the rest of my body. I tumble onto the carpet and lose my grip on the empty ice bucket, which rolls away down the hall. A young nurse, one of Danielle's best attendants, rushes over to lift me up and hustle me to the Family Room before I disintegrate entirely. She has removed me at just the right moment. For the second time in my life, my perceptions of this world become all fire, water, earth, and air, devouring my heart and mind. The nurse holds me as I scream and hiss, battling the realization of news we've known on some level but were not ready to admit.

As my crying subsides, another nurse enters the room to tell me Danielle is asking for me. I straighten up immediately, battle over for now. Danielle needs me. Splash of water across my face and I return to her. For the next two hours, I watch Danielle struggle to breathe as she moves in and out of sleep. During one of her waking moments, she turns to look at me, studying my face in a weary silence. Then she whispers a question, the only indication that she has been thinking about death at all.

"Carol. If he needs to, do you think Eric should help me so I won't have to suffer?"

Just as I did almost twenty-five years ago, when Danielle asked me if I believed Shari would be all right, I speak with all the assurance still remaining in me, and without dissolving into tears:

"Yes, Danielle," looking her directly in the eyes.

Then she quietly says, "Carol. I saw the blue flash. Is Shari here to take me away?"

"Shari is here to help you, Dan. I promise."

As she drifts back off to sleep, I phone Kate and Gemma with the news. As sister intuition would have it, Michele calls from the Los Angeles airport, turns around, and flies back to Santa Barbara immediately; she just had a feeling that she should. Eric, at a routine business meeting in Sacramento and after a phone call from Kate, turns around, too. We are now on the final vigil.

Eric and Michele are on the midnight shift that night, and after watching Danielle's favorite movie, *Crocodile Dundee,* Michele is there for Danielle's last coherent moment. "I love you, Dan," Michele whispers at 2:00 A.M. "I know," are Danielle's last words. Eric comes into the nearby hospital room where Gemma and I are sleeping on cots to wake us. It's nearly time.

Although she doesn't really want to leave the hospital at this hour, Gemma knows she should, to let me stay with Danielle, Eric, and Michele. She braves the darkness and the freeway at 4:00 A.M., getting into an old dinosaur of a car, which has been donated by one of the partners at Danielle's law firm, to retrieve Kate and Anna, who is now ten months old, from Eric and Danielle's house, bringing them to the hospital.

Gemma takes care of Anna in the Family Room as Eric, Kate, Michele, and I find our positions at four contact points around Danielle's body, almost as if they are predetermined. Eric is at her head, Kate on her left side, I am on her right side, and Michele is at her feet.

As the sun begins to come up, Eric removes the oxygen line from Danielle's nose and turns on the soothing Indian music, *Tales of Mullinbimby,* which she has been continuously listening to while in the hospital. Danielle's head has turned and begun to slump down to the right, and the breaths she is taking are now almost imperceptible. I gently rest my right hand on her chest, and beneath my fingers Danielle's heart continues to beat, winding down toward cessation. Tapping with a gentle rhythm on her sternum, I urge her to go.

With the help of Eric and a Dilaudid drip, delivered to her intravenously, there comes a last holy pause, and then the long final exhalation.

Then, Danielle is still.

This is a stillness all on its own, so complete, so loud, so absolute that it sucks up all the air in the room, claiming the breath from each one of us who is left alive. Then, there is a vacuum, a deep void that everything begins to spill into. Hurling, charging emotions and the collapse of our bodies held bricklike for weeks in deferance to

Danielle's unspoken request for no emotional outbursts compel us to fall forward onto her body. Our wailing voices surge up into one blasting voice of piercing anguish. Then one voice becomes distinguished from the rest; high and wild, it is the inconsolable voice of Michele. I hear her huge and smashed-hearted, "NO!" as she flees the room. Once Michele is gone, our circuit of support, which had surrounded Danielle, is interrupted. The life energy is shifting up and away.

I get up to find Michele. She is out on the terrace, facing a brisk wind coming from the west. I put my arms around her from behind, knowing there is really nothing I can do to protect her from the magnitude of her loss. I can only be her big sister. We stand this way for a few moments, not saying anything, simply bearing the weight of our individual pain, together. Then I leave her to the winds and to what the tides will bring in this morning.

Later on that day, I find *David and the Phoenix* lying on the bureau in Eric and Danielle's den. I turn to the last page and, facing the photographs of Danielle, read the final sentence:

> *"The bird launched itself into the air and soared out over the valley, sparkling, flashing, shimmering; a flame, large as a sunburst, a meteor, a diamond, a star, diminishing at last to a speck of gold dust, which glimmered twice in the distance before it was gone altogether."*

~

Two weeks ago you died, Dani. I am having a hard time conceiving of life without you. You gave my life so much meaning. Maybe I was too dependent on you—I need help to deal with this. I'm afraid I will lose my mind. That last week with you haunts me. Watching you weaken and waste away was the hardest thing I've ever had to go through. But I am grateful I could be there and hold your hand as you died. We were all there with you, Dan—you never had to be alone. I think you are in a good place— no more pain or fear. But I have this big void and this deep ache in my heart—at times I don't want to go on— everything is an effort. Our last words to each other, after I kissed you on the forehead and you woke up:

"See you later, Kate."

"I love you, Dan."

"I love you, Kate."

"See you later."

About six hours later you were in a semi-coma, breathing hard, the life slipping out of you. You were waiting for the sunrise, Carol and I told each other. Then, at 6:30 A.M., to your favorite music, you died; stopped breathing, very quietly, very peacefully. . . . I just wish I knew for sure where you were, my dear sweet sister. Yes, *you* were the sweetest.

KATE, JOURNAL ENTRY, MARCH 1993

Some day! A spectacular fest of light and song and the joyous explosion of energy in bud form—the air so sweet it makes me salivate, as if I could bite into it, taste and be nourished by it. Pulling, teasing, and cooling off all of us is the spring wind. But beneath it all, inside of me, pounds a pain so cruel and vibrant, if they took an X ray of my body right now, it would show up on film. Beneath the breastbone, cradling my heart with its black fingers, it lies.

I stretch myself out onto the earth, throwing my head back so it can be held. The earth responds with gentle softening. It is too beautiful a day for such feelings. The warmth and insistence of spring in total contrast to the cold, black place of suffering. I do not know how to assimilate these images of my dying sister into the world I see before me. I do not know how to calmly watch as life opens up before me while behind my eyelids I am still witnessing Danielle taking her last breath of air, her head bald and so white, cheeks hollowed out, so drawn and so old at thirty-four years of age.

I hope she felt us near as sound, sight, taste, and smell faded from her forever. I hope she sensed my hand upon her heart as she let it stop beating once and for all.

Maybe there is no assimilation. Maybe there is only the bold and raw facing up to the images and feelings as they move through. There is a place where life and the death of my sister meet, that place behind the breastbone. They wrestle there. They bear fangs and hiss. Perhaps they will be able to embrace one day.

I look at pictures of you, Dan. Your eyes flat. The two dimensions you play in now. I observe the images and try to conjure your three-dimensional self, how you moved and sounded and felt. I don't want to forget that. You move two-dimensionally into the past with Shari. I HATE THAT! I try to find comfort in knowing you are with others, but what does that mean exactly? Are you *with* them? Do others go by you? Are you even aware of others?

My brain feels twisted and singed. Bruised. Hot. I have this desire to crack the skull and let it all pour out. What to do with such tumult? I need to volcanically erupt.

I need a kinetic escape. An altered state. I'm so tired and crazed by the pain and grief. These endless teachings scrape my heart. Danielle physically ended. My heart tormentedly beats.

This photograph of her in front of me. She was sick then. My hand resting on her shoulder. Beneath my hand, blood, damaged blood, moved through her veins. I didn't feel it. I didn't sense it. She looks so happy. Beneath her skin bubbled the blood that would one day kill her.

CAROL, JOURNAL ENTRY, MAY 1993

Goodbye, New York, my heart cries as the wind blows up Ninth Avenue through the window of my office. The sky is dramatic—gray clouds shaded with blues, deep blues and light, pale blue patches of sky. The birds circle above the buildings, the Empire State Building looming close and familiar.

I have watched that building from varying distances my entire life. As a child from my bed across the river on the cliffs at night, it was lit up and dazzling, a distant promise of excitement in the grown-up world beyond. I saw it in the light of day as my sisters and I played outside into the late afternoon, a tower blazing on fire, lit by the sun. I see it from my terrace in my Cliffside Park apartment, the lights changed for every occasion: Valentine's Day, red; Halloween, orange; St. Patrick's Day, green; and so on. And it stands boldly now before me. It has watched me, too, as I've grown and changed through the years, like a guardian angel.

Now it sees me off to a new life. It says goodbye. It knows it's time for me to leave this New York/New Jersey existence, wrought with pain and sadness, and yes, joy and enlightenment, too. But it's time for me to leave this desk and pack up the photographs that line the windowpane. A photograph of Danielle, Josh, and me taken in February of 1992 on an extraordinary visit and hike up the mountains; this picture orders me to go. "Remember the happy times, for there were many. Go to them; go to the happy times that await you once again, here in this life of darks and light."

And I sit here, winds blowing, guitar music playing on the tape machine, and I am filled with such feelings, for this incredible journey we are all on, together. I want to share this feeling; this pain and anguish, and joy and creativity and the people I have loved, with the depths that go beyond, way beyond, this physical reality. It does. I feel it now. I know it in my soul. Yes, there is soul love deep inside that transcends it all.

And so, at least for now, I leave this New York/New Jersey existence, overflowing. I'll sail off to start a new life, to create a new home among the ocean and trees where I belong. I will love more than I have ever loved and pass on a message of hope, a gift to me from my sisters, my flesh-and-blood sisters, Kate and Carol—and my angel sisters, Shari and Danielle.

MICHELE, JOURNAL ENTRY, MARCH 1994

15

~

CHOCOLATE CAKE

The west-facing porch of our house overlooking Lake Champlain is spreading out into the summer grasses; chairs are set and ready for Kate, Michele, and me.

Coming up and through the last year and a half of grief, the reconvening on my fortieth birthday brings whispered, stilted words of hesitant hope. We sit together, legs touching, feeling our way into being three sisters. All around us, fifty or so friends and relatives are communing with one another and the lovely summer day. Bountiful amounts of food that Gemma made, drinks, and flowers that she arranged swell out of baskets and bowls, opening this afternoon into a celebration, one I requested, wanting a gathering of friends and family to help me greet the next decade.

Kate, Michele, and I have become almost shy with one another, our alliances confused once more by loss. We go for the safe bets, the sure things, subjects that will not raise questions or force us to consider our loyalties. It's back to skirting over any feelings or issues that could be interpreted as controversial. Paul and Anna's constant interruptions are welcomed because we need the distractions from the tension.

I put my arms around Kate and Michele. This is it, again. But this time, we are three. The middle has been eaten out from between us. We are the sides of our sister configuration now, the outskirts, and it feels extremely fragile. *What if it doesn't hold together?*

Looking as far into their faces as I can, past their sad eyes and haunted smiles, I see Shari's and Danielle's features living within the faces of Kate and Michele; I suspect that Shari and Danielle will always be showing up in our faces. Kate takes my hand, and I take Michele's. Our bodies naturally lean in toward one another and the safety and love of sisters. Our heads come together gently. This is it. The angling in of three with the connection of five still harbored within flesh, bone, and blood. We will always be heading in this direction: toward one another, our bodies forever searching for the warmth and familiarity of the original five within the context of three.

The porch door opens slowly as Gemma and our friends bring out the gigantic chocolate cake. O holy chocolate! As I stand next to Gemma, this woman who has already struggled with me through shades of great sorrow and danced with me into waves of bliss, faces turn toward us, and the singing begins. Anna, now two years old, and Paul, just four, creep closer to the cake as a slow rendition of "Happy Birthday" is sent up into the sweet heat of this July day. By the time the song is finished, my niece and nephew are within licking distance of the icing.

There is a moment when we're all looking at one another with anticipatory smiles, moving our eyes toward the cake; everyone imagines their first bite. Wind, sun, cake, family, and friends are all around me. I hold these visions in my healing heart as the next decade of my life begins.

~

I dream that I am waiting for my sisters and their families. The world has gone autumnal, colors all shades of waning earth. I can hear voices coming up from a village nestled in a valley between two mountains. A light wind is blowing in from over the pinnacle of the north slope. I reach deeper into my coat, trying to find some more warmth.

I am beginning to grow impatient, wondering where my sisters could have gone. Then I see and hear people approaching, moving slowly up the hill where I've been sitting. The soft clamor is filled with familiar intonations—my sisters are coming.

I see Kate's face first, breaking through the twilight with a smile of recognition. She is holding the hand of a young girl, who I initially believe to be Michele. But it's Anna, her chin and cheeks covered with marshmallow, as she waves and shouts out, "Hey, Bub," our pet name for each other and everyone else in our family, too. I notice that they are both wearing matching T-shirts, "Peak Experience" emblazoned in red and blue block letters across the chest, just like the ones Shari made for herself, Michele, and me years ago.

Just behind Kate and Anna, Michael appears, wearing a blue hospital hat and gown, the "Peak Experience" letters showing through the thin material. He keeps turning around and stopping, seemingly to check on Paul, who is dragging a red wagon filled with lilacs.

Paul comes to a halt every few feet, allowing Michele, Josh, and their two daughters, Sarah and Isabelle, to take inhalations of the lilacs. They are all wearing "Peak Experience" on their T-shirts as well.

I'm thinking that's it, that's everyone, when I spot three more figures emerging from the valley and out of the lengthening shadows. I see Gemma, her amber eyes illuminated by bright leaves, small orange flames bursting spontaneously as they fall from the trees. She's carrying a staff, carved wood, it is resplendent with feathers, bones, and stones—Gemma has clearly made it. As she lifts it above her head, the staff turns into a torch, lighting the landscape. As the light spreads out in all directions, I am able to identify the final two travelers: Shari and Danielle.

The two of them, arms linked, are dancing up the hill behind Gemma, Danielle wearing a facial expression that makes Shari laugh. Danielle puts her arm around Shari, and they continue on with their antics.

Soon we are all on top of the hill, becoming intertwined, all scooped up together, a pile of hands, bodies, and heads. I can't tell where anyone is, or who is who, until Gemma once again holds up the torch. Shari and Danielle have vanished. The rest of us are left sitting on top of a cliff, looking out over a great view of sea and sky.

Then, Paul spots it.

"Look," he says, pointing.

There is a blip on the horizon, rising up from the white line between ocean and sky. It is gold with tremendous wings, and it is flying toward us. I hear Gemma say, "It's a phoenix." The firebird hovers directly overhead, circles us once, lets out a triumphant cry, and then soars off into the cerulean blue of the sky, disappearing altogether.

Waking from this dream, my eyes are opening to the light.

∼

Can you hear me calling
Softly in your mind
Do you see me smiling
To the eyes that time has taught me to know
I can feel your tears when I cry
Understand that pain can only make love grow
Answers never come before "why."

Well, I know I've hurt you
Now you've hurt me, too
Somehow you're pretending
Love that hurts must never be true.

Hold me in your arms again
And nothing can be wrong
Tell me that you're back again
For I was never gone
In my confusing way I felt I would say
But I never drifted away.

Time has made me stronger
As I've tried to change
Still this love grows longer
Now my heart is slowly bleeding inside
Only you are the one who can heal
I can't really pretend that

This ending is an end
When I can't seem to fight what I feel.

Hold me in your arms again
And nothing can be wrong
Tell me that you're back again
For I was never gone.

SHARON ORTLIP, SONG, 1974

Acknowledgments

~

The thanks I feel stretch out into the distance of a vast gratitudinal plain.

The entire community of Brattleboro, Vermont. As I walked the streets at all hours of the day and night, greetings from many acquaintances kept me pumped.

To everyone at Everyone's Books and Heartstone Books.

Martha Ramsey and the Monday night writing group for your coaching.

Melinda Underwood, who read it and wept, and then helped with the initial editing.

Marion Nesbit, Barney Brawer, and Nan Doty: my team from Lesley University, who lifted my sights to a more expansive view of the possibilities.

The Neighborhood Schoolhouse and community that helped me find my way back to children. Special thanks to Julie Dolan, mentor extraordinaire.

All of my former students, with special thanks to Elias, Julian,

Hannah, Sienna, Kestrel, Shayna, Mike, Jens, and Zeke. We worked through our grief together, and the gift goes on.

Mullen and Hensel Law Associates.

Julie Andrews. Someday you'll know why, I hope.

Susan Grimaldi. For formally introducing me to the phoenix.

Joanne Wyckoff. Thanks for allowing my story to move you, and for asking to see more.

Anika Streitfeld, my totally amazing editor at Ballantine. Thanks for taking these words and making them shine.

Elisabeth Dyssegaard, for taking the manuscript to an almost perfect state of deliverance.

Everyone else at Ballantine Books.

Linda Konner, my dedicated and lovely agent, who kept the manuscript heading out to publishers, completely believing it would land on the desk of the right editor, which it did.

Robin Westen, for helping me get to the truth in my writing. For opening the door and pushing me through it.

Barbara Docktor, for your friendship and photographs, since the beginning.

Elaine Johnson. You truly are the older sister I'd been waiting for. It's the stick, Elaine, with grief to tops.

Sarah Waldo, who continues to provide the most steadfast friendship that there ever was, even from a distance.

Basia, most loyal and understanding of canines. Thanks for getting me outside every day.

Vermont. You saved me.

The woods. You hold me.

The cliffs. You endure within me.

Mom. Whether you know it or not, your decision to leave was the best one. Your encouragement over the last few years is helping us to heal. Forgiveness is certainly an option.

Grandfather and David.

The Champoli clan, for your love and encouragement.

The Ortlip clan, for your support and your genes.

Eric. You're the sweetest, and I know lots of people who would concur.

Michael and Josh—steadfast brothers-in-law.

Paul, Anna, Sarah, Isabelle, and Emma, nephew and nieces. My love for all of you will only grow stronger. You allow me to believe in the promise of new generations.

Mary Louise Ortlip, for being the right Mary.

Dad. Your love and eternal optimism bring me through to the light, every time.

Shari, Danielle, and Dylan, for your guidance from somewhere out there.

Kate, you are and always will be, my first companion.

Michele, you are and always will be, my jewel-eyed baby sister, inspiration central, keeping me honest while those crazy animals continue to cry and wonder why, in Melancholy Valley.

Gemma, you are my connection to what matters most in the world: love, in all its forms.

And holy appreciation for the wild powers of life that rage through mind, soul, and body, en route to their rightful place, on paper.